HENRIETTA SZOLD

Henrietta Szold

Hadassah and the Zionist Dream

━━━━◆◆◆━━━━

FRANCINE KLAGSBRUN

Yale

UNIVERSITY

PRESS

New Haven and London

Yale University Press books may be purchased in quantity for educational,
business, or promotional use. For information, please e-mail sales.press@yale.edu
(U.S. office) or sales@yaleup.co.uk (U.K. office).

Set in Janson Oldstyle type by Integrated Publishing Solutions.
Printed in the United States of America.

Library of Congress Control Number: 2023940418
ISBN 978-0-300-24778-7 (hardcover : alk. paper)

A catalogue record for this book is available from the British Library.

This paper meets the requirements of ANSI/NISO Z39.48-1992
(Permanence of Paper).

10 9 8 7 6 5 4 3 2 1

Frontispiece: Henrietta Szold dancing the hora with children from Youth Aliyah,
1937. Photo by Tim Nachum Gidal. © The Israel Museum, Jerusalem.
Tim Nachum Gidal, Israeli, born Germany, 1909–1996. Henrietta Szold, 1937.
The Israel Museum, Jerusalem, Tim Gidal Collection, purchased through the
gift of Gary B. Sokol, San Francisco, The Pritzker Foundation, San Francisco,
Larry Zicklin, New Jersey, Dr. John Sumers, New York. B02.0382(Is3217-022).

Lioness: Golda Meir and the Nation of Israel

Voices of Wisdom: Jewish Ideals and Ethics for Everyday Living

The Fourth Commandment: Remember the Sabbath Day

Jewish Days: A Book of Jewish Life and Culture around the Year

Free to Be . . . You and Me (editor)

Married People: Staying Together in the Age of Divorce

Mixed Feelings: Love, Hate, Rivalry, and Reconciliation among Brothers and Sisters

Too Young to Die: Youth and Suicide

Freedom Now: The Story of the Abolitionists

Sigmund Freud: A Biography for Young People

To the women of Hadassah,
who have never forgotten their founder

CONTENTS

HENRIETTA SZOLD

---◆I◆I◆---

Introduction

I KNEW THE WOMAN for whom Louis Ginzberg, Henrietta Szold's great love, jilted her.

Szold had met Ginzberg at the Jewish Theological Seminary in New York, where he was an eminent professor of Talmud and she the first woman enrolled full-time in that august institution, which trained men to become rabbis in the Conservative movement. She had wanted to expand her Jewish knowledge, and she'd been accepted on condition that she not seek to enter the rabbinate. At forty-two she was older than the students there and thirteen years Ginzberg's senior. Fluent in German, she felt flattered when the professor asked her to translate his class notes and some of his writings from German into English. During the next several years, she worked closely with him, laboring slavishly on his books, especially his magnum opus, *Legends of the Jews*, a compilation of legends and fables based on biblical origins. In addition to translations, she made editorial suggestions and corrections as the work expanded from one volume to seven. In the process, she fell hopelessly in love with him. Given the many hours they spent together and the letters they shared when they were apart, she assumed he felt as she did, despite their age difference. When he returned from a trip to Berlin at the end of the summer of 1908 and announced his engagement to marry a young woman he had met there, Szold's world fell apart.

Her name was Adele Katzenstein, and she differed in every way imaginable from the plain-looking, shy, and erudite Henrietta Szold. Adele had high cheekbones, beautiful eyes, and a strong, German-accented voice in which she tended to articulate whatever happened to be on her mind. Although sharp, that mind rarely turned to bookish matters; more often it focused on people and events around her. I met her decades after her marriage to Professor Ginzberg, when I was a student at the Seminary College for Jewish Studies (now List College), a division of the Jewish Theological Seminary that supplements secular college educations. She was a presence on campus, known to all as "Mama G," a beloved surrogate mother, who felt no compunction about publicly addressing her dignified husband as "Schatzi," her treasure.

Devastated by Ginzberg's rejection, Szold poured out her heart to almost everyone she knew. The seminary community was nearly as shocked as she—Szold and Ginzberg had long been regarded as a couple. The story soon spread beyond that community, becoming a source of endless gossip. To this day, in rabbinic or Jewish academic circles, her name evokes pitying comments about her unrequited love, even among people who may know little else about her. After her initial reaction, Szold descended into a dark pit of depression that lasted for several years and at times bordered on self-destruction. She began to heal when she stopped blaming herself for what had happened and acknowledged Ginzberg's role in the sorry episode. As she recovered, she emerged a different person, far more independent and assertive, no longer the self-effacing woman behind the scenes she had been to Ginzberg and other men she worked with. Through profound self-examination and sheer will she had transformed herself.

Now, beliefs and values that had been in the background of Szold's thinking moved to the forefront. Zionism, which she had adopted years earlier, became a dominant force in her life, as did issues concerning women's roles and rights. Within a year after regaining her health, she founded Hadassah, the Women's Zionist Organization of America, which under her guidance would become the largest and most influential of all American Zionist groups. She viewed the organization's work as practical idealism, a combined ethical and pragmatic approach to fulfilling Jewish life in the historic Land of Israel. A decade later she would move to that land herself and use her skills to direct the health, education, and social services there. Late in life she took on the task of heading the Youth Aliyah program, rescuing thousands of young people from the Nazi menace and resettling them in pre-state Israel. Through all her activities in Palestine, she sought ways to establish peace and equality with the Arab population there.

How different would Henrietta Szold's life had been if Louis Ginzberg had returned her love? We can never know—that is one of the "what ifs" of history. But it is a fair guess that like Adele's life, much of Henrietta's might have revolved around Ginzberg and the seminary. Adele Ginzberg didn't fully come into her own until after her husband died. She remained involved in the seminary, and became active in supporting rights for women in synagogue rituals. Szold moved away from the seminary neighborhood sometime after her nervous collapse and recovery. While she maintained several of her old friendships, she developed new, closer ones. She never spoke of Ginzberg again or mentioned the episode with him in her vast correspondence. And she never married, although she regretted not having children.

There have been numerous biographies, monographs, and articles about Henrietta Szold. I have read and relied on them all in my own study of her life and works, and have credited them in the endnotes throughout this book. But with her myriad accomplishments, Szold appears in most of these writings as almost a paragon of perfection, so spiritual that, in the words of her longtime secretary, visitors entering her room had "the sensation of entering a cathedral, a holy place."[1] In reality, Szold was a complex flesh-and-blood human being who had to cope with controversy and criticism, a workaholic with an outsized sense of duty and a fierce temper, and an idealist who fought hard for what she believed in, even while she questioned her own abilities. It was that real-life woman I wanted to write about in this book, hoping to uncover the human person behind the idealized icon.

In my search, I gave special weight to Szold's own words. She wrote an incalculable number of letters during her life; she insisted on personally responding to every letter she received, from critics and cranks as well as admirers. Most revealing were the letters she wrote to family and friends over the decades. In them she spoke more openly about personalities and situations than she did in her public talks or published correspondence to the Hadassah community. Consequently, I read hundreds of her personal letters, the bulk of them located in the Hadassah Archives on deposit at the American Jewish Historical Society in New York City, and others at the Central Zionist Archives in Jerusalem. (Marvin Lowenthal collected many of her letters in his valuable book, *Henrietta Szold: Life and Letters*. But the book was prepared during her lifetime and of necessity omits material she did not wish to make public then. As a result, there are significant gaps in the letters' contents, with no indication of where an omission has been made. I therefore thought it best to read and quote from the originals as much as possible, using Lowenthal as a source when relevant.) I also examined the personal journals Szold kept before, during, and after the Ginzberg years. Along with her thoughts on contemporary issues, Szold's writings display her quirky sense of humor, fine insights into people and places, and superb literary style.

With her straight-laced appearance and soft speech, Szold might be said to reflect the Victorian era in which she was born. (She was always called "Miss Szold," even in the pioneer world of pre-state Israel, where everybody used first names.) But behind the modest demeanor and proper manners lived a powerhouse of a woman whose ideas and abilities shaped the world around her. Her life reveals that strength.

1

First Daughter

ON THE NINETEENTH ANNIVERSARY of her father's death, Henrietta Szold, over sixty and living in Jerusalem, wrote to her sisters in the United States: "Out here my recollection of him, his views and his attitude towards all sorts of questions, has become more vivid rather than less. As problem after problem comes up . . . I involuntarily ask myself how he would have met them. . . . At all events, summoning back to my mind his way of dealing with social, human perplexities helps me to serenity better than anything else."[1]

She did not exaggerate. Rabbi Benjamin Szold had been her ideal and her mentor from as far back as memory could take her, and though he had died years earlier, he remained the guiding force of her life. She was much like her mother, she would say, in her organizing skills, practicality, and concern for details. But it was her father who shaped her intellectual and spiritual development, influencing the values she held and the actions she took.[2] From him she had learned to speak several languages, understand classic texts, and turn her thoughts into written words. His stamp on her was such that toward the end of her long life, her assistant could still say of her that she "thinks and speaks of him constantly."[3]

Born in 1829 in the village of Nemiskürt, Hungary, to a landowning family, unusual for Jews of the time, Benjamin Szold came to America at the age of thirty to serve as rabbi of one of the leading synagogues in Baltimore, Maryland, Oheb Shalom. According to family lore, he had been something of a prodigy in the old country, reading the Torah in Hebrew at the age of four and receiving rabbinic credentials at sixteen (some said fourteen). Orphaned at a young age, he and his brother Solomon lived with a kindly uncle for a while. Benjamin moved on after his bar mitzvah to a prestigious yeshiva in Pressburg (today Bratislava, Slovakia) and from there to secular and Judaic studies in Vienna. Along with many of his schoolmates, he supported the Revolution of 1848, and when it failed, he fled back to Pressburg. There and in surrounding rural areas he made a living tutoring Jewish children. In the tiny village of Cziffer (today Cifer, Slovakia), at the home of the well-to-do widow Miriam Schaar—her husband had opened a brewery, which she maintained—he met his wife to be, Sophie, the youngest girl of Miriam's ten living children of the twelve she had borne. But first, supported by Miriam, he accompanied two of her young sons to Breslau, where he supervised their studies while studying himself at the University of Breslau and the Jewish Theological Seminary there.

This was an exciting time to be part of the Jewish intellectual world. The emancipation of the Jews in various European countries and the Jewish enlightenment, which opened Jewish thought to secular Western influences, had brought profound changes to Jewish religious life. The Reform movement, begun in Germany in the early 1800s, sought to modernize the reli-

gion by doing away with many of its rituals, alienating Orthodox Jewish authorities. The Breslau seminary, headed by the
scholar Zecharias Frankel, created a middle ground between the
extremes of an Orthodoxy that clung unchangingly to tradition
and a Reform that challenged almost all traditional observance.
Its "positive-historical" approach emphasized Judaism's ability
to confront modernity while remaining loyal to fundamental
Jewish laws and practices. Many of its teachings would translate
into the centrist Conservative movement in the United States,
whose flagship was the Jewish Theological Seminary of America.
To a great degree, that movement defined the religious behavior of Rabbi Benjamin Szold and later his daughter Henrietta.

After accepting the rabbinic position in Baltimore, then the
third-largest city in the United States, Rabbi Szold married
Sophie Schaar and the young couple set off for America in 1859,
bringing with them one of Benjamin's cousins and one of Sophie's brothers. They settled in a small house on South Eutaw
Street in the German section of town, a few blocks from the
new synagogue building at Hanover Street. Like the rabbi, most
of its congregants had emigrated from central Europe, spoke
German as their first language, and were generally known as
"German Jews." Slim and dark-eyed, with a black beard and pitch-
black hair that curled around his ears, the young clergyman impressed his flock both with his appearance and his Jewish knowledge. The synagogue had joined the central Reform governing
body, the Union of American Hebrew Congregations (UAHC),
but many of its worshipers leaned toward more traditional observance. They accepted the rabbi's moderate views, with his
emphasis on the Sabbath, dietary laws, and other rituals.[4] At first
he preached solely in German, but over time, he interspersed
the German with English sermons. Eventually he also created
a new prayer book, *Abodat Yisrael*, which had a Hebrew text and
German translation. In his congregation and several others, it
replaced the strictly Reform *Minhag America* that had been in use.

On December 21, 1860, a little over a year after the Szolds arrived in Baltimore, their first daughter was born "amid the booming of the first guns found ushering in the Civil War."[5] They named her ritually Chaile, after Benjamin's mother, and called her Henrietta, in honor of Henriette Herz, a beautiful eighteenth-century scholar who ran a brilliant salon in Berlin (and about whom Henrietta Szold would later write an article in the *Jewish Encyclopedia*). Henrietta would have few memories of the war that raged during the first four years of her life. One that became iconic for her was of being held up high to watch the funeral cortege of the slain President Abraham Lincoln as it moved slowly through town, past her home. She would never forget that moment, surrounded by sadness and silence.

As a border state, Maryland had been torn between Northern and Southern sympathizers, and Rabbi Szold's community was as divided as the rest of the state. Although the rabbi personally opposed slavery, his public position in the battle between North and South mirrored his centrist religious positions. Unlike the firebrand Reform rabbi David Einhorn, who had to flee town because of his passionate preaching against slavery, Benjamin Szold placed the preservation of the Union above all else, speaking regularly against the secession of Southern states and emphasizing more than anything the need for peace and unity.[6] Along with so many of his teachings, those lessons left a lasting impression on his eldest daughter.

Rabbi Szold differed from many Baltimoreans in that he admired and supported Lincoln. On one occasion he traveled to Washington to plead with the president for the life of a Jewish deserter sentenced to death. Lincoln sent him on, with a letter of introduction, to General George Meade, who turned down the appeal. The rabbi went to see the terrified soldier, recited psalms and prayers with him, and stayed by the condemned man's side until he and four other deserters were executed by firing squad.[7] Henrietta Szold spoke with pride of her father's compassion in that incident, as she did of his membership after the war in the Baltimore Association for the Educational and Moral Improvement of the Colored People, an organization that helped freed black men attain an education.

Sophie Szold gave birth to seven daughters after Henrietta, two of whom died in infancy. Henrietta helped care for her sisters and became especially attached to one of the younger ones, Johanna. When that child died of scarlet fever at the age of three, a distraught Henrietta became ill with a nervous disorder, St. Vitus' Dance (now known as Sydenham chorea). The birth of the last girl, Adele, born when Henrietta was almost sixteen, comforted and helped heal her. By then everyone in the family recognized Henrietta's place as the daughter closest to the rabbi, treated by him as he might have treated an eldest son being groomed to follow in his footsteps. Intellectually gifted, serious, and devoted, she received an education from her father equaled by few other women of her time. She even loooked like him, with her intense dark eyes and somewhat sallow complexion, different from her mother's blue eyes and pink cheeks, traits that some of the other girls inherited.

The elder Szolds spoke German at home, and Henrietta became fluent in the language. By the age of eight, she was reading Goethe in the original with her father. Sitting at his side, she also mastered French and Hebrew, becoming knowledgeable in biblical and Talmudic law and lore. She read voraciously in English, from Dickens's novels to the scholarly encyclopedia articles her father favored. As the years went by, she became his confidante and amanuensis, editing his work, translating his papers into English, and helping with his sermons. He came to depend on her and she, shy and self-conscious, blossomed with his attention and teaching. She gained confidence in her abilities to form opinions and express ideas, to write and speak her mind.

She also developed a massive sense of duty that hovered over her throughout life. She personally responded to the thousands of letters she received during the course of her lifetime, for example, almost invariably beginning her letters—whether to friends, family, or others—by apologizing for not having written sooner or more fully. "I don't forgive myself . . . my conscience on the subject of correspondence debts keeps me from enjoying life," she wrote to an acquaintance. And in spite of consistently assuming more responsibilities than she realistically had time for, she rarely refused a new request. The world, she once wrote to her sister Adele, "is always jabbing some goad into me, as they do into the donkeys in the East. That keeps me trotting, just as the donkeys do." She would attribute much of her sense of duty to the example of her mother, who reared five children to adulthood and cooked, baked, and ran the household with great efficiency. Yet the many hours she spent with her father, working hard to please him, had the most powerful impact. Indeed, as she grew older, she felt guilty, she said, for not having devoted herself exclusively to scholarship, as she believed he would have wanted her to.[8]

To some extent, Henrietta Szold's dedication to duty prevented her from going to college. Her formal schooling began in the basement of her father's synagogue, where she studied religious and secular subjects, and continued at a public grammar school until, at the age of thirteen, she entered the Western Female High School, the only Jew there. She graduated as class valedictorian in 1877, with the highest grades ever before achieved at that school. Johns Hopkins University had recently opened for men, but there were no schools of higher education in Baltimore that accepted women. Henrietta longed to attend Vassar College in Poughkeepsie, New York. Financial considerations were an issue, but the strongest barrier to her going there was the need for her at home, to help her mother with the younger girls and aid her father in his work, which now included writing a commentary on the biblical book of Job. Within a few years, three of those younger sisters would get the college education denied her, and Henrietta would contribute to their tuition. But she herself had to divert her desire for a higher education into attending public lectures at Johns Hopkins and the Peabody Institute.

Instead of continuing her formal schooling, she began to teach after high school, serving briefly on the staff of Western and for the better part of the next fifteen years teaching French, German, Latin, algebra, and a variety of other subjects at the Misses Adams' English and French School for Girls, an elite academy. Some afternoons she also commuted to Oldfields, a boarding school for girls outside Baltimore. At the same time she taught in Oheb Shalom's religious school on Saturday mornings and Sundays, and gave a Bible class for adults on Saturday afternoons. For all that, she would label herself a "humbug" of a teacher because she had not had any official training.[9]

She enjoyed the teaching and she enjoyed the writing she had begun to do around the same time. Before she was eighteen she became a correspondent for the *Jewish Messenger*, a weekly paper published in New York, writing columns under the heading "Our Baltimore Letter" and using the pseudonym Sulamith—too modest, as a proper Victorian lady, to sign her own name. Some of her early articles sound like echoes of her father's sermons. "Why need we adopt the Xmas tree, ridiculously baptized a Chanucka bush? Have we not the Menorah?" she scolded the Jewish community, as rabbis have done and would do for decades.[10] Or, targeting Baltimore Jews for their "indifference," she complained that synagogue services were "woefully neglected on Friday Eve, when there is usually a ball at one of our principal club-houses."[11] When she found her own voice it was straightforward, a little self-righteous at times, but also alive with verve and humor. Responding to antisemitic comments in a newspaper called the *Standard*, she labeled the author a Russian cur who might go mad and bite his editor.[12] And when a critic called her "a pan and pot scourer," a lowly woman, she proudly embraced domesticity, lobbing back that she would never "neglect the peculiar privilege of women to attend to the physical comfort of their more awkward fellow creatures."[13]

"I have a pretty big capacity for righteous indignation," she later said of herself.[14] After a while, her *Jewish Messenger* column, which had been at the back of the paper, was moved to the middle pages, printed under a boldfaced headline.

By her early twenties Henrietta Szold had branched out to write for various American Jewish newspapers and a few secular ones. In some articles she used pen names; in others she wrote anonymously. One of her anonymous pieces, published in the magazine *Education* in 1883, could well have been her cri de coeur, starved as she was for a college education. In it, she called for an endowed women's college in Baltimore whose best students would be admitted for special study at Johns Hopkins University. In an editorial supporting her ideas, the *Baltimore American*, a local newspaper, advocated for a women's college in Baltimore that would parallel the undergraduate training men received at Hopkins.[15] Both articles caught the attention of the ardent feminist M. Carey Thomas. From a well-to-do and prominent Baltimore family, Thomas had studied at Sage College, the women's school at Cornell University but, prohibited by Johns Hopkins from attending graduate classes with men, she went abroad to attain a doctorate at the University of Zurich. Soon afterward she became dean of the newly established Bryn Mawr College for Women in Pennsylvania and then its second president. Together with several friends she founded Bryn Mawr School in Baltimore, a rigorous institution to prepare young women for college. Most biographies of Henrietta Szold describe the two women becoming good friends as a result of Szold's article, a prestigious friendship for her.[16] Their closeness is questionable, however: extensive research into Thomas's writings and letters have shown her to be a virulent antisemite and racist, who worked hard to keep Jews from joining Bryn Mawr's faculty. In fact, she lobbied against accepting Henrietta's younger sister Sadie as a student at Baltimore's Bryn Mawr School because she was Jewish.[17] Sadie was accepted despite Thomas's objection, and so was the next youngest, Bertha, who would also attend Bryn Mawr College.

It's unlikely that Henrietta Szold knew of Carey Thomas's behind-the-scenes manipulations. The two women probably met in Baltimore's social circles, becoming politely friendly through their mutual concern about women's education. But Henrietta's article held more importance for her than winning Carey's friendship. It represented her first foray into publicly presenting women's interests as extending beyond home and family life, a position she would develop fully in years to come.

Henrietta was about thirteen years old when the family moved from their house on Eutaw Street to 702 West Lombard Street. (By then the two relatives who had come to America with her parents had gone their own ways.) She would dwell in that home until she was thirty-three, and it would live on in her memory for the rest of her life, an almost Proustian symbol of idyllic youth and family closeness. When she was settled in Palestine in her seventies, she found the scent of the fig trees in Nablus evocative of the Lombard Street garden. And Bertha's laughter and "constant babble" during a recent visit was "so reminiscent of the years on Lombard Street . . . that I can't believe in the flight of time from twenty-seven to seventy-two," she wrote Adele.[18]

The three-story redbrick building on Lombard Street was designed in typical Victorian fashion, with a formal parlor on the first floor. But the most beloved room was the second-floor sitting room, which held Henrietta's desk. There the family gathered informally, and there on Sunday evenings they entertained their closest friends—many of them eligible males. The five Friedenwald boys, whose father, Dr. Aaron Friedenwald, was a noted ophthalmologist, lived nearby and exchanged frequent visits with the five Szold girls. The two sons of Rabbi Marcus Jastrow, a distinguished Philadelphia scholar and good friend of Rabbi Szold, came to town regularly to be with the family. Joseph, the younger, lived with the Szolds for a time while he attended Johns Hopkins. Other students from the university, who took Rabbi Szold's course in theology there, dropped in for dinner and discussion. Among them was Cyrus Adler, a brilliant scholar and expert in Semitics, whose life would cross Henrietta's in myriad ways, and who would come to hold major positions in the Jewish community, including president of the Jewish Theological Seminary of America.

"Miss Henrietta," as she was known, held serious, intense conversations with the young men who called on the family. One by one, her sisters married them. Rachel, probably the prettiest of the Szold girls, and the sister Henrietta had been closest to, married Joseph Jastrow. The couple moved to Madison, Wisconsin, where he became a highly acclaimed professor of psychology at the University of Wisconsin. Henrietta broke down in tears at that move, so far from her and the family home. "I don't know what I am going to do without you," she wrote to Rachel. "The lump in my throat . . . has become stationary."[19] Bertha later married Louis Levin, a prominent Baltimore lawyer, and Adele wed Thomas Seltzer, an editor and book publisher.

To be sure, Henrietta formed warm friendships with several of the male visitors, but those relationships never seemed to move beyond the intellectual. To take one example, the elder Jastrow son, Morris, who attended the University of Pennsylvania, wrote her long letters—some twenty pages—on whatever current subjects interested him, and she responded in kind. In 1881, after college, he went to the Breslau seminary, presumably to prepare for the rabbinate, with the intention of eventually taking over his father's prestigious pulpit in Philadelphia's

Rodeph Shalom synagogue. During the next four years, he opened his heart and shared his most pressing thoughts with her as he agonized about whether that was the path he really wanted to follow.[20] In letter after letter, he analyzed the American Jewish community and his place in it. He finally decided, with her sympathy, on an academic career at the University of Pennsylvania. For all the confidences they exchanged, however, no further intimacy grew from that relationship.

Her bond with Harry Friedenwald, eldest of the Friedenwald brothers and some four years her junior, may have been more serious to begin with. The two kept up a lively correspondence when he went to Germany to follow in his father's footsteps and continue his ophthalmology studies after completing medical school. Sensing a possible romance, his controlling mother quickly moved to squelch it. In a letter she wrote to Harry soon after he left, she warned, "Henrietta is much older than you, and if that does not look so much now, as you both grow older it will probably show itself more. A woman ages quicker than a man." A year later, still worried about her Harry's intentions, she minced no words: "She is too old for you, not only in years but in ideas, and is stubborn and moody. Remember how angry she made you at times?" she wrote after he mentioned anticipating a reunion with Henrietta on his return. "I admit that she is as good as you say, and that it is a great pity that she cannot get as good a husband as she deserves. Through her singular disposition she repels everyone who approaches her, and she has done this since she was young."[21] The anger she was referring to was probably Henrietta's forthright defense of positions she held, making no concessions to the young men visiting her home.

Harry returned from his studies in 1890. He had been looking forward to Sunday evenings at the Szolds' again, but somehow the enchantment had vanished for him. Henrietta seemed tired out from her many activities, and old.[22] Within a year, he became engaged to marry pretty, vivacious Birdie Stein, two years younger than he and the daughter of a banker. He and Henrietta would remain lifelong friends.

Years later, Henrietta Szold reflected on her unmarried status. Had she met happily married women in her "young womanhood days," she wrote in her diary, she might have learned the "secret of a woman's life, her true life," and then "all might have been different."[23]But whatever regrets she would have in the future, in these childhood and young adult years, her emotional energy was wrapped around her father's needs and expectations, guided as well by the weight of responsibility she felt as the first daughter in her large and demanding family.

2

◆│◆│◆

"I Eat, Drink, and Sleep Russians"

IN JUNE 1881, when Henrietta was twenty-one, her father took her on a three-month trip to Europe to visit relatives and friends, most of whom she had not met before. They went to the Hungarian towns where her parents had been born, to Pressburg, where her father had studied in a yeshiva, and to Berlin, Hamburg, Vienna, and other parts of Germany and Austria-Hungary that were sprinkled with relatives—her mother's Schaar family and her father's Szolds. Forty years later, living in Jerusalem, she met a young pioneer, a recent immigrant from Galicia with the surname "Sold," who wondered whether they were related. After examining a family tree sent by the man's uncle with all the branches until 1755 and looking through her own family papers, Henrietta discovered that they shared a great-great-great grandfather named Jacob, who had been a paid government official in Galicia, a rare position for a Jew. When Emperor Joseph II insisted that Jews take family names, Jacob

18

proudly called himself "Sold," from *besoldeter,* meaning wage earner. Later, the Hungarian branch of the family added a "z" to maintain the "s" sound in their language. The origin of the name, unknown during Henrietta's youthful visit to the Szold relatives, became family lore in the years after she wrote of her discovery to her sisters.[1]

The trip itself held a tinge of sadness at its start. Rabbi Szold had been asked by his wife's family to oversee the dedication of a tombstone honoring her mother, Miriam, the woman at whose home he and Sophie had met. Henrietta had been writing to that grandmother since her childhood, but had never met her. She cried at the dedication and her father's talk, as did many of the relatives who came from distant towns to honor Miriam and meet the rabbi and his eldest daughter. Some of the aunts called Henrietta "the stout niece," for she had grown heavy and, unlike her younger sisters, paid little attention to her appearance. Some of her cousins found her dark eyes and hair exotic in a family where fair skin and light eyes were the norm. But she felt accepted and loved by the large, sprawling family.[2]

A highlight of the trip for her was a visit to Prague's Alt-Neu Shul, the oldest active synagogue in Europe. According to Jewish lore, the synagogue's attic holds the remains of the Golem, a creature made out of earthen materials centuries ago to rescue the Jewish people from their enemies. Looking up as she stood in the sanctuary, Henrietta noticed a small round window on one wall, darkened except for a thin beam of light. It opened, she learned, into a hidden gallery, the women's section, where during services one woman relayed to all the others what was taking place in the men's synagogue below. It struck her that she could become a teacher of women, a bridge between their world and the men's world, conveying to them the Jewish learning she had absorbed from her father and her own studies.[3] It did not yet occur to her that she could do more, that she could guide women out of the dark, narrow places that constricted many of them toward the more expansive spaces men inhabited.

In Vienna, she spent time with several male cousins, who pleaded with her to stay on at least for a few months. She especially enjoyed the company of Ignatz Kien, her mother's sister's son, a handsome young man studying at the Vienna Institute of Technology to be a chemical engineer. He squired her around the city in an open carriage, and promised her that if she stayed with his family in Vienna for a year, he would take her on a trip to Italy during the winter. The offer sorely tempted her; she'd had a wonderful time with Ignatz seeing the city sights and attending the opera and theater. She looked to her father for a response. "The little ones will miss you," he said, his mind most likely on himself and his need for her at his side.[4] She packed her bags without a word of dissent, and off they went for short visits to Paris and London, and finally home.

Back in Baltimore, both Szolds became caught up in the plight of new immigrants swarming into the city, part of a vast wave of Jews fleeing eastern Europe. Many of the newcomers had left their lands to escape the vicious pogroms that followed the assassination of Tsar Alexander II in 1881. Although revolutionaries masterminded the bombing that killed the tsar, many in the lower classes blamed the Jews, unleashing a spate of beatings, murders, and rapes in Jewish communities on a scale unmatched before. Other Jews who left eastern Europe were driven from their homes and property by the ever-expanding Christian church. But the great majority of the new arrivals came to seek a way out of the bitter poverty that, more than ever ground them down in the ghetto-like Pale of Settlement where they had been confined. More than 2 million Jews poured into the United States between the 1880s and early 1900s. The vast majority settled in New York; others went to such large cities as Boston, Chicago, and Philadelphia. And some eight thousand landed in Baltimore's Locust Point Harbor, with large numbers making their homes in the poorest sections of the city's eastern district near the harbor, turning the area into its own poverty-ridden "ghetto."

These "Russian" Jews, as they were called—although they included large numbers of Lithuanians, Poles, Latvians, and other east Europeans—arrived in America at a vulnerable time for the established German Jews who had preceded them. Those earlier arrivals had long since been Americanized, becoming prosperous department store owners, respected judges and physicians, and formidable politicians. In the Reform Judaism many of them practiced, they had moved ever closer to their Christian neighbors. Men sat bareheaded in their "temples," rabbis debated substituting Sunday for Saturday as the Jewish day of rest, and Christmas stood out as the most celebrated holiday on the calendar for Jews as well as Christians. Even so, in recent years, the scourge of antisemitism had touched them as it had their ancestors throughout history, in many instances precisely because of the Jews' prominence and financial status. In one of the most notorious incidents, in 1877 Judge Henry Hilton barred the well-known banker Joseph Seligman from the posh Grand Union Hotel in Saratoga because he was Jewish. Two years later, railroad magnate Austin Corbin announced that "Jews as a class" would be banned from his Manhattan Beach resort in Coney Island. In a Sulamith piece on the Corbin affair, Henrietta included a character based on her father who suggested that the Jews simply ignore Corbin as being beneath contempt, and that, in fact, was how much of the community dealt with the man.[5] Still, the insult cut deep. In Baltimore, as in other parts of the country, Jews increasingly found themselves excluded from prestigious social clubs and unable to buy homes in the finer neighborhoods.

And now came the Russian Jews, with their Old World clothes and lack of social graces, their Yiddish expressions grating on the ears of German-speaking people. Feeling responsible

for their co-religionists, the German Jews began to create charitable institutions and rescue associations to aid and support
them. But they also felt embarrassed by the foreigners, fearful
that their numbers and visibility would exacerbate the balloon-
ing antisemitism.[6]

The Szolds were among a handful of Baltimore Jewish
families who took a different view of the immigrants. Father and
eldest daughter went down to the docks to meet boatloads of
east European arrivals, and on many occasions invited the newcomers to their home to aid them in finding jobs and living
quarters. The Szold family quickly discovered that these people
were not the ignorant, uncouth boors many German Jews took
them to be. They were passionate in their beliefs and outspo-
ken in their opinions. Many had strong Jewish backgrounds and
knew Hebrew fluently, in contrast to the assimilated Reform
Jews who, as the Szolds saw them, constantly whittled away at
basic traditions. For Henrietta, the vitality of the Russian Jews
and their commitment to Jewish values touched something deep
within, and she responded to them with affection and admiration. "I feel very much more drawn to these Russian Jews than
to the others," she wrote to her sister Rachel. "There is something ideal about them. . . . I have no greater wish than to be
able to give my whole strength, time, and ability to them."[7]

Within a short while she and her father became closely associated with a group of intellectual young Russian immigrants
and involved in a literary society these men had formed. Called
the Isaac Baer Levinsohn Hebrew Literary Society, after a leading light of Hebrew culture in Russia, it met regularly to discuss
modern Hebrew literature, and sponsored debates and lectures
for the broader Russian community. Both Szolds delivered talks
from time to time, and by 1890, Rabbi Szold had become a kind
of spiritual mentor to the society, heading a study group that
read and analyzed portions of the Hebrew Bible.[8]

Henrietta moved in a different direction, toward the pragmatic, as she would throughout her working life. She suggested that the society start a night school to teach the immigrants English, their key to fully entering American life, and she volunteered to help organize it.[9] It was a bold move for her; she had been teaching in established schools but had no experience in creating one of her own. Yet almost instinctively she knew what to do. In November 1889, after months of preparation and with the help of a Baltimore lawyer, Benjamin Hartogensis, she scraped together enough money to rent space for the new school in the rear of the second floor of a rundown store on Gay Street. Members of the literary society sanded floors, painted walls, secured kerosene lamps for illumination, and put out the word that the new Russian Night School was open for registration at a fee of 30 cents a month (Szold would not hear of a charity school; paying for learning motivated students). Thirty men and women showed up for classes on the first night. On the second, so many more people clamored to be admitted that another class was formed. Two volunteer teachers soon joined the staff, but it quickly became clear that volunteers could not be counted on for the steady work needed, and additional teachers were hired at modest salaries (Szold herself never took a penny for her work). Students learned English by being required to speak only in that language. For the more advanced, American history books became basic texts, pathways not only to language but also to an understanding of the country and its values. As the weeks went by, streams of Russian immigrants turned to the night school as their key approach to being educated in their new land. By the end of the first semester 150 men, women, and children had enrolled. At the beginning of the second season that number jumped to 340.

This was a heady enterprise for Henrietta. "I eat, drink, and sleep Russians," she wrote to Rachel.[10] She taught a class of her own, hired and supervised teachers, and planned much of the curriculum. In a little black notebook, she kept a list of the dozens of details that also demanded her attention—"admission cards," "dirt in cellar," "slate sponges," "umbrella stands," and many more.[11] And then there was fund-raising, crucial for the burgeoning school, and one of her most difficult tasks. In the spring the literary society held an evening of musical entertainment that netted enough to allow the school to rent an entire building, but so much more was needed for teachers, books, and equipment. The Jewish community remained "cold and indifferent" to her appeals for money, Henrietta wrote.[12] But she did manage to acquire contributions from the Baron de Hirsch Fund, a vast philanthropy with wide-ranging causes. A year after receiving a small grant from the Baltimore branch of the fund, she traveled to its main office in New York, leaving with $700 for the Russian school.[13] It was not a great deal of money, but with that sum and other funds collected by a financial committee she had put together, the school moved to a large residential house on East Baltimore Street, its final home. After the Baron de Hirsch's death, his wife, more interested in the school than he, sent Henrietta a check for $2,000 to aid it.[14]

At Rachel's urging, Henrietta wrote a long article for the *Baltimore Sun* about the school and the immigrants who attended it, noting that they now included not only Russian Jews but also Catholic Russians and Poles, and even some Americans. She described poignantly how husbands and wives sat on the same bench "side by side" with their children, the young ones as intent as their parents in developing their English reading and writing skills. She also suggested that the city establish its own night schools.[15]

Anyone reading the article in the paper that day might have assumed that the Russian Night School filled all Szold's time, so consumed was she by it. In fact, that work came in addition to her regular teaching jobs at the Misses Adams' school, Oldfields in Glencoe, and her father's congregational school. Then there were the clubs she belonged to: in the Baltimore

Botany Club, high on the list, she organized weekly meetings and periodically delivered papers on her botanical explorations. She loved learning the names of plants and flowers, the more exotic the better, and discovering all she could about them, an interest that would last throughout her life. At the Women's Literary Society, formed in 1890, where she was one of only two Jewish members, she served on the executive board and also gave regular talks. As she described it to Rachel, a typical day for her began at 5:30 in the morning and didn't end until 11:30 at night, with barely time for breakfast and none for dinner. Indeed, she said satirically, maybe if she limited her dinner eating to just Friday, Saturday, and Sunday evenings, she might be able to fulfill all the demands made of her. Yet, she admitted, almost grudgingly, "I enjoy this after a fashion."[16]

It was a pattern she would follow all her life: overworking, sleeping four or five hours a night, feeling exhausted and frequently put upon, with demands coming from all directions, yet driven to keep going. The sense of duty she imbibed from childhood never left her, pressing her to meet the expectations others had of her—and pressing her even more strongly to meet those she had of herself. But there was also something else. As she admitted to Rachel, a part of her basked in the pressure and the challenge of trying to keep up with the demands made of her. A part of her felt excited at discovering her own abilities and mastering areas she had not attempted before. And more: while she could be genuinely self-effacing and shy—exceedingly nervous about speaking in public, for example—beneath the insecurity lay the strong-willed conviction that she knew how to get things done correctly and probably better than anyone else, a kind of self-confidence in spite of herself.

All these factors came into play in her work with the Russian immigrants. It was their school, she said, and she made a point of letting them run it. Yet not a detail escaped her scrutiny. She had organized the curriculum, hired and fired teachers

("I told her that her services were no longer needed," she wrote Rachel in the same letter of a teacher who had disappointed her, proud that she'd had the confidence to let the woman go), supervised the overall operation, and raised money to keep it going, all new skills for her. So, while she complained of the overwork and difficulties now, as she would time and again about future projects, she found what she did exhilarating, as she often would, even if the most she would admit to was enjoying it "after a fashion."

In the case of the Russian immigrants, whom she called affectionately "my Russians," additional things gave her pleasure. She admired the immigrants' spirit after all they had suffered, and she had high regard for their attitude toward Jewish education, far greater respect than she had for American Jews in that area. "They have their children taught in the tenets of their faith by men of learning and knowledge," she wrote in one of her columns—not seriously taught in Sunday schools, which were no more than "a pastime" for the American Jewish children who attended them.[17] And she was moved and emotionally drawn to their commitment to the Jewish people and the nationalism that would soon become widely known as Zionism.

Szold had long been an admirer of Emma Lazarus, the poet best known for her sonnet "The New Colossus," with its famous words, "Give me your tired, your poor, your huddled masses" inscribed on the pedestal of the Statue of Liberty. Lazarus, who grew up in a wealthy, aristocratic family of Sephardic origins and fit comfortably into elite New York literary and social circles, found herself drawn to Jewish issues during the latter part of her life. Profoundly touched by the plight of Jewish immigrants streaming into New York during the 1870s and 1880s, she became a powerful advocate for a Jewish haven in Palestine. As she envisioned it, the ancient Land of Israel would be a safe retreat for east European Jews and others suffering from persecution and pogroms. Henrietta spoke of feeling "very near"

to Lazarus "as a woman and as a Jewess" in a talk she gave to a
non-Jewish club in a Baltimore suburb.[18] She also chose Lazarus as the subject of her first lecture to the Hebrew Literary
Society.

It was within that society that she came to formulate her
ideas about Zionism not only as a form of escape for Europe's
downtrodden Jews, as Lazarus imagined it, but also as an ideal
that could be embraced by every Jew. "Zionism converted me
to itself," Szold said, meaning that once she came into contact
with the idea, she quickly made it part of her.[19] For the Russian
intellectuals, Zionism held a central place in Judaism as a whole.
They immersed themselves in studying the Hebrew language
and reading Hebrew literature. They supported early groups like
the Hovevei Zion, Lovers of Zion, pioneers who had gone to
Palestine to build agricultural settlements. And they regarded
nationalism not in narrow, chauvinistic terms, but as a pathway
to a more meaningful life for Jews everywhere. That outlook
fit directly into Szold's own way of thinking. Her father had
taught her that Judaism was "not a faith, not a creed, but a way
of life." You cannot have Judaism in "full flower," she said, un-
less you have a normal human life built around Jewish principles.[20] By reconstituting the Jewish nation in Palestine, she held,
Jews could revitalize Judaism and reclaim a life of wholeness
and dignity.

Some evenings while the night school classes met, Henrietta and literary society members would sit together and talk
quietly about Zionist ideas and how they might make their
thoughts more widely known to Baltimore's German Jewish
community.[21] For the most part, that community identified with
Reform Judaism, which opposed Zionism. The Reform movement regarded Jews as a religion, not a nation. For them, America, not Palestine, stood as the longed-for Zion, a land of liberty
and the fulfillment of Jewish ideals. To spread the Zionist idea,
the literary group formed Hevrat Zion (Zion Association), one

of the first Zionist societies in the United States, and drew Henrietta and Harry Friedenwald into its fold, hoping their presence would inspire others. Rabbi Szold, who, like the Reform movement, had opposed Zionism earlier, became so attracted to it now that the society invited him to be its first speaker.

Two years later, in January 1896, Henrietta gave her first lecture on Zionism to the Baltimore section of the National Council of Jewish Women, a progressive organization dedicated to social service in the Jewish community. It seemed, in some ways, an odd venue. She had earlier turned down a national position in the organization, uncomfortable with the largely Reform orientation of its members. After its convention in November she wrote disapprovingly to her friend Elvira Solis that some members had spread "propaganda" for a Sunday instead of Saturday Sabbath—something she strongly disapproved of. But she also criticized the organization's leaders who entered a resolution calling for better observance of the traditional Saturday Sabbath. "But, holy horrors," Henrietta wrote, "is the observance of the Sabbath a fit matter for a resolution?"[22] Wasn't the Sabbath so central to Jewish tradition that it did not require resolutions or votes? And why didn't these women know that? Still, she agreed to deliver lectures to several council chapters; perhaps she could influence this women's organization.

She called the Baltimore chapter talk, the first in the group, "A Century of Jewish Thought." In it she traced what she regarded as stages of Jewish thought over the past hundred years. They began with "self-respect," introduced through the enlightened teachings of the German Jewish philosopher Moses Mendelssohn, moved on to "self-knowledge," gained from such scholars as Leopold Zunz delving deep into Jewish history, and culminated in "self-emancipation," which referred to the Zionist ideal of her day. That ideal pictured Jews living freely according to Jewish belief and ethics in their historic homeland, with the Hebrew language at the center of their activities. Hebrew, first emphasized by Mendelssohn and his circle, made up an essential component of Zionism, she maintained, for it provided the "key" not only to traditional Jewish texts but also to the "vast literary storehouse" that represented the "treasures" of the Jewish people.[23] Erudite and abstract, the talk fell on mostly deaf ears among the non-Zionist National Council women. After its publication by the Zion Association, one critic found it "almost too profound for an American woman."[24]

Szold always took pride in the fact that she delivered that Zionist talk a month before Theodor Herzl published his Zionist tract, *Der Judenstaat* ("The Jewish State"), and that she had been "converted" to Zionism even earlier. The fiery Herzl, born in the same year as Szold, came to Zionism via a totally different route than she. An assimilated Viennese Jew and correspondent for the *Neue Freie Presse*, a major newspaper in Vienna, he'd had little interest in Jewish affairs until he discovered the fierce antisemitism that existed in France and other European countries. With a great deal of energy, unrelenting determination, and natural charisma, he convened the first World Zionist Congress in Basel, Switzerland, in 1897. The program that emerged called for the establishment of an autonomous Jewish state that would be recognized by the international community.

The Basel congress stirred interest in Zionism among American Jews, whose membership in Zionist organizations had been exceedingly low. The story goes that when a delegate to that congress was asked if he knew of any American Zionists, he responded that there were only two: Rabbi Stephen Wise, a prominent New York Reform rabbi, and Henrietta Szold of Baltimore. "And they are both mad," he said.[25] In later years, Baltimoreans would boast that one of the only two official American delegates to that first congress came from their city—Rabbi Shepsel Schaffer, representing the Zion Association, in which Henrietta and her father were active.

Szold followed the proceedings in Basel and the congresses

that came afterward with great intensity and would actively participate in the American Zionist organizations that grew from them. But her brand of Zionism differed from Herzl's. Whereas he strove for a political state as a haven for the persecuted Jewish people, she spoke of the spiritual renewal of the Jewish nation on the soil of their ancestral lands. Her approach has been compared to that of Ahad Ha'am, pen name for the Hebrew essayist Asher Ginzberg, whose writings she had translated and greatly admired. Ahad Ha'am disagreed strongly with Herzl's political goals, preaching a form of Zionism in which the Land of Israel would serve as a center for the revival of a Jewish national culture. But Szold's insistence on the importance of maintaining traditional religious practices diverged from Ahad Ha'am's secularism. She also pictured broad Jewish settlement in Palestine, not limited to an elite community that would establish a cultural center.[26]

Szold's ideas about Zionism would be expanded and refined in the years ahead as she became ever more involved with life in Palestine. At their core, however, would remain the ideal she shared with the Russian intellectuals who occupied so much of her thoughts and feelings during this period: Judaism is more than a religion. It represents a complete system of living that could have its greatest fulfillment in the Land of Israel.

Henrietta Szold left the Russian Night School program in 1893, but it continued to operate until 1898. By then more than five thousand students had passed through its doors, and it had become a model for similar establishments in other parts of the country. In 1905, the Baltimore city government opened its own immigrant night schools as part of its public school system, as Szold had suggested in her *Sun* article. Decades later, on the steps of New York's City Hall, Mayor Fiorella LaGuardia ceremoniously gave Henrietta Szold the keys to the city in honor of her seventy-fifth birthday. "If I, the child of poor immigrant parents, am today mayor of New York, giving you the freedom of our city," he said, "it is because of you. Half a century ago you initiated that instrument of American democracy, the evening night school for the immigrant."[27]

Life as Henrietta had always known it changed in unexpected and difficult ways during the 1890s. After more than thirty years as spiritual leader of Oheb Shalom, Rabbi Szold was forced to retire, his pulpit taken over in 1892 by a young English-speaking rabbi. The now-prosperous congregation built an imposing new synagogue on Eutaw Place and aligned itself with the more extreme beliefs of the Reform movement that Henrietta and her father had tried so hard to keep at bay. Services were shortened, English translations substituted for Hebrew liturgy, and the prayer book Henrietta had helped Rabbi Szold develop replaced by the American Reform *Union Prayer Book*.[28] With his retirement came a substantial cut in salary, and three years later a chronic and painful bladder illness transformed the once vibrant rabbi into an invalid. A year after his retirement, tragedy struck the family, with the death of Sadie, the third of the living sisters. She had suffered for years from a debilitating form of rheumatic fever but had managed to live as normally as possible, even planning a wedding just before she became ill with pneumonia and passed away.

Helping her parents cope with their sadness and steeped in sorrow herself, Henrietta began nevertheless to look ahead to her future. She did not want to be a teacher forever, nor did she regard writing as a career, even though she had gained a name and a following for her many essays. For the past several years, she had been serving from her home as a volunteer on the publication committee of the Jewish Publication Society (JPS). Formed in 1888 after several earlier false starts, the society aimed to make Jewish literature and culture accessible to American readers. It had been put together by several Philadelphia Jewish leaders, known as "the Philadelphia group," and had headquarters in that city. But its major financial backing came from a New Yorker, Jacob Schiff, head of the banking firm Kuhn, Loeb & Company, one of the wealthiest Jews in America and, because of that wealth, one of the most powerful. Although he held no official position in the society, he had broad influence over the books it published and the directions it took. With his backing, Mayer Sulzberger, a prominent Philadelphia lawyer and judge, became chairman of the publication committee.

In her work as a voluntary member of that committee, Szold helped with translations and editing. Together with her old friend Cyrus Adler, also a committee member, she wrote a chapter on American Jewish history for the society's first publication, *Outlines of Jewish History*, by Lady Katie Magnus. She also edited the first volume of a popular five-volume *History of the Jews*, by Heinrich Graetz, which had been translated from German into English.[29] It was a logical step, then, for her to accept the society's offer in 1893 to become the first salaried secretary of the publication committee in charge of editorial responsibilities. She resigned from her various teaching positions, cut ties with the Russian night school, and, with great trepidation, left her beloved parents and the home she adored. A thirty-three-year-old single woman (a "spinster" in the parlance of the day), she moved to Philadelphia, now on her own for the first time in her life.

3

"Miss Szold" and "Dr. Ginzberg"

IN A LECTURE she gave to the immigrant women of Baltimore's Hebrew Literary Society, Henrietta Szold emphasized that above all, a woman's role was "to help your sons, your brothers, your husbands, to lead a noble, true life." Responding a few years later to a questionnaire titled "Woman in the Synagogue" published in the *Reform Advocate*, she stated her unequivocal belief that a "woman can best serve the interests of the synagogue by devoting herself to her home." If, however, there was not a man available to handle necessary administrative duties, a qualified woman could take on those responsibilites.[1] She hit a similar note in her talk to the Jewish Women's Congress at the Chicago World's Fair of 1893. Titled "What Judaism Has Done for Women," the talk extolled the spiritual values of biblical women such as Sarah and Rebekah, praising their traditional role in educating their children. But Szold also assured her audience that Judaism does not forbid women from assuming whatever duties and responsibilities they feel capable of. Only, she warned, "beware of forfeiting your dignity."[2]

As she embarked on her new career in Philadelphia, Henrietta had mixed feelings not only about leaving Baltimore but also about her position as a woman entering a man's world. Her lectures made clear that she believed in a woman's traditional role as the keeper of hearth and home and a helpmeet to the men in her life. But she did not have a son, brother, or husband to care for—or to care for her—or a home to maintain. Like other unmarried women she needed to enter the workforce and earn her own keep. She was well aware of her capabilities, but in the Victorian world she inhabited, she was also aware of the thin line she walked, fraught with the danger of appearing undignified.

Accordingly, she did not rent a room of her own, but lived with her parents' good friends Rabbi Marcus Jastrow and his family. The correspondence she'd had earlier with the eldest son, Morris, never materialized into the match their respective parents might have hoped for, but Rachel's marriage to the younger, Joseph, made the Jastrows almost relatives of Henrietta. From their Germantown home in Northwest Philadelphia, she took a train into town early every morning, usually returning late in the evening.

To her mind she maintained her dignity also by accepting a salary of only $1,000 a year (low even for those days) without quibble, although society records show she could have won at least $200 more had she bargained.[3] For that remuneration, her contract called for her to prepare manuscripts for publication, correspond with authors, do translations as needed, keep the society in the public eye, proofread, maintain schedules, work with the printer, and perform the dozens of other duties an editor assumes. In fact, in subsequent years, people who held that position at JPS did bear the title of "editor," as did heads of contemporary publishing houses. But Szold didn't object to being the "secretary"—somehow it went with her womanhood—any more than she did (at least openly) to the fact that she rarely received credit for the long hours and hard work she invested in every book published. Moreover, she accepted the arrangement in which the publication committee, and not she, made final decisions about books published. She attended the committee's monthly meetings and wrote the minutes, while each member assigned a suggested book reported on it and the committee as a whole decided whether to publish it. Then the manuscript was turned over to her to put into publishable shape.

"If I were a man," she wrote to one of her relatives, "I would make my voice heard." Instead, when she felt especially put upon, she complained to friends and family members but considered herself "bound by sexual limitations" from speaking out to the society leadership.[4]

Szold reported directly to Mayer Sulzberger, chairman of the publication committee. A brilliant attorney, Sulzberger had a short temper, a large dollop of arrogance, and the unwavering conviction that he was never wrong. Szold called him "the Grand Mogul." It took eight years of her working at the society before he had a word of praise for her. Those words came at the society's tenth anniversary celebration in 1898, when, to her surprise, the organization honored her. Sulzberger spoke glowingly of her excellence in the many areas of her work, from editing to translating to dealing with authors. Thrilled with his compliments, she wrote home: "To me, it was the reward of my work, reward sufficient for two times as much work."[5] At this point in her life, a pat on the head from a difficult boss could make up for many of the job's deficiencies.

That job spanned a wide range of projects. Outstanding among them was the 492-page index she prepared for Graetz's *History of the Jews*. She had already improved the English translation of the five-volume work, and this masterful sixth volume, complete with tables and maps, made the popular history more accessible than ever to both scholars and laypeople. Similarly, she published several books on Zionism that familiarized the general public with that movement. Altogether during her years at the society, she edited more than sixty books. They included children's textbooks along with works of Jewish history, ethics, and philosophy, at least ten of which she also translated from German or French into English. Aside from her own assignments, she participated voluntarily in preparing the JPS Bible translation from Hebrew into English, a huge project that extended over several years. According to historian Jonathan Sarna, she proofread the entire text no fewer than twelve times.[6]

Much later she would say that the books the society chose to publish were "pedantic" and "behind the times" because the organization was "afraid of life" and did not fully use its "possibilities."[7] In spite of such criticism, she derived much satisfaction at the time from the work she did. She especially enjoyed meeting authors, many of whom expressed gratitude for her help. And while she rarely made demands for herself, she did not hesitate to speak out in defense of her authors. When the *Nation* ran a negative review of Richard Gottheil's book *Zionism*, she sent a long letter to the editor pointing out errors in the review. The book was part of a Jewish Publication Society series (never completed) analyzing major movements in Jewish history. Gottheil, son of a well-known Reform rabbi, Gustav Gottheil, and a professor at Columbia University, had written an essay on Zionism for the *Jewish Encyclopedia* that he expanded for the book. Criticizing the reviewer's use of the term *anti-Zionism* for those who disagreed with Gottheil, Szold wrote that "though there may be non-Zionism, there cannot be anti-Zionism. Anti-Zionism is assimilation and assimilation is Jewish self-negation."[8]

The chore Szold found most onerous required preparing the annual *American Jewish Yearbook* for publication. A vast reference work, the *Yearbook* presented a smorgasbord of information about life in the North American Jewish world. Among other things, it included hundreds of pages of directories of local and national Jewish organizations, statistics about every American Jewish community, lists of periodicals, and long articles about contemporary issues. Szold wrote several of those articles as well as a regular feature reviewing the year's major events. As important as each volume was, its production could be sheer drudgery, "hack work," Szold told a friend, requiring dozens of hours of extra labor and skipped vacations, with no extra pay for any of it.[9]

Cyrus Adler's name appears as editor of the first volume, 1899–1900, with no mention of Szold, although she probably prepared most of the material in it. In the next several volumes, as editor, he thanks her for her help but does not share the title with her until volume 6, 1904–5, when they are listed as co-editors. She became sole editor in 1906 for the following two years. After that, the American Jewish Committee took over preparing the *Yearbook*. Even so, she continued to help the subsequent editor for several years.

"You are a chump," her youngest sister, Adele, wrote to her, referencing the many things Henrietta did for the society without pay. "Do stop killing yourself."[10] But "killing herself" was how Henrietta worked: no task was too small for her attention, no toil too difficult, whether she was compensated for her labor or not.

Rabbi Szold became seriously ill in 1895 and would remain incapacitated for much of the next seven years, spending most of his waking hours in a wheelchair. At first Henrietta took time off work to help care for him, but as she gradually spent more and more time at his bedside, bringing editorial material with her, she eventually moved back to work from the family home permanently. Circumstances required her to be in Baltimore again, no longer on her own but with her parents, where she always felt most comfortable. She was there in 1898, assisting her mother in relocating to a new, smaller house on Callow Avenue, where the air was better for the rabbi than downtown on Lombard Street, and she was there a year later when Rabbi Szold's former congregation turned out to honor him on his seventieth birthday. But she was not in the room when his life ended in July 1902, in the summer cottage the family rented in Berkeley Springs, West Virginia. She had been tending him day and night but had gone to bed for a short rest when her mother woke her to say that he had died.

The death of her father, her mentor and the center of her universe for so much of her life, shattered Henrietta, and the fact that she had not been with him in his last moments tortured her for months. Overwhelmed with grief, she could barely function. Her mother, who over the years had coped stoically with the death of four daughters, handled the loss of her husband with the same inner strength, but she was concerned about her elder daughter's unending despair. She suggested that Henrietta edit the articles and books her father had not completed, and perhaps prepare them for publication. Henrietta jumped at the idea, but with reservations. She did not feel qualified to work on the rabbi's scholarly writings without further training in the Bible and various areas of rabbinics. The two agreed that the place to gain the education she needed was the Jewish Theological Seminary of America in New York, training school for Conservative rabbis. Founded in 1886, the seminary had been reorganized in 1902 with financial backing from Jacob Schiff and other wealthy New Yorkers. Rabbi Szold had worked with some of the scholars there, and through her position at the Jewish Publication Society, Henrietta had her own connections— Cyrus Adler presided over the seminary's board of trustees and Mayer Sulzberger served on it, as did several authors whose writings she had edited. Most important, she had a warm relationship with Dr. Solomon Schechter, head of the reorganized seminary.

A renowned scholar at Cambridge University, Schechter had discovered the Cairo Genizah, a hidden storehouse of hundreds of thousands of fragments of early Hebrew manuscripts and scrolls that opened up a world of knowledge of ancient and medieval Jewish texts. His presence enhanced the seminary's prestige, and his strong personality and vast knowledge shaped it for many years. Henrietta had met Schechter in 1895, when he was lecturing in Philadelphia. He invited her to supper and then offhandedly invited himself to stay at her parents' home in Baltimore, where he was to speak at Johns Hopkins University. Taken by surprise, Henrietta wrote to her parents apologetically, "I made no advances to Dr. Schechter about coming to our house. He did all the talking about it, and consequently will come with me Tuesday evening." She went on to say that he would be a "troublesome" guest because he demanded attention "all the time," and was so absent-minded that he had been seen wearing "one grey and one brown stocking." Nevertheless, she assured her parents that he was a "lamb" and they would enjoy him.[11] For his part, after his visit, Schechter wrote to his wife, Mathilde, that Henrietta was "an excellent Jewish scholar, but very nice and feminine."[12] The two corresponded after that, and when Schechter decided to leave Cambridge and become president of the Jewish Theological Seminary, he wrote to Henrietta to tell her that news.

It made sense, then, for her to request permission from Schechter to study at his all-male institution as a special student. He agreed, but noted that he would have to consult his board of trustees. That body also gave its consent, with the understanding that although she could take a full course, she could not pursue a rabbinic degree.[13] It might seem strange for an institution that would not even raise the issue of ordaining women as rabbis for another seventy years to suppose that she might consider entering the rabbinate there. But the subject was in the air at this time. In 1890, on the eve of Yom Kippur, a charismatic woman named Ray Frank preached at a religious service in Spokane, Washington. Even though she was not a rabbi, the press dubbed her "the girl rabbi of the golden west." A few years later, when she enrolled in Hebrew Union College, the Reform rabbinical school, to further her education, its president, Rabbi Isaac Mayer Wise, encouraged her to study for the rabbinate. However, she showed no interest in doing so, leaving after only one semester, although she continued preaching.[14] The 1897 symposium "Woman in the Synagogue" in which Henrietta Szold had participated followed in the spirit of Frank and the Reform movement. That questionnaire had actually been devised by a well-known Reform rabbi and publicist, Emil G. Hirsch. Henrietta Szold had never expressed a desire to be a rabbi, but with the concept floating around, the seminary leaders wanted to distinguish themselves definitively from American Reformers on this subject as on so many others.

Szold, who always regretted not having had a college education, looked forward to this opportunity to study Jewish texts at the graduate level. In 1901, she had addressed the graduating class of Western High School, her alma mater, recalling how rare it had been twenty-four years earlier for members of her class to continue their education, compared to the many college choices currently opening up for female high school graduates. She appealed to these young women to get as thorough an education as they could to equip them for the complex world ahead of them, but to pay attention also to their spiritual education, meaning their way of living in that world.[15] Now she herself was to receive an advanced education and needed to find her own place in the rarified scholarly world she was entering. She received permission from Judge Sulzberger to continue her JPS duties in New York, although he cautioned her that she was undertaking a heavy load.

In the fall of 1903 she, her mother, and her sister Adele— who lived with them until she married in 1906—moved into an apartment on the third floor of a building with a brownstone front on Morningside Heights and 123rd Street—528 West 123rd Street—diagonally across from where the seminary then stood. They would soon be joined by their housekeeper, Anna. The Schechters lived nearby and Henrietta saw them frequently, often as a luncheon or dinner guest at their home, or at seminary Sabbath services. She became close to Mathilde Schechter, a learned and talented woman who had translated the works of the poet Heinrich Heine from German into English and helped her husband translate his books. For all her education, however, Mathilde centered her life on her family and domestic responsibilities. Known for her hospitality, she made the Schechter home a gathering place for scholars, students, and select community members, where "so many, many of us basked and were transformed," Szold wrote to the Schechters' son years later.[16]

Solomon Schechter recruited as his faculty the elite of European Jewish scholars, among them Louis Ginzberg, a brilliant Talmudist, Israel Friedlaender, an expert in biblical studies, and Alexander Marx, a noted historian. Marx became the seminary's first librarian and, with Schechter, assembled a collection of rare books and manuscripts that gave the seminary the most important Judaica library in America. Whereas wealthy German Jews like Jacob Schiff and Felix Warburg, who had helped finance the seminary, were part of a group known to each other as "our crowd," the seminary faculty made up a different kind of "crowd."[17] Its members stood at the pinnacle of New York Jewish scholarship. Highly respected in the academic world, they produced articles and books that would become classics in their fields. Yet, with their thick foreign accents, these lionized professors had trouble communicating in English with their students.

Henrietta Szold, who understood their German perfectly, came to their rescue. Soon after enrolling at the seminary, she began holding informal classes in the English language for Marx and Friedlaender in her home on Saturday evenings. Eventually Ginzberg also joined the group. Schechter did not become part of the class, but he gave Szold letters he wrote to edit and translate into English, and she helped him in preparing the second series of his book *Studies in Judaism.* As with the Jewish Publication Society, she expected no special recognition and asked for no payment for her work or for the many hours of assistance she gave faculty members.

She was a model student, diligently attending classes during her three years at the seminary, just as full-time rabbinical students did. In the words of scholar Mel Scult, with her knowledge and education, she became in essence the first female rabbi in the Conservative movement, although, of course, she was not ordained.[18] Indeed, with her extensive background, she found the lectures almost too easy at first, writing to Elvira that "one almost feels as though one could have delivered them oneself."[19] With time she learned to pick the lectures that most interested her, skipping a class by Israel Friedlaender, for example, to attend one on theology by Solomon Schechter. Mordecai Kaplan, who would become principal of the seminary's Teacher's Institute (and later the founder of Reconstructionist Judaism), remembered with some pride sitting next to her in that and other Schechter classes. He believed that she had recommended him for his position at the Teacher's Institute.[20]

She seemed to enjoy herself during those early seminary years. In her forties, some twenty years older than most of the other students, she still fit easily into their circles of friendship. One graduate of the seminary, a Boston rabbi, recalled that he and the others regarded her as a "savant" and looked upon her with "awe" because of her knowledge, yet they also saw her as "one of the boys," with her "unassuming and endearing manner" and her willingness to help them with their studies when needed.[21] She was as comfortable with the students as they were with her. She did not, however, attend the formal dinners the seminary held for students, probably feeling it was not quite proper for a woman to be in a social situation with all men.[22] But she did participate in the informal study groups several professors held. One of the groups she joined, led by Israel Friedlaender, focused on the essays of Ahad Ha'am, one of her Zionist heroes.[23] A member of that group, Judah Magnes, then a young Reform rabbi, would become her close lifelong friend and collaborator.

And she enjoyed living in New York. "I do some Seminary work daily, and every evening I take a walk along Riverside [Drive]," she wrote Elvira one summer, "a walk whose beauties seem to me to be inexhaustible. . . . I love New York, the mild pleasures of the softly-lighted view, and the cozy comforts of our tiny tenement."[24]

During all the years Szold taught school and her early years working at the Jewish Publication Society, she continued to write essays on a wide range of subjects. She contributed fifteen biographical articles on Jewish women throughout history to the monumental *Jewish Encyclopedia* that Funk and Wagnalls was developing, wrote numerous pieces for the *American Jewish Yearbook* she also edited, and published a variety of book reviews in Jewish journals. Then, during the seminary years, most of the original writing stopped. She wrote an article for the *Hebrew Standard* on the history of Jewish women's liturgy called "What Our Grandmothers Read," but did not follow through on Schechter's suggestion for a broader study in book form of Jewish women's literature during the Middle Ages. Certainly, holding a full-time job and being a full-time student was more than enough pressure for one person. Yet there seems to have been another barrier stopping this woman for whom overworking was a way of life. Always self-conscious about her lack of a college degree in spite of her prodigious intellectual abilities, she might have felt especially insecure surrounded by world-famous scholars. So, instead of writing her own works, she translated those of faculty members, edited their letters, and tutored them in English.[25] And for one professor, Louis Ginzberg, she also translated and organized lecture notes and book manuscripts, and assisted in creating his magnum opus, *Legends of the Jews*.

Much has been written about Henrietta Szold's love for Louis Ginzberg, and there is still disagreement about whether he behaved toward her as a cad, callous and self-serving, or if she imagined feelings he did not pretend to have. The matter may never be resolved. But at the time, her preoccupation with him consumed so much of her emotional and mental life that little remained of either for original writing, except in the letters she wrote him and the journal she kept from 1908 to 1909, obsessively reviewing every detail of their relationship.[26]

Perhaps he evoked memories of her father, with his slight frame, full head of somewhat unruly hair, and expressive eyes (Ginzberg's blue). Or perhaps his reputation for brilliance drew her to him even before they met—genius can be as much of an aphrodisiac in intellectual circles as power is in the political sphere. But from the moment she laid eyes on him, she was smitten, and puzzled by her own impulsive behavior. Why, she asked herself over and over, instead of simply nodding, had she extended her hand to him on only their second meeting, a familiarity a proper woman would not ordinarily do? Why had she almost brusquely turned him down when he asked her to translate the eulogy he had written in German on the death of Rabbi Marcus Jastrow, her close family friend, but then soon thereafter agreed to do so? Why had she avoided attending his Talmud class, assuming he did not want a woman there, although he had not said that, and indeed welcomed her into it when she did go? Was she so frightened by the "strange attraction" he exerted on her that she found herself behaving irrationally?[27]

Forty-three years old when she entered the seminary, Szold was like a naive teenager with her first crush in regard to Ginzberg; excited, confused, and self-reprimanding. She'd had male friends before; she'd had long and intricate correspondences with Harry Friedenwald and Morris Jastrow. But never before had she felt herself in love the way she did now, never before experienced that stirring sense of her own sexuality. Sadly, at age forty-three she was also thirteen years older than the man she loved, a fact she reminded herself of again and again. I'm too old, she told herself. My hair is turning gray, my face is lined. I lack the "round contours, the fresh color, the light laugh" of young women.[28] And still, she suffered at every attention he paid to a young woman, even to her sister Adele, even after Adele's marriage. She felt jealous of Adele's youth, of all youth, and was ashamed of herself for those feelings.

Adding to the turmoil within her, the seminary faculty members she liked most began to marry. "Both Dr. Marx and Dr. Friedlaender will return with their wives," she wrote to Elvira a bit wistfully at the beginning of the 1905 semester. "The Seminary circles are growing considerably."[29] Only Louis Ginzberg remained a bachelor, seemingly making him more available—yet, she warned herself, unavailable to her.

She had been glad in her early seminary months that Ginzberg was not in the informal English class she held for Marx and Friedlaender. But one spring Saturday, after she did not appear at seminary services in the morning because of an earache, the two professors called on her, bringing Ginzberg with them. She felt obliged then to invite him to join the others for supper and class in the evening, and after that she accepted him in her class as a regular. She dated her difficulties from that time on— her struggles, as their friendship grew, to control her emotions, or at the least conceal them from the man she adored.

On his end, with their expanding friendship, he felt comfortable turning to her for help. One day he asked her to write a letter for him in English. Another time he gave her his lecture notes to organize and put into good English, a practice he would then repeat often. A little later he requested that she meet with him regularly at the end of class to correct errors he had made in speaking. Eventually they worked together on articles and books he was writing, she translating for him from Hebrew or German, reading proofs, editing and sharpening what he wrote or dictated, and having his manuscripts typed for him. Sometimes he borrowed money from her to buy cigars or pay a typist, forgetting to repay her.

With each request he made of her—without ever saying thank you—she thrilled to the intimacy she imagined it represented. She happily labored long hours for him, even if that meant going without sleep to complete her JPS work. Rarely did she indicate to him just how long those hours were.

She spoke to no one about her feelings for him. One day, however, Adele found her weeping after he had left for a summer trip to Europe, and Henrietta poured out her heart. And one day she put her feelings in a letter to him. "Dearest Friend," she began. Then she told him that "my whole happiness lies with you" and that until he had awakened her soul "it had known only filial passion." She told him that a woman's love was an "opportunity for self-effacement," that she more than loved him, she worshiped him. Even so—in a tsunami of self-pity—she offered to give him up for a "sprightly young creature" more appropriate to his age, although in doing so she doomed herself to unhappiness for the rest of her life. She wrote all these things, and more, in her letter, dated it July 1905, folded it neatly, and put it in a drawer, never to be sent.[30]

Over the course of time she and Ginzberg developed personal routines. At first he came to her home on Tuesdays to work with her on his lectures, usually staying for dinner or having lunch before his classes and returning afterward. Soon Tuesdays expanded into Wednesdays and then almost the entire week. On

Sunday afternoons they took long walks on Riverside Drive overlooking the Hudson River. On one cold windy day, she could not keep a veil she wore on her head. He asked her to sit down on a bench, leaned over, and tied the veil tightly to hold it in place. When she returned home, she carefully took the veil off without opening the knot he had made, putting it away in a drawer where she could stroke it from time to time.

The walks expanded later; it became routine for them to stroll on Shabbat after services at the seminary synagogue. During the services, his eyes would seek her out, she would nod, and both would leave together at the end to head toward Riverside Drive or to Morningside Park east of the seminary. Sometimes while they walked, he read to her from a manuscript in progress. Often they ambled along quietly or sat on a bench saying nothing, a silent meeting of minds, as she saw it, that required no speech between them.

During the summer, Ginzberg vacationed in Tannersville in the Catskill Mountains in upstate New York or traveled abroad to do research in various European archives or to visit his parents in Amsterdam. He wrote to Szold regularly when he left town and she responded immediately. In several of his letters he lightheartedly demeaned women: they frequently changed their minds; they couldn't master more than one strong feeling at a time; they—specifically in this case "well-fed and well-dressed Jewesses" he saw vacationing—strutted around in an ostentatious way.[31] None of these descriptions seemed to distress Szold, whose heart simply leapt at every communication from him.

Nor did it bother her that Ginzberg did not exhibit as strong a passion for Zionism as she did. She had longed to attend the Zionist Congress in Basel in 1905, but could not get away from her JPS duties. He had been elected as a delegate but chose not to attend because he did not belong to any Zionist organizations. He did join her, however, in criticizing the wealthy Jacob Schiff who, like other Reform leaders, opposed Zionism as anti-American. Can anyone "dare remain a Zionist," she wrote sarcastically after the congress of 1907, "since the great and only Mr. Schiff has spoken." Ginzberg responded, describing Schiff as "a great financier and a small man."[32]

In later letters Ginzberg encouraged Szold to speak up about how the Jewish Publication Society overworked her, and to demand that she have her duties more clearly defined. She should not be expected to be a *maedchen für alles* (a woman for all jobs): secretary, translator, author, and so on, he advised.[33] He did not suggest, however, that she limit the number of hours she devoted to the JPS's major project, his *Legends of the Jews*, which she was translating, and which grew over the years from one volume to a prospective seven.

For three years, as best she could, Szold kept a lid on her feelings, accepting the idea that if she and Ginzberg could continue as just friendly companions forever, that would be fine with her. In 1906, she left the seminary but remained part of its milieu. She continued to devote many hours to helping Ginzberg with his lectures and books. A year later their relationship seemed to change. Ginzberg's father became severely ill with cancer of the throat, and Ginzberg decided to spend five months in Amsterdam with his family. Brokenhearted at the long separation ahead, Szold could barely hold back her tears as she and others walked him to the dock before he left. But their correspondence became longer and more intimate during his absence, and he let her know how much her letters meant to him in this difficult period.

When his father died in July 1907, she wrote to him every day during the seven days of shiva and, as his son Eli would later say, "his defenses broke."[34] Torn with grief and guilt, Ginzberg bared his soul to Szold. His father had hoped his son would become a *gaon*, the learned leader of a great yeshiva, and not the modern scholar he was, he told her. Pious in the extreme, the older man also had been disappointed in Ginzberg's laxity in religious observance—had, in fact, once caught him with money in his pocket on the Sabbath. Now Ginzberg wondered sorrowfully whether his presence had helped or hurt his father in the dying man's last days. Szold tried to comfort him, writing of her own beloved father's death and how, in her grief afterward, for a while she could not even recall the features of his face.[35]

After Ginzberg returned to New York in the fall, the two drew closer than ever—their meals at her home, their long walks and shared silences, their constant work on his lectures and books increased and intensified. Szold felt a difference in their relationship now. She saw in his face a softer look when he gazed at her, a "lovelight," she called it, and after all the years of exerting as much self-control as she could muster, she gave in to her deepest yearnings. "He loves me!" she concluded, no matter her age.[36] Throughout the winter and spring she carried that secret joy within her. In the summer, he went abroad as usual, and though his letters were not as plentiful as they had been in other years, she found sufficient warmth in some of them to keep her heart singing. He also sent her a book about Jewish literature, inscribed "To my dear friend, Miss Szold." She was transported by the word *dear*. It seemed more significant here than in their ordinary exchange of letters.[37]

On the Tuesday of his return he came to see her. It was October 20, 1908. He asked her to accompany him into another room, away from the desk where she had been working with an assistant. "You will be surprised to hear that I am engaged," he said, and the room began to whirl around her as she tried to keep from falling or fainting. Years earlier, whenever he went abroad she would imagine him returning engaged to be married, and she would steel herself for that possibility. But not this year, not when they had spent so many wonderful hours together, not when she had seen the lovelight in his eyes. Somehow she managed to mumble the right responses, and when he asked her to write to his fiancée—cruelly, she later decided—she agreed, not knowing what else to do.

He had first seen Adele Katzenstein sitting in the women's gallery of the synagogue in Berlin he attended with his friend Isadore Wechsler. Later he saw her again at the Wechsler home. She was beautiful, from an Orthodox family, domestic rather than intellectual, lively, and twenty-two. Within two weeks he had proposed marriage and she had accepted. In Henrietta's congratulatory letter (written in German because Adele knew no English), she wrote of how fortunate Adele was to have "won the love of such an extraordinary man," and indicated that she, Henrietta, could speak from knowledge, because she had been "in almost daily contact with him for five years."[38] She secretly hoped Adele would read between the lines and understand how great a sacrifice Henrietta was making in giving up this "extraordinary man." And Adele probably read Henrietta's letter just as it was intended; even at her young age, she was not a naïf. When Ginzberg first told her about Henrietta, she immediately asked whether there was anything more than friendship between them. Now, in a return letter, she told Henrietta to ask Ginzberg for a photo of the engaged couple she had sent him for Henrietta to have. And she referred to him in the letter as her *Schatzilein*, her small treasure.[39] She was taking no chances in securing her turf.

For three weeks after his revelation, Ginzberg continued to eat at the Szold home, invite Henrietta for walks, and take for granted her devotion to his works in progress, as if nothing had changed. All the while she suffered and agonized. Had he ever loved her? Had he not seen how she felt about him? And—in days of deepest despair—how could she go on living? When she finally arranged a meeting to confront him with her feelings, he seemed utterly surprised. Yes, he had regarded theirs as an extraordinary friendship, he said, but not a romance. Had the situation been reversed, he insisted, he would have been happy for her, his best friend, as he had believed she would be for him. Even now he would be content to continue their friendship on the same basis as before. When he realized that would not happen, he assured her that with her moral strength she would "get over it." Then he left.

"Today it is four weeks since my only real happiness in life was killed by a single word," Szold wrote about a week later, beginning the journal that would chronicle in minute detail every aspect of her relationship with Louis Ginzberg.[40]

What, then, are we to make of that relationship? Was Ginzberg a cad? Had he deceived and exploited Szold? Certainly Ginzberg's engagement took the seminary community by surprise. Over the years, faculty members had frequently invited Szold and Ginzberg to their homes together, treating them like a couple. In fact, when Alexander Marx learned of Ginzberg's engagement, he assumed it must have come about only after a rejection from Szold. The Schechters, to whom Szold detailed her misery, proffered constant sympathy, and it was to distract her that Solomon Schechter suggested she write the book on women's devotional literature, an idea she turned down. As Szold told more people her story and word spread throughout the seminary and beyond, the overarching feeling was that Ginzberg had led her on, used her shamelessly to further his own work, and humiliated her with his sudden engagement to another woman. Szold's family shared that outlook. Her mother, whose hospitality and cooking Ginzberg had enjoyed, felt betrayed and pained by her daughter's suffering.

Ginzberg's family saw the matter differently. While expressing sympathy for Szold, his son Eli described the relationship as an "exceptional friendship" and nothing more in the biography he wrote of his father. Louis Ginzberg had turned to Szold for solace after his father died, but as a cherished friend, not a potential marriage partner, Eli maintained.[41] Other relatives have pointed out that through five years of friendship and a far-reaching correspondence, the two never went beyond "Miss Szold" and "Dr. Ginzberg" in addressing one another or included any intimacy in their letter closings. While it is true that strict protocol governed personal relations in the early 1900s, they argue, one might have expected Ginzberg, at least, to write some words of endearment if he felt that way about her. In contrast, from the first, Adele's letters to Ginzberg (which remain within the family) brim with passion and sensuality. She never addressed him, either in writing or in speech, as Dr. Ginzberg. To her he was always Schatzi.[42]

About two weeks after Szold's confessional meeting with Ginzberg, she received a note from him requesting permission to thank her publicly for her "kind assistance" on his book *Geonica*, a work she had labored on through the years, translating, editing, and proofreading. She had done the work on her own time—the seminary, not JPS would publish the book—but like so much else she did for Ginzberg, she regarded it as a labor of love. Now she turned him down. She did not want her name to be associated with his in any way. Later, but only after a great deal of persuasion by her family, she agreed to have her name included as the translator of the first volume of Ginzberg's *Legends*, which she had slaved over.

In the early spring, Szold asked the Jewish Publication Society for a six-month leave of absence. She felt emotionally drained from the Ginzberg affair and needed time away. She recognized also that she had exhausted herself with the heavy burden of work she had been carrying for the society and from the many tasks she had undertaken gratis for the seminary faculty and students while she attended classes there—"the more fool I," she wrote in one of her journal entries.[43] It would be some time before she became strong enough to stand on her own, free of exploitation and with the dignity she deserved, but the seeds of a renewal existed.

The JPS board approved her leave, with pay, and she and

her mother began planning a tour of Europe. Some weeks before they were to leave, the society gave her a gift of $500. In a
heartfelt thank-you letter to Cyrus Adler, she labeled the money
her "Palestine Fund," to be used to extend the European trip
on to Palestine.[44] The two women left on July 30, 1909. Alas,
because of scheduling needs, she would be sent the uncorrected
proofs of Ginzberg's second volume of *Legends* to be reviewed
while they traveled.[45] She was far from liberated from him.

4

Travels and Travails

DURING SZOLD'S YEARS in New York, she received proposals of marriage from three men, the most recent just a few months before she and her mother, Sophie, sailed to Europe. The men were respectable enough, all widowers seeking companions for themselves and/or mothers for their children. She turned each of them down without a second thought; to her mind she had become an *agunah*, the abandoned "wife" of Louis Ginzberg. No other man interested her. Now, on board the S.S. *California* en route to Glasgow, she hoped the lovely stateroom she and her mother shared and the attractive array of passengers would heal the self-torture about Ginzberg she had endured for months. Yet not long into the journey, she wrote in her travel diary that the "vast unity of the sea has not yet brought serenity, as all predicted."[1]

From Glasgow and then Edinburgh, the two women traveled to England, stopping at Cambridge, where they saw the house Dr. Schechter had lived in, before going on to a boarding house in London, which made Henrietta think of Dickens, whose writings she had consumed as a young woman. But even as she enjoyed the city and its surroundings, her mind fled back to her sorrow. She had brought with her the corrected proofs of a book she was editing about the first-century philosopher Philo Judaeus that Norman Bentwich had written. His parents, prominent British Zionists, had invited her and her mother to their luxurious country house near the ocean, along with their daughter Lilian and her husband, Professor Israel Friedlaender, both of whom Henrietta knew well from the seminary. Ginzberg had been married quietly in London in May, aware of the seminary gossip and disapproval of his treatment of Szold. The Friedlaenders, among the small number of his New York acquaintances invited to the wedding, reported their impressions of the event to the Szolds. Adele, the bride, they said, was attractive and clever enough to question the seriousness of Ginzberg's intentions when he began his whirlwind courtship of her, something Henrietta berated herself for not having done in the days when he took up so much of her time. Friedlaender also criticized Ginzberg's hasty engagement, and Henrietta wondered to herself whether the haste had been to get away from her.[2]

Back in London, the proofs of Ginzberg's *Legends* volume arrived for her to correct. "I cannot stand the sight of his handwriting," she wrote in her diary.[3] Still, she could not shake his image from her head as she and her mother made their way through Europe. Sometimes she would dream about him, and sometimes she seemed actually to hear his voice telling her she would "get over" her feelings for him. Fortunately, as they moved on to Paris, Vienna, and various parts of Hungary, where their many relatives lived, she managed to distract herself with the sights and with family sagas. She remembered the trip she had made twenty-eight years earlier with her father, going to some of the same places, seeing some of the same people. At that time a cousin, Ignatz, had tried to prevail upon her to stay on for a year after her father left—there had even been some speculation in the family that the two cousins might marry one day. But when her father reminded her of her duty to her younger sisters, she had left with him. Now all the cousins were married, with large, bustling families of their own, and nobody remembered the possibilities of long ago.

Henrietta had planned the women's trip from Europe to Palestine with visits first to Constantinople, Beirut, Damascus, and other cities of the East to get a flavor of the "Orient" before moving on. Touring in those places she remarked about the "unspeakable filth and disease that meet the eye at every turn in the cities," but also marveled at "the riot of costumes, colors, and jewels that fills the courts."[4] As picturesque and colorful as these scenes were, she worried that she might discover little difference between Arabs in these Middle Eastern towns and Jews in the Holy Land. When she did get to Palestine she concluded happily that in spite of rampant poverty in a number of Jewish areas she visited, the people there had within them a "new spirit," a concern about Jewishness that would "hearten the Zionist."[5] This was a land, she would report when she returned to the States, "of living workers," "a land of idealists," "a land of hopers," "a land where there are men . . . who are building up the possibilities of human life there."[6]

Most of her enthusiasm and optimism came from going to agricultural settlements spread throughout the country. Following a different route from the one tourists to the Holy Land usually took, entering through Jaffa and going directly to Jerusalem, the women entered from the north, the Galilee, and worked their way south so they could visit numbers of those settlements and see the countryside before arriving in Jerusalem. Many of the settlements they saw had originally been created in the late 1800s by groups of dedicated young people. Some of the first people to arrive came from Russia with an association

called BILU, an acronym for Beit Yaakov Lechu Venelcha—
"House of Jacob Let Us Go Up." Larger groups belonged to the
Hovevei Zion, Lovers of Zion, the organization Szold's Baltimore Russians had supported. These early pioneers—"colonists,"
as Szold called them—were indeed the "idealists" and "hopers"
she so admired. Unfortunately, large numbers of them lacked
agricultural training or preparation for the hard physical labor
needed to cultivate the desolate land. Many became disillusioned
or sick with malaria and returned to their homes; many others
died of exhaustion or hunger and illness. Those who remained
depended to a great extent on the largesse of the Parisian banker
Baron Edmond de Rothschild to sustain them. Still, by dint of
courage and determination, the early settlers managed to establish some thirty permanent agricultural villages. Szold and
her mother visited fourteen of them during their trip.

Their guide was Israel Shochat, one of the creators of
Hashomer, a defense group of Jewish watchmen to protect the
settlements. Szold had met his wife Manya in the States a few
years earlier, and the two had become fast friends in spite of
very different personalities. A radical feminist and labor union-
ist, Manya had been a revolutionist in Russia. One of the few
female members of Hashomer, she became a familiar figure in
the country, riding on her horse from place to place dressed in
the flowing headpiece and robes of a Bedouin man. Israel seemed
colorless next to her, yet he had his own story: when a university student in Russia, he had run away from home to live in
Palestine, earning his living in the settlements as a day laborer.
He and Manya had established the collective of Sejera in the
Galilee.[7] She was currently in Europe trying to raise money for
it, so Israel took the women to see it. They traveled there and
during the rest of their journey through the settlements in a
horse-drawn wagon, an uncomfortable and potentially dangerous mode of transportation as it careened around pitted, muddy,
or rock-filled roads. Sejera was tiny, its small farmhouses dot-

ting each side of the one street running through it. The settlement was surrounded by cultivated fields where its inhabitants worked, growing wheat and barley and raising cattle.

At Zichron Yaakov, one of the largest agricultural settlements they visited, they attended Shabbat services in a good-sized synagogue and left impressed by the intensity of discussion among the settlers afterward about some points of Jewish law. A man in the village looked so much like the late Rabbi Szold, that Henrietta almost fainted when she saw him, but she could not summon up the courage to speak to him and ask if they might be related. A rather depressing-looking settlement on the whole, Zichron had poor housing and an unclean hospital, but it boasted vineyards planted by Baron de Rothschild, as did Rishon le Zion, the second settlement built in the country (Petach Tikva was the first) and one of the more developed ones. The Szolds spent time at Petach Tikva, Hadera, Meir Shfeya, Rehobot, and other settlements that would become legendary in Israeli history. At one stop, a settler said to Henrietta, "What right have you to live in America? You are interested in Palestine. Your place is here."[8] American Jews would hear sentiments like that for decades to come. Szold would be among the minority who responded to them with action.

Henrietta found the "obstinacy" of the settlers in speaking Hebrew, a language few had grown up with, deeply moving. On the negative side, she felt deeply disturbed by the settlers' use of fellaheen, Arab laborers, to work their fields. "That was my purest disappointment in the colonies," she wrote to Mayer Sulzberger, "the small number of Jewish workmen, the large number of fellaheen."[9] It would take the next wave of pioneers— people like David Ben-Gurion and Yitzhak Ben-Zvi—to make "Hebrew labor" fundamental to their ideal of building the land, insisting that Jews do their own hard labor on the farms and kibbutzim that soon started sprouting everywhere. At the time of their visit, Henrietta and her mother witnessed only the beginnings of Jewish settlements and the many difficulties that came with them.

In the cities they visited, particularly Jaffa and then Jerusalem, their final destination in the Holy Land, problems revolved mainly around unclean conditions: open-air markets with filthy stalls dense with flies; homes lacking basic sanitary facilities; children blinded by trachoma because of the swarms of flies that flocked against their eyes. Sophie wept several times at the unnecessary blindness and the uneducated townspeople who paid little attention to fundamental matters of cleanliness and health. In words that have often been credited with influencing the direction her daughter's life would take, she suggested more than once that a woman's study group Henrietta belonged to should devote its attention to practical work in Palestine rather than reading Jewish writers and discussing Zionism in the abstract as it did. Reinforcing her suggestion, when the women visited the four major hospitals in Jerusalem they were shocked to discover that even the best of these, such as Shaare Zedek, lacked a maternity ward and basic laboratory equipment, including microscopes and X-ray machines.

In the course of their travels in Palestine, the women met men who would become some of the movers and shakers of Israel. Dr. Boris Schatz, founder of the Bezalel Art School, hoped Szold would use her influence in America to help him raise money for his institution. Others had heard about her and wanted to meet her. Prominent among them were Arthur Ruppin, a major land developer for the Jewish National Fund, Meir Dizengoff, one of the founders of the city of Tel Aviv and its first mayor, and Yitzhak Ben-Zvi, future president of Israel. Henrietta Szold would become a leader of women and have close female friends, but always she also built friendships with powerful men, whom she might call upon if needed—Mayer Sulzberger and the Jewish Publication Society group, Solomon Schechter and the seminary faculty, and the many men she met on this trip.

Henrietta and Sophie spent six weeks in Palestine before moving on to Italy. Henrietta took great delight in visiting the major cities—Venice, Milan, Florence, Rome—with their museums and cathedrals, their monuments and vistas. Looking at the classic works of the Renaissance she marveled at how deeply paganism had invaded Christianity and how Judaism, although so often under attack, had nevertheless withstood that seduction.

But her real passion remained the Holy Land they had left, with its "pulsating life," its "idealism, enthusiasm, hope."[10] She had fallen in love with everything about the land. She had held hunks of fertile soil in her hands in the settlements, reveled in the flowers that bloomed everywhere—mimosa, narcissus, oleanders, maidenhair fern; she could name them all. She had shared the settlers' pride in their vineyards and orange groves, their olive, almond, and apple trees. And the moon, the sky, the mountains, the caves, the air, she wrote in her letters, are all "beautiful with an indescribable beauty."[11] Above all was Zionism, the force behind so much of what she had seen. From Milan, Henrietta wrote to Elvira Solis that as a result of her travels in Palestine, she now thought Zionism "a more difficult aim to realize than I ever did before," but, at the same time, she was "more than ever convinced that if not Zionism, then nothing—then extinction for the Jew."[12]

In a letter to Mayer Sulzberger, Szold described her stay in Palestine as a series of "revolutionizing experiences." Had she been younger, she said, those experiences might have shaped her attitudes and work. But—in what may be one of the most understated predictions in Jewish history—given her current life, she imagined that those experiences would probably amount to nothing more for her than "a very stimulating memory without much result in action."[13]

For the moment, the most practical result of the trip for her was the ability she believed she now had to put Louis Ginzberg out of her mind. Not completely, as she confessed to Elvira: "I still have sleepless nights and inwardly to myself I know now that I shall never be the same as I was." Nevertheless, she felt convinced that physically and mentally she had far more strength than before. "I am strong," she wrote, "and I have myself under perfect control."[14] With that attitude she arrived in New York in late January 1910 after six months abroad. And with that attitude she soon entered into a whirlwind of activity.

Mathilde Schechter and others had arranged an elegant dinner party at the Hotel Premier in New York to welcome the women home. Friends and family from New York, Baltimore, and Philadelphia celebrated not only the women's return but also Sophie's seventieth birthday and Henrietta's forty-ninth, both of which had been in December. Henrietta spoke at length to the assembled guests about the women's travels, particularly in Palestine. Soon after that, she undertook a heavy public-speaking schedule, spurred on, perhaps, by the fact that she no longer felt constrained by Ginzberg, who had disapproved of women speaking in public. Her basic lecture, repeated often, mostly to women's groups such as the Young Women's Hebrew Association (YWHA), Council of Jewish Women, and temple sisterhoods, had a new, almost militant, tone. She still equated women's work with domestic activities, but when she described working women in the Jewish settlements she had visited in Palestine, she criticized philanthropic organizations for focusing only on the men and paying little attention to the women's needs. Why, for example, should the women be burdened with old-fashioned ovens that made cooking so much harder? Moreover, the women in the settlements were too willing themselves to accept inadequate conditions. They needed Western women to push them to demand better sanitation and better living standards. They needed to be roused to what she called "noble discontent," dissatisfaction with their lives and an active desire to improve them. She was challenging American Jewish women as she never had before.[15]

She kept herself constantly busy. While continuing her full-time work for the Jewish Publication Society, she piled on new responsibilities. A few weeks after her return, she agreed to serve as secretary of the Jewish Agricultural Experimental Station, which was a kind of go-between connecting an agricultural project in Palestine and its American financiers. She had met the brains behind the project, a young, personable agronomist named Aaron Aaronsohn, sometime earlier. Aaronsohn had discovered wild emmer wheat in the Galilee, an ancient form of wheat that became the forerunner of modern strains. Well known because of his work, he had come to the United States to seek financial aid for an agricultural research station at Atlit, near Haifa. Always intrigued by botanical and scientific subjects, Szold also admired Aaronsohn's intellect, energy, and Zionist commitment. During her trip to Palestine she had visited his parents' home in Zichron Yaakov and noted its sparkling cleanliness and beautiful garden.

Aaronsohn managed to get the wealthy non-Zionists Jacob Schiff and Julius Rosenwald interested in his project, largely because they believed his discoveries would be useful for American agriculture. As Szold recorded in her diary, some Jewish leaders argued that Aaronsohn could not be trusted, and that Schiff and others were being manipulated into supporting Zionism against their will, becoming "the tail to the Zionist kite." She regarded such arguments as "most childish" and continued to aid Aaronsohn and enjoy his friendship.[16] A few years later, during the First World War, Aaronsohn organized a spy ring called Nili to help the British against the Turks. While Szold considered herself a pacifist, she never lost her fondness for him. In turn, he regarded her as "the greatest Jewess" he had "ever had the opportunity to meet."[17]

Her friendship with Judah Magnes led to another new responsibility, her position as secretary of the education committee of the New York Kehillah, an umbrella organization put together by Magnes of hundreds of Jewish community groups and associations.[18] Although a Reform rabbi, Magnes leaned toward the more traditional Conservative Judaism of the seminary, where he and Szold had become friends, and unlike many Reform leaders, he had a passionate commitment to Zionism. As associate rabbi of New York's Temple Emanu-El, the wealthiest Reform congregation in the United States, he was expected to uphold the viewpoints of most of his congregants, "uptown Jews" like Jacob Schiff, who deemed Zionism incompatible with Jewish loyalty to America. Discarding that outlook, Magnes preached Zionism and nationalism—and soon lost his position at Emanu-El. Meanwhile, he took the lead in organizing the Kehillah, which featured a twenty-five member executive board and committees in such areas as religion, Jewish education, and philanthropy. On the education committee, Szold worked closely with Israel Friedlaender, its chairman, and at her urging, the committee hired Dr. Samson Benderly, an educator she knew from Baltimore, to form the Bureau of Jewish Education. As Benderly's power grew, seminary head Solomon Schechter resented the influence the bureau had on Jewish education and especially on the seminary's own Teacher's Institute. Szold continued to back Benderly even while maintaining her close relationship with Solomon and Mathilde Schechter. Her faith in him paid off. Benderly went on to become a giant in the field of American Jewish education, and the students he trained (mostly male) became known as the "Benderly Boys."[19]

The messiest extra work Szold took on was as secretary of the Federation of American Zionists. (It should be noted that no matter how significant her contribution to the organization she worked for, Szold always held the position of "secretary." The titles "president" or "chairman" invariably went to men.)

Made up of Zionist groups throughout the United States, the federation, or FAZ, was formed after the first Zionist Congress convened in Basel by Theodor Herzl in 1897. About a year later, Szold became a member of its executive committee, and in 1904, her old friend, Harry Friedenwald, became its president. The organization began to deteriorate precipitously after Herzl's death that year, but Friedenwald, busy with his medical practice in Baltimore, had little time to devote to it. As the situation worsened and member groups fell away, the board turned to Szold for help. Tied up as she was with her own work, she declined, one of the few occasions in her life when she refused such a request. She changed her mind a few years later, however, when Joseph Jasin, the salaried executive secretary hired by the federation at Friedenwald's suggestion, proved totally inept and the organization faced steep financial losses. Although Szold was packing her life with one commitment after another, trying hard to push away memories, she gave in this time when a committee from the FAZ pleaded with her to become secretary. (Actually, she became "honorary secretary," meaning without pay.)[20]

In July 1910, at the height of a scorching New York summer, she began working at the federation building on East Broadway, arriving late in the afternoon after spending the day on JPS work and other duties, and often laboring through the night to sort out jumbled paperwork that had piled up: neglected correspondence, unacknowledged donations, bank statements, membership receipts.[21] Gradually she began to impose order, admitting to Elvira that once again she had become caught in the kind of "senseless generosity" she had "resolved" not to do.[22] To Solomon Schechter she wrote how sorry she felt to have allowed herself to be "entrapped" in this way. "I cannot flatter myself that I am doing Zionist work; cleaning up other people's Augean stables is too far removed from Jewish ideal hopes to be a solace," she lamented.[23]

And then everything fell apart.

Hard as she had been trying to avoid Ginzberg in the months after her return, his presence, both real and imagined, seemed to haunt her at every turn. When she went to synagogue, he appeared, arm in arm with his young wife. "He came in particularly gaily with his wife" just before the prayer for the new moon, she recorded in her diary. "I fled."[24] She knew that dinner party hosts made sure not to invite her at the same time as the Ginzbergs, no matter how important the occasion. However, when she herself organized a farewell dinner for Solomon Schechter, who was going on sabbatical, she found herself facing Adele Ginzberg—in spite of the hours she spent planning the seating arrangement.[25] Because Louis Ginzberg wrote prolifically, she had constantly to confront his works, either at editorial meetings of the JPS or in correspondence with him about them. "I broke my glasses over a letter of his, the second or third this week," she noted in her diary. The letters concerned expanding his *Legends* once again, this time to five volumes. "He now seems to notice that a change requires a number of changes," she added sarcastically.[26] In earlier days she would have handled those additional changes for him without his even being aware of them. Now, when he sent her a preface in German, she returned it to him with a request that he submit it in English, and then felt miserable, knowing how easily she could have translated it herself. Another time she returned notes that had been misnumbered, aware that his wife had probably committed the error.[27]

In an act of self-preservation, she determined that she could not edit one more volume of the *Legends*, could not look at that material again. "I must give up the position with the Publication Society because I cannot, cannot, cannot bear the handling of his book, and more than that, I cannot do my duty to the Society," she wrote in her diary.[28] She did not leave the society for another six years, but she did give up Ginzberg's book. On June

8, 1910, in a letter to Mayer Sulzberger that must have been humiliating to write, Szold asked to be relieved of any further work on volumes 3 and 5 of the *Legends,* offering to employ someone at her own expense as a substitute. Admitting that she was placing personal feelings above responsibility and loyalty, she wrote, "Let that be the measure of my present embarrassment. What it should indicate further is, that, being a human woman besides a proofreader, I may not be in a condition to do my literary duty to the author properly."[29] Sulzberger unquestioningly accepted her request.

Szold packed her diary in 1910 with obsessive details of her history with Ginzberg and her current anguish, as she had her journal of 1909 after his rejection. Rather than blaming him, most of the time she turned against herself, as she had before. "I am filled with ugly envy," she wrote. She envied women who seemed happily married and she envied women she saw enjoying their children. She even envied her sister Rachel, who had been ill, because the illness elicited additional tenderness from her husband. "I hate myself and my life."[30] She described in another entry meeting Marx and Ginzberg as she strolled in the neighborhood. Marx raised his hat in greeting to her, as a gentleman would; Ginzberg ignored her. Pained but not angry, her mind flew instead to "how differently he and I would have spent a radiant spring Tuesday two years ago."[31] For all her recognition that the relationship had ended permanently, she could not stop herself from writing, "And yet I love him still."[32]

When, in early 1911, it became clear within seminary circles that Adele Ginzberg was expecting a baby, the torment became unbearable for Henrietta. The round-the-clock work that continued unabated—she had even added the extra chore of indexing the first ten volumes of the publications of the American Jewish Historical Society—the lectures, the diary writing: in the end none of it could block out the depth of despair she had come to feel about her life. Physically exhausted and emotionally drained, she collapsed. In April 1911, she entered Baltimore's Hospital for the Women of Maryland for surgery to alleviate excruciating pain she experienced on her right side, from her head to her feet. Several of her biographers believe the surgery was a hysterectomy.[33]

A more enduring problem was that she had become close to blind in both eyes, a condition that had begun slowly a year earlier and then engulfed her. No matter how many eye doctors she consulted, including her good friend Harry Friedenwald, none could find a medical cause for the blindness. In those days the condition might have been labeled "hysterical" blindness.[34] Sigmund Freud and Josef Breuer wrote extensively about hysteria as a diagnosis for psychogenic symptoms that have no physical origin, based largely on Breuer's treatment of a patient he called "Anna O."[35] While Szold didn't use that term, she might have been familiar with the syndrome, just as she was with many psychological concepts, through her closeness to her brother-in-law, Joseph Jastrow, who had become a distinguished psychologist and expert on Freud. However she understood what had happened to her, she felt trapped by being unable to read, her favorite pastime, or write in her diary. It would be six months before she recovered from the surgery and the eye trouble, literally groping her way back to health.

She spent much of that time in Mount Desert, Maine, where her sister Bertha had rented a home for the summer. When she began to recuperate and felt able to correspond with friends again, she wrote to Elvira that the pain she'd suffered even after the surgery was beginning to diminish, but even so, on her surgeon's orders, she was to do nothing until the fall. She hoped that as her body became stronger, her eyes, too, would improve, although they had not yet "revealed the secret of their malady."[36] With time and rest, she slowly began to see again, allowing her to read a little and start answering letters. No known record exists of her thinking during this long, dark period of

convalescence, and never again would she speak of Louis Ginzberg or the painful drama that had turned her life upside down.
But a hint about how her mind worked as she struggled toward
recovery can be seen in a letter to another friend, Alice Seligsberg. She had spent three years after her European trip trying
to "bluff" herself into believing that the trip itself or the hard
work she undertook afterward would restore her to "sanity,"
she wrote, only to discover that "the body rebelled as the soul
had before." She was determined now, she wrote, to "blot out"
what had happened in the past and "leap into a new existence."[37]

The person making that leap had moved far from the one
who had been steeped in misery and self-blame. This was no
longer the person who had regarded a woman's love for a man
as "an opportunity for self-effacement," no longer the woman
who felt bound by "sexual limitations" from speaking out at work,
no longer the lecturer who cautioned women to "beware" of
forfeiting their dignity as they moved ahead. In blotting out the
past she began to take a clear-eyed look at the future, and with
steely resolve shape it into "a new existence." In that existence
women had purpose in life and shared the platform equally
with men. Years earlier, when she and her father had visited the
Alt-Neu Shul in Prague, she dreamed of one day becoming a
conduit between the closed-off world of women and the more
expansive, freer one of men. The woman who emerged now from
months of soul-searching would go further. As a leader of other
women, she would guide them into her new world and out of
the shadows of the men around them.

"I am cheerful and even optimistic," she wrote Alice.[38]

5

Hadassah

THE TRANSFORMATION DID NOT HAPPEN out of the blue. Even at the height of Szold's passion for Louis Ginzberg, and in spite of her conventional attitude about gender roles, she had begun to question the place of women in Judaism. In 1907 she wrote an article called "What Our Grandmothers Read" based on the *tehines,* traditional prayers in Yiddish that Ashkenazic wives and mothers had recited for hundreds of years. Touched when Ginzberg later gave her a collection of his own mother's tehines, she nevertheless voiced a complaint as an unmarried woman: "But do not speak to me of the progressiveness of Judaism! Why isn't there one Techinnah [*sic*] in all the books to fit my modern case—not one to raise up the spirit of a so-called emancipated woman."[1] Even before that she had acknowledged women's widespread capabilities, demanding that they receive higher education, recognizing their competence in the synagogue, and noting their facility in any duties they chose to undertake—always, however, assuming their activities would be subject to the leadership of men. Most recently she had encouraged American Jewish women to urge Jewish women in the Holy Land to improve their lives by making greater demands on the men in control. Kernels of thought germinating deep in her mind after her return from abroad came together to form a coherent whole during her long period of soul-searching. Following the radical break with her past that resulted, women and their potential would be at the core of her thinking for years to come.

She was aided by new friendships with women she had made during this period. She and Elvira Solis had been friends for a long time and that relationship continued, but she became especially close to two strong, creative women, both younger than she, and both of whom would adopt her Zionist outlook in addition to their common concern for women's issues. She met Alice Seligsberg, with whom she would correspond extensively, in 1908, a short time after her breakup with Ginzberg. From a wealthy assimilated Jewish family and one of the first graduates of Barnard College, Seligsberg began her career as a social worker on New York's Lower East Side. She and Szold quickly became confidantes; it was to her that Szold revealed much of her heartache about her lost love. Jessie Sampter, whom Szold met a few years later, grew up, like Seligsberg, in a well-off German Jewish home with little Jewish identity. A poet and writer partly crippled by a childhood disease, she spent many years finding her way to Judaism. Greatly influenced by Szold, she embraced Zionism and eventually opened a school for Zionism for women. Although they met in America, all three women would live a large part of their lives in Palestine and support each other emotionally and intellectually until their deaths.[2]

For Szold and her friends, as for many other women, changing times brought changing attitudes toward society and women's place in it. The Gilded Age of the 1800s, with its vast industrial

advances and its breed of wealthy business tycoons, was giving
way at the end of the nineteenth century and into the twentieth
to the Progressive Era's concern for workers and farmers, for
the poor and displaced. Women led many of the reform movements sprouting up at the time. Chicago's Hull House, established by Jane Addams in 1889, became a model for settlement
houses across the country. In New York, Lillian Wald began a
visiting nurses service, which later influenced Szold's thinking,
and founded the Henry Street Settlement House, a haven for
hundreds of thousands of immigrants flowing into the city in
the early 1900s. During this period, the women's suffrage movement, having gained steam in the late nineteenth century, became a powerful force in society, culminating in the Nineteenth
Amendment of 1920, which gave women the vote. And everywhere, women were gathering in clubs—to read together, hold
broad cultural discussions, and in many cases do good works in
philanthropy and education.[3]

Against this background of women's clubs and progressive
ideas, Henrietta Szold had joined a small Zionist study circle before her trip to Palestine. Such groups began forming in New
York City after the Second Zionist Congress in Basel in 1898.
The prominent Zionist and Columbia University professor of
Semitics Richard Gottheil—whose book on Zionism Szold
would later defend in the *Nation*—had attended that congress
as a delegate, accompanied by his wife Emma. Responding to
a request from Theodor Herzl to organize American Jewish
women in support of Zionism, on her return to the States Emma
held a meeting with a group of women in her apartment on
New York's Fifth Avenue to study Zionism and various Jewish
subjects. Soon afterward other study circles began gathering in
Harlem, a center of Jewish life at the time. Many called themselves Daughters of Zion, some adding Hadassah or the names
of other heroines of Jewish history. Around 1907, Szold's friend
Judah Magnes, then still a rabbi at Temple Emanu-El, suggested

to his secretary, Lotta Levensohn, that she invite Henrietta Szold to join her Harlem Daughters of Zion group as an honorary member. Intimidated by the idea of approaching the renowned Szold to become part of her much younger set of women, Levensohn asked Magnes to extend the invitation. He did, and Szold agreed to join, but only as an active, not honorary, member. Years later Levensohn recalled that "wherever she sat, Henrietta Szold became the head of the table."[4]

Emma Gottheil's study circle fell apart after a short while, and Szold's came close to dissolving by the fall of 1911. But it was Henrietta's group her mother had in mind when she suggested the need to do practical work in Palestine, and it was her membership in that group that led Szold to the much larger goal of a national women's Zionist organization. Back in 1897, after speaking at the National Council of Jewish Women convention, she had written Elvira about her disapproval of strictly women's organizations—"You know how seriously I object to Jewish women segregating themselves," she wrote. "Well, then, is it absolutely necessary for us to have a Women's Council?"[5] Now, after laboring through the messy files of the men's Federation of American Zionists—the "Aegean stables," as she wrote Solomon Schechter—and working through her own thinking about women, she changed her mind. She envisioned an important place for women Zionists, and looked to the non-Zionist National Council of Jewish Women as an organizational model.

For the time being she also enlisted the aid of the FAZ, in spite of its faults, and for practical reasons planned to affiliate her national women's group with it while still maintaining the women's autonomy. In early 1912, fully recovered and with the Ginzberg affair behind her, she held several meetings with Bernard Rosenblatt, a young lawyer and member of the FAZ executive committee whose wife, Gertrude, was an active Zionist. A core of women from several early study circles, including Szold's, joined her at these meetings. Seven in all, they included

Lotta Levensohn, Emma Gottheil, and her old friend Mathilde Schechter. Guided by Rosenblatt, the women created two constitutions, one for a national organization and the other for its first chapter.[6]

With the documents in place, the women wrote to prospective members, proclaiming that "the time is ripe for a large organization of women Zionists," and inviting them to a meeting on February 24, 1912, to be held in the vestry of Temple Emanu-El. Its purpose: "the promotion of Jewish institutions and enterprises in Palestine and the fostering of Jewish ideals." The seven women who initiated the meeting and signed the invitation to it are all, in that sense, the founders of Hadassah, the national women's Zionist organization that would emerge from it. But Henrietta Szold's vision shaped the enterprise from the start and dominated that first meeting, where she was elected president of the new organization. From that time on she has been known as *the* founder of Hadassah.[7]

Some thirty-eight women attended the February 24 meeting, and a record nineteen of them were elected officers or directors. Henrietta Szold spoke about her trip to Palestine in 1909 and urged the group to seek a single "definite project," a Zionist project, that would define them and their mission. Years earlier her father had taught her that for whatever end she sought in life, she should adopt a central idea and relate everything else to it.[8] Her insistence on a definite project for the women's group fit that mode. During the discussion, ideas for projects ranged from a girls' lace-making workshop in Palestine to sending nurses to that land, with no agreed-on conclusion. Because this group formed the first and only chapter at the time, it called itself Daughters of Zion, Hadassah Chapter, after the name of Szold's earlier Harlem circle and—more so—in honor of the holiday of Purim, which fell about the time the group met. Hadassah was the Hebrew name of Queen Esther, heroine of the Purim saga. As other chapters came into existence, the national organization that developed, like the New York chapter, was referred to as Hadassah, causing some confusion.

The name mix-up would smooth out later, in June 1914, when the national organization held its first convention, in Rochester, New York. Delegates voted to drop the cumbersome Daughters of Zion and adopt Hadassah as the organization's official name. By then the group had its motto, suggested some time earlier by seminary professor Israel Friedlaender: *Aruchat bat Ami*, "the healing of the daughter of my people," from a verse in the book of Jeremiah (8:22): "Behold the voice of the cry of my people from a land that is very far off. . . . Is there no balm in Gilead? Is there no physician there? Why then is not the healing of the daughter of my people accomplished?"[9] The emblem the group commissioned featured a Star of David with the Hadassah motto connected by two myrtle leaves (*hadassah* means myrtle). Its designer, Victor David Brenner, well known in the field, had created the Lincoln penny.

"Daughter of my people," a poetic rendering of "my people," pointed to the direction the organization would take. The "definite project" Szold decided on, reinforced by her good friend Dr. Harry Friedenwald, called for a district visiting nurses service in Palestine along the lines of what Lillian Wald had done in New York City. Szold convinced the others to accept the idea, although it seemed rather foolhardy for a new organization with almost no money to undertake such a far-reaching project. Shortly afterward, and almost miraculously, the philanthropist Nathan Straus appeared on the scene, as interested in public health as Szold. Straus had a moving background. He and his older brother Isidor had been co-owners of R. H. Macy & Co. and other department stores. In April 1912, after spending time together in Europe, Nathan and his wife, Lina, traveled to Palestine while Isidor and his wife, Ida, boarded the *Titanic* for their return to New York. As the ship was sinking in the North Atlantic, Ida climbed out of a lifeboat, demanding to remain on board with Isidor, who had insisted that women and young people be rescued before him, and the couple perished together. Deeply affected by his brother's death, Nathan, who had already financed health projects in the United States and Palestine, including a center in Jerusalem for treating malaria and trachoma, retired from business and devoted the rest of his life to philanthropy.[10]

In December 1912, Henrietta Szold met with the Strauses, and on January 1, 1913, at a historic gathering in Emma Gottheil's home, Szold submitted a proposal Nathan made to the Hadassah board. He would pay traveling expenses and four months' salary for a trained nurse to go to Palestine if the organization would pay the remainder of her salary for a two-year period. He estimated the cost of the nurse to be $2,500, and she would have to be ready to leave for Palestine on January 18, when the Strauses planned to go. With less than $300 in the treasury, Henrietta and Emma used all their rhetorical skills to persuade the others that somehow they could raise the money and find a nurse in time. Lillian Wald, whom Szold consulted about hiring a nurse, doubted that Jewish nurses would be willing to go to primitive Ottoman Palestine. The more than twenty women who applied for the job proved her wrong, and after interviewing them, Szold hired Rose Kaplan, a nurse from Mount Sinai Hospital in New York. Meanwhile, Eva Leon, Emma Gottheil's sister, came up with a grant of $2,000 a year for five years, raised from wealthy non-Zionist friends in Chicago. A second nurse was hired, Rachel Landy from Cleveland, and the two set off with the Strauses on January 18, 1913, after enjoying a farewell party hosted by Szold and her mother two days earlier. The nurses rented a stone house with a lemon tree in its courtyard in Mea Shearim, the poor, Orthodox section of Jerusalem, and in March of that year, opened their visiting nurses clinic. On the iron gate entrance to the house, they hung a sign in Hebrew and in English that read: American Daughters of Zion

Nurses Settlement HADASSAH. It was the organization's first step to heal Palestine's people.

While the nurses launched their mission, fighting to combat illness and ignorance, the small, struggling Hadassah group that sponsored them began building new chapters and recruiting members for what would in a matter of years become the largest and most influential Zionist organization in America. For the most part, the principles that guided the organization as it moved ahead stemmed directly from the ideas and iron will of Henrietta Szold. Or, as everyone called her, Miss Szold.

From the outset, Szold decided that women's Zionist work needed to differ from men's if the women were to find their place and make their mark in the Zionist world. So, whereas men's groups generally concentrated on building up the Land of Israel through farms and agricultural settlements, Szold focused women's attention on the cities—the unsanitary, fly-infested, disease-plagued urban areas that she and her mother had witnessed on their trip to Palestine. The women she organized would provide community health and social welfare programs to those areas, much like those provided by general women's groups throughout the United States. Influenced by the American settlement movement, in which social workers and nurses concentrated on aiding women and children, Hadassah made women and children its first priority. It later expanded its services to providing medical care to the broader community, but the initial goal of helping women and children in Palestine, the most vulnerable members of society, drew American Jewish women to the organization. From its beginnings also, and led by Szold, Hadassah made a point of extending its health services to people of all religions, races, and nationalities without discrimination—Muslim and Christian women and their children would be treated along with Jewish ones. With that policy, a woman who joined a Hadassah chapter in America could feel that she was spreading goodwill in the Holy Land, and even, in her own way, helping to create better understanding between the Jews and Arabs there.

The women who became members of Hadassah in those early days felt drawn to the practical nature of the organization's work. Mostly middle class, many of them homemakers, they responded to rhetoric that reflected their personal experiences. Unlike male Zionists, with their often grandiose political and nation-building objectives, these women could identify with the down-to-earth goals and skills associated with family life that Hadassah emphasized: patience, attention to details, and responsibility. And they felt comfortable with the maternal terms frequently used to describe their Zionist activities. They understood when Szold spoke of healing and helping the population in Palestine as "motherhood work" or labeled the land itself a "Joyful Mother of Children."[11] Eventually, those terms, along with the emphasis on separate gender roles, would be dropped as the organization expanded and as more women entered the workforce. But in the beginning years, such images appealed to women's sense of nurturing a population that needed them, much as they nurtured their own families. Ironically, by attracting growing numbers of women, maternal language, so closely associated with women in their private domestic roles (the "little woman" at home with the children) became the very source of Hadassah's power.

For the women themselves, Szold said many times, Zionism enhanced lives. "We need Zionism as much as those Jews do who need a physical home," she wrote to Alice Seligsberg.[12] She firmly believed and taught that doing good works for the Jews in Palestine would also bring spiritual renewal to American Jewish women. By raising money for the medical care of Palestinian Jews, sewing clothes for the poor of that land, as they did in their Hadassah sewing circles, and working with other Jewish women toward a common goal, they enlarged their own lives. More than that, by devoting themselves to restoring a homeland for the Jewish people, they also restored Judaism into their own homes—and, Szold would say, their hearts. Toward that end, she took pride in the "cultural work" Hadassah groups did, with women reading aloud at their meetings from the Zionist writings of Leon Pinsker, Theodor Herzl, Ahad Ha'am, and others. From the attention they gave to Jewish and Zionist culture, there emerged, she said, a "Hadassah spirit," an aura of harmony within the organization as a whole that enriched each individual.[13] In Szold's teaching at this time, Hadassah women did not need to live in Zion to be good Zionists. They needed to absorb Zionist ideals within themselves, while doing the pragmatic work of sustaining the organization's mission in the Land of Israel.

Beyond anything else, perhaps, the example Szold herself set drew members to Hadassah. The slight woman (she had thinned over the years) with graying hair topped by a frumpy black felt hat, a pince-nez often perched on her nose, seemed tireless as she traveled from city to city carrying her Zionist message to women in Philadelphia, Boston, Cleveland, Baltimore, and Chicago. Sometimes the audience was sparse, the woman who organized the event embarrassed before her distinguished guest. It didn't matter. Szold delivered her talk to large or small crowds, occasionally adding clunky lantern slides with blurry pictures of Palestine she had lugged with her to round out a lecture. She was not an eloquent speaker, one of her admirers would recall. She kept herself distant, a bit austere, her talks cerebral and somewhat academic.[14]

But she had presence. The women she addressed heard authenticity and passionate commitment to the Zionist cause she so greatly believed in, and they were inspired. Years later, a woman who had devoted herself to Hadassah but had recently lost her husband and questioned whether she should keep going wrote to Szold: "Dear, dear Miss Szold, perhaps without your example I would not have found the answer. . . . Again I experienced the conviction of the great life force which gives me strength as it flows through you to others."[15] Szold's talks might have been less than dazzling, but the resolution behind them streamed outward to her listeners. Nor did she limit her recruitment efforts to talks; she involved herself in every aspect of a new chapter. When the Reading, Pennsylvania, chapter held its first meeting at the Young Men's Hebrew Association (YMHA) on February 29, 1916, for example, its sixty-four members voted to send a telegram to Henrietta Szold informing her of its organization. At its second meeting, held in its new president's home, Szold showed up to formally accept the new chapter, a pattern she repeated again and again as chapters formed.[16] Often she asked friends or acquaintances to start new chapters in the towns or cities where they lived; then she followed through with a personal visit.

With her skills—one might say her genius—for organization, she set strict rules: only one chapter in a city to avoid competition, and each a composite of rich and poor, elite German Jews and recent east European immigrants, educated and non. Members learned together and from each other—women who had never spoken in public discovered their voices; women who had scrimped to balance their family budgets became educated in the intricacies of fund-raising and fiscal responsibility. In the process of working out the complexities of organizational life, many developed new confidence and a sense of self-worth.

By 1914, Hadassah had 519 members in eight chapters. Three years later it had 2,710 members in thirty-three chapters across the United States—and counting.[17]

It would take some time for male Zionist organizations to tip their hats to Hadassah or its founder. The relationship was bumpy from the start. "The men looked upon us as organizers of strawberry festivals," Szold told an interviewer years later, meaning lightweights, in no way as serious as the men in their goals.[18] In fact, the FAZ liked the idea of a women's auxiliary to their organization, but for them that meant a women's group subordinate to them that would espouse their goals, help them raise money, and serve tea and coffee at their social functions. They did not like the independent stance Szold and her group had adopted even as affiliates of the FAZ, and Louis Lipsky, chairman of the board of the FAZ and a major Zionist leader, told her so in a letter—but she continued doing what she had set out to do with her women's organization.[19]

The complaints mounted as Hadassah grew in numbers and deeds, arousing the Zionist men's envy along with their condescension. Although they acknowledged that Hadassah members helped the Jews of Palestine in practical terms, they accused the organization of not contributing to the Zionist ideal of building the land. They labeled Hadassah work "charity," evoking images of the old *halukah* system Zionists despised—of doling out funds to poor, mostly elderly, religious Jews in Palestine who wanted to live out their lives in the Holy Land but had no interest in nation building. And they mocked the women's work as narrow and amateurish, concentrating as it did on women and children, on health issues and social welfare. "Diaper Zionism," they called it. Through their own work in supporting agricultural projects, the men pointed out, they were part of the noble, historical Zionist goal of creating the "New Jew," the strong, sun-kissed pioneer, filled with confidence as he (rarely did they speak of women in this category) turned his back on the beaten-down, pale, ghetto Jew who had emerged over the centuries.[20]

Sometimes Szold defended Hadassah against the relentless attacks: "Not charity, I deny it," she wrote in the Zionist magazine the *Maccabaean*. "We go to Palestine equipped . . . with the purpose of bringing to Palestine the results of American healing art. . . . If we can bring order to that land of chaos, that charge cannot be brought against us, that we are a charitable society."[21] Sometimes she just threw up her hands in despair at the "constant criticism because [Hadassah] was not political enough, or because it was too political, either it didn't think or it thought too independently."[22] More important than answering the male attacks was supporting the health-care work being done in the Land of Israel.

When Szold interviewed Rose Kaplan, the first nurse she hired for that work, Kaplan told her, "I am a nurse, but not a Zionist." To which Szold replied, "What we want is a nurse. We want a woman with initiative, with love, with desire to adapt herself; and we think that when you have worked with your own people you will become a Zionist."[23] Kaplan more than filled the role Szold laid out, and the prediction came true. She and her co-worker, Rachel Landy, devoted themselves body and soul to bring medical care to the sick of Jerusalem in what seemed not only a thankless task but an almost impossible one. The doctors at hospitals and clinics there expected nurses to be assistants: taking orders, not initiating practices. The people the women tried to help were suspicious and set in their ways—nobody had ever seen nurses going around, seeking out the ill and trying to help them. Adding to their difficulties, these nurses followed American models and techniques; Szold had been adamant about having them look at all Palestinian matters from an American point of view. Jane Addams, the famous American social worker, had even come to visit them soon after they settled in.[24] Rumors spread that perhaps these women were Christian missionaries, like other medical personnel who had come to Palestine from America, looking to convert people in return for the care they offered. But the women persisted, attaching themselves to Dr. Albert Ticho, an ophthalmologist, who ran a clinic for eye diseases. By September they could write to Szold and the Hadassah central committee that they had treated thousands of children with trachoma. Having witnessed the miseries of persistent maternal deaths, they were also preparing to branch out and begin training local midwives in Western techniques.[25]

Slowly, slowly, the two women began to gain people's trust. With time and hard work, tall, blond Landy and short, dark-haired Kaplan became recognized as a team: "the tall one and the short one," people called them. They were warmly greeted wherever they went, and schoolteachers sought them out to examine children's eyes. About a year after the nurses came to Jerusalem, the Uzbekistan-born Jewish doctor Helena Kagan, right out of medical school in Switzerland, arrived, brimming with idealism. Discovering fairly quickly that she had little opportunity to offer her medical services—the Ottoman authorities would not even grant a medical license to a woman—she joined the nurses in their maternity and trachoma work. Still, she went on struggling to be recognized as a physician, and eventually succeeded.

With the women making headway in Palestine, Szold began planning to send two more nurses to join them; in the back of her mind, she was developing strategies to raise money for a nurses' training school and perhaps a maternity hospital. She and the central committee also realized that they needed to be the final arbiters of all Hadassah work taking place in Palestine, and they needed to receive regular reports. They wanted it clearly understood that this was an American-based Zionist enterprise, devoted as it nevertheless was to the welfare of the Jews of the Holy Land.[26]

The First World War turned all plans upside down. "The war makes joy impossible," Szold wrote to Jessie Sampter soon after the guns of August 1914 began robbing her, as she said, "of confidence in the perfectibility of human kind."[27] She opposed the war with all her heart, as did many Americans, hoping it would end quickly and the United States would not get involved. Like many German American Jews, she felt ambivalent about the Triple Entente, the alliance that pitted Britain and France against Germany but made an ally of tsarist Russia, a country that so badly mistreated its Jews. That alignment of countries caused havoc among Zionists, she wrote, with some leading members of the Actions Committee, the administrative arm of the World Zionist Organization headquartered in Berlin, "serving in the Russian army, one in the German and one in the Austrian."[28] Then too, Dr. Shmarya Levin, a Russian writer and Zionist executive who had become stranded in the United States because of the war, had organized a new administrative body in New York, but could not get the old files out of Berlin, an illustration "of how destructive this outbreak of passion and greed is of all the works of peace," Szold wrote.[29]

In Palestine, the situation grew worse by the day. After Turkey entered the war in October 1914, joining with Germany and Austria-Hungary against the Entente powers, it expelled all non-Ottoman citizens from the land. Thousands of Jews were brutally deported from Tel Aviv and Jaffa; others swarmed out of Jerusalem and various parts of the country, most fleeing to Egypt and refugee camps the British had set up in Alexandria. Those who remained, accepting Ottoman citizenship, were forced to serve in the Turkish army. In the Jewish community, the Turks shut hospitals, turning some of them into military bases, and cut off food supplies, exposing the population to disease and starvation. As dangers mounted, the agronomist Aaron Aaronsohn warned Hadassah that the two nurses should leave the country. Rachel Landy stayed on for some months, then returned to the United States at the insistence of her parents. Rose Kaplan, suffering from a cancer she kept hidden at first, received permission from Hadassah to assist the Jews in the Alexandrian refugee camps. She continued to work there, particularly with the children, sending optimistic reports to Hadassah's central committee, until she died in August 1917. Szold eulogized her, remembering the courageous woman who had not considered herself a Zionist but had given her all to Hadassah's work.

With the nurses gone and their settlement building closed, Dr. Helena Kagan, courageous in her own right, opened a small clinic for women and children in Jerusalem under Hadassah auspices. She bought a cow that she kept in her backyard so she could give a little milk to her young patients as she struggled to sustain as many as possible in the starving, dying city.[30]

In New York, Szold did what she could to keep her organization growing. Along with her travels to set up new chapters, she made a point of reaching out to non-Zionist women with the goal of drawing them into Hadassah or at least having them affiliate in some way. With the war ravaging Palestine and European Jewry suffering from the fighting, she recognized that even those individuals who did not agree with the Zionist viewpoint had come to "think with pity of our little sanctuary," as she wrote to Augusta Rosenwald, whose non-Zionist husband, Julius, owned Sears Roebuck.[31] By appealing to that sympathy for Palestine she managed to get financial backing and with it moral support for Hadassah and its Zionist goals from outside the mainstream. As she was fond of saying in encouraging Hadassah leaders to recruit non-Zionists, "Where money goes, the heart follows."

At the same time, she continued to promote her Zionist ideas in lectures to both Jewish and general audiences. In a typical talk, this at the prestigious Cooper Union in New York City, she developed themes she had touched on before and would return to. Like Theodor Herzl, she spoke of the "Jewish problem" that stalked European countries, an antisemitism that had not been eradicated by emancipating the Jews any more than it had been earlier by herding them into ghettos. Nor, for Jews themselves, would the solution come from regarding Judaism as a religion only and drawing inward, or from assimilating and trying to disappear into the general population. The solution to the Jews' place in the world could come from only one source: the recognition that "Jews are a nation—that all the Jews together, be they religious or not—are a people." As such they needed a Jewish center, and that center, Szold emphasized, lay in "the old home of the Jewish people," Zion, which "runs like a red thread through Jewish history." The goal, however, was not "to go back to Zion" but "to go forward to Zion," to rebuild the land while also refashioning life there on the traditional values of Judaism.[32] Despite pulling non-Zionists into the Hadassah fold, Szold never compromised her belief in the centrality of Zionism to Jewish existence.

In this belief she found an unexpected ally: Louis D. Brandeis, the renowned Boston lawyer. Brandeis is one of those figures in history whose sudden conversion to a cause has never been fully understood. What made this aristocratic attorney who had no Jewish background or education, belonged to no synagogue, and had few Jewish friends become at the age of fifty-eight a devoted Zionist? The shift has been attributed to his admiration for his uncle, Lewis Naphtali Dembitz, an early Zionist, whom he had adored since childhood, or to the influence of the east European Jews he met when he helped mediate a garment workers' strike in New York City in 1910, or—much like Herzl—to the antisemitism he saw expanding around him, or, as his biographer Melvin Urofsky holds, to his American progressive outlook.[33] Whatever the reason for his metamorphosis, he emerged in 1914 as the unquestioned leader of American Zionism.

The change came about after the war broke out and Jewish leaders in Palestine desperately appealed to Americans for relief funds. Dr. Shmarya Levin, the World Zionist leader who had been visiting America and could not return to Europe because of the conflict, called an emergency meeting with the Federation of American Zionists on August 30, 1914, at the Hotel

Marseilles in New York City. Brandeis had joined the FAZ a few years earlier at the urging of his friend Jacob de Haas, but he had taken no active part in it. He was invited to chair this meeting in the hope that his prestigious name might attract others to the cause. Nobody expected much more from him. To the amazement of the FAZ and many others, he left the meeting as head of the newly formed Provisional Executive Committee for General Zionist Affairs (PEC), openly committed to Zionism and ready to take charge of the Zionist movement in the United States.[34]

He would surprise the FAZ also by viewing Henrietta Szold and her Hadassah organization far more seriously than they did. A Hadassah president later wrote that Brandeis considered women equal to men in "intellect, ability and judgment," and he had great respect for Szold.[35] She became a member of the Provisional Executive Committee along with Judah Magnes and such prestigious associates of Brandeis as Julian W. Mack, a prominent U.S. circuit court judge, Felix Frankfurter, a professor at Harvard Law School, and Rabbi Stephen S. Wise, one of the most influential American rabbis of the time. Brandeis's Zionism differed from Szold's. He viewed the concept in secular terms, as an extension of both the vision of the prophets and American democratic ideals. She saw it as informing Judaism as a whole, secular and religious. But they also had much in common that made it possible for them to work well together. As native-born Americans (Brandeis grew up in Kentucky), they understood American ways, and through the examples of their own hard work they were able to reach American Jews.

Moreover, they both admired efficiency and valued practicality. Szold could agree with the Brandeis motto "Men! Money! Discipline!" (although she would expand the "Men" part to include women)—the idea that membership numbers mattered, as did the ability to raise money and spend it in a disciplined manner. She had been disgusted by the slovenliness of the FAZ when she worked for that organization, and was impressed by the way Brandeis brought order to the Zionist movement. And he greatly appreciated Hadassah's practical work in Palestine. In a letter to her about a Hadassah speaking engagement he had accepted, he wrote, "I am particularly impressed with both the spirit and the efficiency of the work of the Hadassah under your wise guidance."[36]

It stood to reason that when in 1916 the World Zionist Organization appealed to the Provisional Executive Committee for medical help in devastated Palestine, Brandeis called on Szold and Hadassah. From its beginnings the organization had been hoping to develop enough resources to send a medical unit to the Holy Land. Now Szold offered to ship over a unit of ten doctors, two nurses, and a supply of drugs at a cost of $25,000, which Hadassah would provide. Within a few months that cost rose to $30,000 as the need for more doctors and nurses became clear. When Hadassah leaders, aghast at the figures, wondered how the organization could handle such a financial burden, with just $3,000 in its treasury, Szold suggested—only in part facetiously—that if every Hadassah member walked instead of taking streetcars, each could contribute up to $15, giving the group the money it needed. Hadassah members dutifully started saving nickels and dimes for the cause.[37] On her end, Szold barnstormed eastern cities to raise funds, and began negotiating with the Joint Distribution Committee, a worldwide Jewish relief organization, for its financial help. Sadly, after the United States entered the war in 1917, the Turkish government shut Palestine's doors to the Hadassah medical corps, known as the American Zionist Medical Unit (AZMU). Aid for the ill of the Holy Land would have to wait.

By the time Szold had begun organizing the medical unit, her life had changed again drastically. Judge Julian W. Mack, a great admirer of Szold's, put together a lifetime annuity for her so that she would no longer have to work for a living but could devote herself to Zionist activities. Brandeis contributed to the fund, as did such prominent American Jews as Julius Rosenwald, Irving Lehman, and Mary Fels (of the Fels-Naphtha soap fortune). Somewhat "bewildered" at the generous offer, as Szold wrote Cyrus Adler, she accepted it gratefully, and soon after resigned her position as secretary of the Publications Committee of the Jewish Publication Society. In her letter of resignation she compared herself to "a mother when she stands on the threshold of her home" and watches her son go off on his own, knowing she will no longer be a primary influence on his life. It was an interesting analogy; her unfulfilled hopes to be a mother in the true sense of the word had caused her great pain during a large slice of the more than twenty-two years she had served the society. But she had gained much from her work there and contributed a great deal toward shaping Jewish thought and culture through the books she translated and edited. Now she was ready to close the door behind her, move on, and accept that she "will have no direct part" in the society's future.[38]

In her private life, her own mother lay gravely ill in December 1915, when she wrote her letter of resignation. A month earlier, her good friend Solomon Schechter had died, a loss she still grieved. Mrs. Szold had become ill with a lung disease sometime before that, and the two women had moved away from Morningside Heights to Pinehurst Avenue on the edge of the city, where large, open spaces offered clear, fresh air. Henrietta tended her mother throughout the illness, grateful, as she wrote to Elvira Solis afterward, that she had been with the older woman until the very end. Writing that, she probably remembered the pain and guilt she had felt at having been out of the room at the moment her father died. She hoped, she said, to be able one day to put aside the picture of the dying woman and to recapture the healthy image of her "dear mother with her rosy cheeks and blue eyes."[39] When Henrietta was little she sometimes wondered, as children do, whether she belonged to this mother whose coloring so differed from her own swarthy skin and dark eyes. But those attributes were like her father's, and he remained the great spiritual guide of her life. Nonetheless, she had come to appreciate her mother's influence on her own pragmatic ways and organizational skills. The two had become close during the many years they shared a home, and Henrietta would miss their companionship.

After her mother died in August 1916, a family friend, Haym Peretz, offered to say the memorial *Kaddish* prayer for her, following Orthodox Jewish tradition in which male children recite the prayer for almost a year in honor of their parents. If there are no male survivors, an outside male often acts as a substitute. Szold responded, in part, by thanking him warmly, then turning down his offer: "I believe that the elimination of women from such duties was never intended by our law and custom—women were freed from positive duties when they could not perform them, but not when they could. It was never intended that, if they could perform them, their performance of them should not be considered as valuable and valid as when one of the male sex performed them. And of the *Kaddish* I feel sure this is particularly true. My mother had eight daughters and no son; and yet never did I hear a word of regret pass the lips of either my mother or my father that one of us was not a son. When my father died, my mother would not permit others to take her daughters' place in saying the *Kaddish*, and so I am sure I am acting in her spirit when I am moved to decline your offer."[40]

Henrietta Szold wrote probably thousands of letters and gave hundreds of lectures in her lifetime. But of all the things she wrote or said, the words in this letter are the most often cited. For her and for generations of women after her, they were and remain an affirmation of Jewish women's religious rights.

6

Palestine:
The Great Adventure

"YOUR NOTE . . . CAME when I longed to have someone stroke me and pet me and soothe me," Szold wrote to Jessie Sampter on March 8, 1917. "Nothing has happened—nothing at all. But holiday times are so bare to me nowadays. So your note came just at the right moment."[1]

It was the holiday of Purim. On her own since her mother had died some eight months earlier, Henrietta felt lonely and sad. In a few days she would be off on another long, exhausting speaking tour to nine or ten cities, recruiting Hadassah members and raising much-needed funds. A loving letter from her good friend Jessie helped sustain her in the difficult work of developing Hadassah into the premier Zionist organization she envisioned.

She ended the letter with a subject much on her mind, as it was for most Americans—the war being waged in Europe. Woodrow Wilson's second presidential campaign boasted of keeping

America at peace while the world was at war, yet every day seemed to draw the nation nearer to the conflagration. Just a month earlier, Wilson had cut off relations with Germany after German submarines had threatened American merchant ships, an ominous sign for the future. "If only America were not being drawn into the bloody maelstrom," Szold wrote.[2]

Szold had declared herself a pacifist from the very beginning of the Great War. In some respects, her position carried on her father's determined peacemaking efforts during the Civil War. While he had opposed slavery, his sermons dwelled on preserving the Union, not on abolition; he spoke against secession and for unity and peace under all circumstances. In larger measure, she fit into a list of pacifist progressives—Jane Addams and Lillian Wald prominent among them—who lobbied for the United States to maintain its neutrality. In Hadassah, several Central Committee members, including Jessie Sampter and Alice Seligsberg, joined Szold in her stance.

Through the years, Szold's longtime friend Judah Magnes had been making a name for himself as a pacifist spokesman. In May 1917, about a month after the United States entered the conflict, Magnes addressed a mass antiwar meeting of fifteen thousand people in Madison Square Garden, and afterward helped found the People's Council for Democracy and Peace. Its leaders, mostly non-Jewish, included such well-known socialists as Eugene V. Debs, Norman Thomas, and Scott Nearing, who became the council's head.[3] Szold and other pacifist Hadassah women joined the organization in September, only to quickly find themselves embroiled in a war of their own.

With American men fighting overseas, sentiment in the country had turned against any form of pacifism. Patriotism was the order of the day, and Szold and her antiwar cohorts came under fire from several other Hadassah leaders, including Emma Gottheil, once a good friend. The situation worsened when the pacifist women objected to a proposal by the Provisional Executive Committee to attach the American Zionist Medical Unit to British expeditionary forces in Palestine as a way of speeding up medical help to that region. Regarding such an attachment as an unacceptable "endorsement of militaristic action," the women threatened to withdraw Hadassah's participation in the unit.[4] Matters came to a head when Szold and Sampter met with a group of male Zionists from the Provisional Executive Committee. Brandeis led the way in denouncing the women's pacifist affiliation and actions. A year earlier, when he had been appointed to the United States Supreme Court, he resigned his position as chair of the Provisional Executive Committee, but he remained the most powerful American Zionist leader. He also served as a close adviser to President Wilson and fully supported America's joining the Allies. If the Germans were to win, he said, "it will put back civilization one hundred years."[5]

At the meeting, he emphasized the importance for American Jews, and Zionists in particular, to support the administration if they wanted U.S. backing once peace came. The antiwar, essentially socialist, People's Council the women had joined was "hostile" to the American government, he admonished, and the women's position itself "very harmful to the Zionist cause."[6]

Szold agonized over the committee's attitude, and especially that of Brandeis. She knew he could be aloof and autocratic—she had seen that at the meeting—but she admired him greatly for his intellect and his wholehearted commitment to Zionism. When he spoke to an audience, she would say, there was a "prophetic spark" in his words.[7] Without giving up her pacifist convictions, she reluctantly decided to resign from the People's Council, as did the other Hadassah women. From then on, she expressed her feelings about the war only privately in letters to friends. After a visit with her sister's children in Baltimore, she reflected sadly about the "virus of misunderstood patriotism" the children were being fed in school, "consisting chiefly of hatred and prejudice." And, agreeing with Sampter that she was "not happier for having relinquished my pacifism," she was glad, she wrote, that soldiers' uniforms had high collars, because she could not bear to look at the strong young necks of marines. "I see them mangled and gory."[8]

Szold was pulled into another painful conflict within the Jewish community during these fraught years. This one centered on Professor Israel Friedlaender, her friend from seminary days, who had given Hadassah its motto. In 1918 the Joint Distribution Committee (JDC) recommended Friedlaender as a representative of the Jewish community to accompany a Red Cross expedition into Palestine. Two major Zionist leaders, Richard Gottheil and Rabbi Stephen S. Wise, opposed the appointment, accusing Friedlaender of having had pro-German sentiments throughout the war. Friedlaender denied the charge but bitterly resigned from the expedition. In the midst of the uproar that followed, he accused Henrietta Szold and others on the Provisional Executive Committee of being too fearful to support him in the face of the Gottheil and Wise's opposition. She acknowledged the power of the two men, but tried to smooth over Friedlaender's anger with expressions of warm personal feelings.[9] To Sampter she wrote, "The Friedlaender incident bowled me over. . . . I can't bear strife."[10] Tragically, Friedlaender died two years later, when he was sent to Ukraine as an emissary of the JDC and murdered by Bolsheviks, who might have mistaken him for someone else.

The Russian Revolution itself excited Szold when it began in 1917, as it did Jews throughout the world. The tsar was overthrown and a new, free life for Russia's Jews appeared to be opening up. Writing to Jessie, Henrietta was thrilled to be the "contemporary" of the "Russian awakening" and was sorry she was not in New York to join others in celebrating it. A year later, with German forces invading Russia, she felt better about no longer being an "orthodox pacifist" in these complicated days. "I was ready to fight for the people," she wrote Sampter, "though I could not fight for the kings." She could have supported the Entente's alliance with the Russian people, but had resented backing the tsar. And though she disapproved of America's sale of Liberty War Bonds, which she regarded as a form of taxation, with Russia out of the conflict, she felt comfortable giving her support to the American war effort.[11] (The Russian Revolution she so approved of lasted only two years, and a new dictatorship under Lenin and then Stalin made Jewish life in Russia miserable again.)

She had some reservations about the Balfour Declaration, the other big event of 1917 for world Jewry. Like Jews everywhere, she celebrated the declaration, which had been stated in the form of a letter from British foreign secretary Alfred Balfour to the Zionist financier Lionel Walter Rothschild, that the British government "views with favour the establishment in Palestine of a national home for the Jewish people." In fact, irritated by the low level of interest in Zionism she found among Jews in Texas when she visited Galveston, she wrote Sampter that the declaration had simply passed over the heads of the Jews there, who didn't even know that "something epoch-making had just happened."[12] Later, however, during the Arab riots against the Jews in Palestine, she spoke more negatively of the declaration as an extension of British imperialism leading up to "the sword," the British military conquest of Palestine. Still, she never renounced the declaration. Carried out simply, it would not have hurt the Arabs, she wrote home, describing a long car trip she took to Haifa. "For five hours and a half we flew through an empty, deserted country. What harm to the Arabs if Jews develop it?"[13]

After the Balfour Declaration and General Edmund Allenby's capture of Jerusalem from the Turks a month later ("the sword," in Szold's terms), the Zionist dream of a homeland in Palestine suddenly appeared real and within reach. The time had come, Brandeis and other leaders decided, to put the American Zionist movement in order, with special attention to the weak Federation of American Zionists and the various clubs and societies that over the years had clung to it. Accordingly, in 1918, toward the end of the war, the FAZ and its affiliates were merged into the newly formed Zionist Organization of America (ZOA) with a national executive board headed by Judge Julian Mack. At the time, Szold approved of the reorganization. Although Hadassah was to remain a separate affiliate, she agreed to merge some of its activities with the new agency, in that sense making it an equal partner with the Zionist men. The *Hadassah Bulletin* of August 1918 spelled out several financial transactions between the two organizations, continuing, albeit with a touch of sadness, that this would be the last *Bulletin;* henceforth it would be "the news-bearer of the whole Zionist Organization." Before dissolving, the *Bulletin* outlined Hadassah's history and achievements as if to emphasize that, for all the changes taking place, Hadassah was still Hadassah.[14]

Szold was appointed secretary of the Department of Education of the new organization, the only woman to fully lead one of its departments (again "secretary," again the only woman). The work involved organizing adult education programs as well as Hebrew schools and clubs for young people, creating various publications, and initiating other projects. Along with Jessie Sampter and Rose Zeitlin, a Hadassah friend, two outstanding young educators joined her: Emanuel Neumann and Alexander Dushkin, one of the "Benderly boys" trained by Samson Benderly, whom she had hired years earlier to work in the New York Kehillah. Neumann, named educational director in her department, remembered being intimidated at first by the almost sixty-year-old Szold, who arrived at meetings a few minutes early and waited silently—to Neumann it seemed reproachfully—for others to show up, most of them invariably late. With time, he came to love and respect her, as did the other young staff members, who found that once she knew them, she relaxed, gave them more responsibility, and became easy to work with. Sometimes she held little informal soirees for the staff at her home—she had moved to a small apartment in the Hotel Alexandria on West 103rd Street—where she entertained them with humorous mimicry; she specialized in imitations of people taking snuff.[15]

That camaraderie did not carry over to the men who ran the ZOA on an everyday basis, Jacob de Haas and Louis Lipsky. De Haas had helped bring Brandeis into the Zionist movement and remained close to him, although his sharp edges irritated many other people; Lipsky, formerly with the FAZ, dominated the Zionist landscape. Neither man regarded Hadassah or Szold with any greater respect now than they had during the group's formative days. Moreover, they wanted the ZOA to take over Hadassah's Palestinian work, namely, the medical and health-care services that had distinguished the women's group from its beginnings. These men's brashness triggered Hadassah's disillusionment with the Zionist organization fairly quickly, and the next several years would involve a tug of war, with Szold and Hadassah pulling hard to take their organization back from the ever-encroaching grasp of Lipsky and the ZOA. Under the pressures of their grappling, Szold had to take time off work at her doctor's orders, her heart "in bad condition," as she wrote Alice Seligsberg, and "I need not tell you why."[16] She spent the summer of 1919 recuperating at Booth Bay Harbor in Maine.

Meanwhile, the AZMU, the unit of doctors and nurses that had become Hadassah's special project, had taken on new life after Allenby's capture of Jerusalem. By March 1918, the British embassies in Washington and London had authorized sending it to Palestine. And by then, it had become something far different from the two nurses, two doctors, and a handful of medical supplies with which it began. It was now planned as a corps of some twenty nurses and twenty doctors, covering a range of medical fields from dermatologists and gynecologists to pediatricians and dentists. Its four hundred tons of supplies, to be shipped separately, held ambulances, eight vehicles, an assortment of medical equipment, and piles of linens and clothing—in short, a fully equipped hospital in the making. Its first year's budget alone had mushroomed to $450,000, not the kind of figure Hadassah women's nickels and dimes could amount to. For much of the money, Szold and others turned to the Joint Distribution Committee, which provided about $200,000. Nathan Straus gave another sum for the specific use of Muslims in the Holy Land, Brandeis allocated a good part of the American Zionist funds to the unit, and Hadassah managed to raise the rest. For Hadassah women, fund-raising now became targeted on the medical unit more than any other project.

Some of the money raised went toward uniforms to distinguish the unit members. The nurses' summer uniforms consisted of gray crepe blouses with white collars and cuffs, long skirts that ended just above the ankle, Panama hats with veils, and on the sleeves a red Star of David encircled by the words "American Zionist Medical Unit." Similar winter uniforms were made of gray wool and velour hats. The men wore khaki cottons and woolens. After many delays and with the war still raging, on June 11, 1918, members of the unit, in their uniforms, boarded a troop ship carrying three thousand soldiers and military personnel, some American Red Cross workers, and a sprinkling of other passengers. Alice Seligsberg, a member of Hadassah's Central Committee, headed the unit while Szold remained in the States to raise funds for it. At the last minute the medical director, Dr. Israel E. Hirsch, withdrew because of family pressure, and Szold quickly replaced him with Dr. Isaac M. Rubinow, about whom she knew little other than his good reputation. He signed on without great enthusiasm.

The unit spent two weeks crossing the Atlantic, many members suffering from seasickness, all fearful of German submarines. After time in Paris, London, and Rome, the group arrived in Lod (now Lydda) in August 1918. Soon afterward they set up headquarters in the Rothschild Hospital in Jerusalem, which the Baron Edmond de Rothschild had agreed to turn over for their use and to help finance. Both Jews and Arabs had suffered terrible losses from malaria and famine in that city. As the war moved toward an end and the Turks were pushed out of Palestine, the team expanded, setting up emergency hospitals and clinics in Tiberias to fight the cholera epidemic there; in Safed, where typhoid raged; and in Jaffa, struck by bubonic plague. Much later, these and other hospitals would grow into the Hadassah Medical Center complex on Mt. Scopus. In the same year, 1918, the Hadassah Nurses' Training School opened in Jerusalem.[17]

Dr. Harry Friedenwald, who spent much of his time working in Palestine, wrote to his friend Henrietta Szold about the AZMU on June 11, 1919, exactly one year after it had set sail for the Holy Land. Looking at the work it had accomplished, he assured her that she and Hadassah had a great deal to be proud of. But he also mentioned difficulties and mistakes that had been made.[18] In the States, Louis Brandeis had become aware of those difficulties and mistakes, of infighting among doctors in the unit, finances in disarray, and struggles between the unit and the Zionist Commission, a liaison group between the Jewish population and the British administration in Palestine founded by the World Zionist Organization. He asked Henrietta Szold to go to Jerusalem to straighten things out, especially to make sure the AZMU remained under American control. Both excited and frightened by the prospect, she accepted the assignment. She stored the belongings she would not need on this trip in Bertha's home in Baltimore. They included her journals and correspondence with Louis Ginzberg, and the veil he had knotted about her head on that cold, windy day long ago.[19]

On February 21, 1920, she boarded the S.S. *Giuseppe* bound for Naples, embarking on the first lap of what she would call "the great adventure of my life."[20]

* * *

A year and a half after Szold began her journey, another woman would leave America, also destined for British-controlled Palestine: Golda Meir (Meyerson at the time). The two would become the most famous American Jewish women of the twentieth century to make their homes in that land. Their lives would differ greatly: Szold, approaching sixty, would always regard herself as an American, although, unexpectedly for her, she would live much of the rest of her life in Palestine. Meir, only twenty-three when she left the United States, shed her American citizenship almost immediately, although she would return to that country regularly to fund-raise and attend meetings. Both would contribute greatly to the development of the Yishuv, the pre-state Jewish community in Palestine, Meir through politics (eventually becoming Israel's fourth prime minister), and Szold through health, education, and social services. On the tenth anniversary of Szold's death, Meir delivered a talk commemorating her. She recalled that in her own early days in Palestine, when she lived on a kibbutz, she planned to visit Szold to discuss some matter. She knew no Hebrew yet, and a colleague warned her not to go. She would make a bad impression on Szold if she spoke to the older woman in English, the colleague said. In Erez Israel, Szold expected to be spoken to in Hebrew.[21]

Hebrew was much on Szold's mind as she sailed across the sea. Before leaving, she had written to Alice Seligsberg that she would have "a little more confidence" in herself if she spoke Hebrew as easily as she spoke English.[22] Consequently she had her books with her for studying on the ship, and on part of the voyage, she would be tutored by a young man. Years earlier she had written to Rabbi Joseph Hertz, a family friend (who later became chief rabbi of Britain) about the close connection between Zionism and Hebrew and how frustrated she felt not to have had time to master the language, although she was not going to give up.[23] Over the next several years, she struggled through the difficult Hebrew in the essays and novels of Peretz Smolenskin and other Jewish nationalist writers, observing that through modern Hebrew literature "the secular is elevated and consecrated."[24] But she fretted because she had not become proficient in spoken Hebrew. That would change within a year after arriving in Palestine when, with hard work, she was able to give lectures in Hebrew, albeit haltingly. As Golda Meir found out, she also expected new immigrants to the land to make an effort to learn the language.

On the ship carrying her to Naples Szold shared a cabin with Julia Aronson, a young dietician who was off to join the AZMU. The two would remain close friends in Palestine, but on this trip, Aronson went ahead to the Holy Land while Szold remained in Naples waiting for a permit to enter the land that she had postponed getting in New York. She had expected the permit to be at the British consulate, but when days passed without it, she left Naples for Florence, where she spent Passover at the home of a Sephardic rabbi, Samuel Hirsch Margulies, whom she and her mother had met during their 1909 trip. Among the guests at the Margulies home were Herbert Samuel and his wife and son. An aristocratic British Zionist and former cabinet member, Samuel would soon be knighted and named high commissioner for Palestine. Like the friendships Szold made with powerful men at every stage of her career, this one placed her on a level with the elite of the society she was now entering.

She loved Florence, with its churches and Renaissance paintings, so much so that steeped in that culture, she kept aware of world events only as a faint "tinkling" in her ears.[25] Yet momentous things were happening. Samuel, in fact, was on his way to San Remo, where the League of Nations would award Britain a mandate over Palestine, incorporating in it the provisions of the Balfour Declaration. With the First World War over, the United States had made peace with Germany. And in Jerusalem, Arab mobs had attacked the Jewish Quarter in the Old

City during Passover. The Jews called the violence a "pogrom," a term carried over from their experiences in eastern Europe. The militant Jewish Zionist Vladimir Jabotinsky was thrown in jail while fighting back, and in the northern village of Tel Hai, a beloved pioneer leader, Joseph Trumpeldor, was killed in the rioting. Szold would later experience Arab violence herself in Palestine. After some time, she boarded the S.S. *Umbria* for Alexandria and finally picked up her permit in Cairo. Two long, steaming train rides later she entered Lod. Alice Seligsberg, Nellie Straus—a Hadassah friend, recently married—and Dr. Rubinow greeted her there with an automobile to take them all up to Jerusalem. Seeing Alice, who "represented home" gave her a feeling of serenity, Szold wrote her sisters. "At once this whole adventure of mine seemed right and normal."[26]

The serenity would vanish fairly rapidly as she coped with conflicts within the unit and disagreements outside it. As always, she overworked and complained about demands made of her, feeling herself pulled and pushed in dozens of directions at the same time, but, as always, she would turn chaos into calm and on some level take pleasure in her accomplishments and the adventure that brought her to them.

Seligsberg had arranged for her to stay at the home of Dr. Kagan and her mother. Dr. Kagan had gone to Europe for several months of rest and study, and Szold received a bedroom, sitting room, and maid's room occupied by a young woman named Rivkah Cohen, who not only served Szold but also helped her practice conversational Hebrew. Aside from breakfast, Szold would take her meals at the Hôtel de France, living headquarters for the unit. On her first day in her new home she received visits from Alex Dushkin, who had worked with her in the ZOA education department and would become one of her best friends in Palestine; Norman Bentwich, attorney general of mandate Palestine, whom she had last seen when she and her mother went abroad; and other friends and acquaintances. By the next day she felt ready to plunge into work. Within a few hours she had almost drowned in the sea of problems that turned up.

She met with Dr. Rubinow, the unit's director, who spelled out his troubles about the money shortages he faced. American organizations had not come through with promised funds and consequently, the Zionist Commission had cut off his credit. Prices had risen since the AZMU had arrived, and the Arab riots, forcing numbers into the hospital, drained needed funds. He and his staff lived hand to mouth, he said. But the troubles went far beyond money. Many of the doctors had turned against him, refusing to accept his authority. All demanded raises in their salaries; some, from Europe, who joined the unit in Palestine, accused him and the American physicians of being highhanded, as if they possessed the only medical knowledge among staff members. When Szold met later with the staff, she discovered an even worse situation than Rubinow had described. Relations of the unit members to one another and to the director were strained "to the breaking point," she wrote home.[27]

Matters became worse yet within the next few days. Rubinow resigned in a huff after newspaper reports gave the impression that Szold had come to Palestine to investigate him and take over the medical unit. The unit's medical council, an advisory group, resigned in sympathy with him, leading also to the resignation of the chief pathologist, the unit's star. At the same time, student nurses in the Jerusalem hospital went on strike for better conditions, stalking out of the wards. And everyone—doctors, nurses, and patients—complained about the hospital food.

Although the resignations were retracted and the strike recalled shortly afterward, Szold realized that she had almost lost her balance that first week under the "storm of gossip, rumors, complaints, grievances, charges, malice, and distortions."[28] Looking back after several months, she told Harry Friedenwald that she had been ready to return to America in those days, driven by a voice within her that kept shouting: "These are not your people. You have no part and parcel in them."[29] But she determined to persevere, and began to examine the workings of the unit systematically. She came to respect Dr. Rubinow, "a tired, nervous man," who had never received the budget promised him but still managed to have the medical unit do crucial work.[30] Now that she had arrived, he informed her that he was going back to America to vacation for several months and could not promise that he would return. Rumor had it that he had fallen in love with his Russian secretary, and was going home to his wife and children to try to sort out his life.[31] Under the circumstances, Henrietta Szold would become acting director of the AZMU—a woman with no medical training in charge of a string of hospitals with a staff of four hundred, dozens of whom were physicians, nurses, pharmacists, and other medically related personnel. "If Dr. Rubinow stays away three months, I may have time enough to wreck the whole thing," she wrote sardonically to her family.[32]

To familiarize herself with the operation before Rubinow left, she set out with him and Julia Aronson in an old Ford automobile to visit the hospitals outside Jerusalem. What she saw in Jaffa delighted her—a small hospital with beds for children and surgical cases and a clinic for eye trouble, dental work, and other medical issues. What she saw in Tiberias appalled her. The hospital occupied a small house with barely any medical equipment, and her first reaction was simply to close it up. Yet after seeing the crowds of people seeking medical aid, where absolutely none had existed before, her second impulse was to keep the facility going despite its inadequacies. The same held true in Safed, whose hospital had such dirty and decrepit kitchen and laundry areas they deserved to be condemned. And Haifa, a city she found as filthy and unsanitary as it had been ten years earlier, had a hospital and clinic that required at least twice the amount of money they presently had in order to function decently. But here, as in the rest of Palestine, illness ran so rampant, and the numbers of people needing help appeared so enormous, that the hospital filled a crying need. "Just as the stoniness of the soil doesn't kill one's confidence in the fertility," Szold wrote in a moment of optimism, "hope is not blighted" by the shortcomings of the cities' hospitals. Somehow they would continue to serve the population.[33]

After spending time in Haifa, she and her party visited Jabotinsky and twenty of his associates, jailed at the nearby fortress prison of Acre during the Arab uprising and sentenced by the British to fifteen years of hard labor (later reversed by Herbert Samuel). She found Jabotinsky fascinating and defiant, and although she could not sympathize with his aggressive outlook, she left the visit impressed by his intelligence and charisma. She made a sorrowful visit over the weekend to the family of Aaron Aaronsohn at the settlement of Zichron Yaakov in the area. The agronomist, with whom Szold had struck up a warm friendship during his visit to America in 1910, had been killed in an airplane crash in 1919. At the time of the tragedy, Szold wrote a eulogy for him suggesting that building up the land would be the most fitting monument to the man who had devoted himself to creating a scientific agricultural station at Atlit.[34] Now the cases holding samples of ancient wild wheat he had collected and exhibited stood in disarray and the station itself had gone bankrupt, with no possibility of continuing the experimental work Szold had enthusiastically encouraged.

On her return to Jerusalem, and while preparing for Rubinow's departure, Szold had to contend with the Zionist Commission's attempts to take over the AZMU. She had been sent to safeguard the identity of the unit as a professional American organization, Hadassah's project. To do so, she needed to negotiate with the commission members. The current president and toughest of them all was Menachem Mendel Ussishkin, a man who thought so highly of himself that even Jerusalem's civil governor, Ronald Storrs, spoke of him as "Czar Menachem." Born in Russia, Ussishkin had been one of the founders of Hovevei Zion, the Lovers of Zion group that had first drawn Szold toward Zionism. Authoritarian and single-minded, he brooked no objections to goals he wanted, and in this case he wanted, Szold realized, "unconditional surrender," meaning complete control of the unit, with no hint of compromise.[35] The struggle over the AZMU would continue and become tied up during the next year with a larger battle between the American Zionists, who provided much of the money for Yishuv development, and the European Zionists, who wanted authority over everything that took place there. In the meantime, Szold did manage to have Hadassah funds go directly to her rather than through the commission. They amounted to only a fraction of the money needed, but it was still a small victory.

Once Rubinow left for vacation in mid-June, Szold's focus became fixed on running the unit. Her day began in the office at 6:45 in the morning and usually extended far into the night. She had hoped to be able to take a short nap in the afternoon or a walk in the evening, but that would not happen. All day long, people sought her out with their problems—doctors, nurses, midwives, students—each claiming also to have been promised a raise by Dr. Rubinow. In between she delved through voluminous files of the doctor's correspondence, checked on agreements with workingmen's societies, and familiarized herself with government regulations. She discovered quickly that every division of the AZMU lacked the funds necessary to operate efficiently. Throughout the day, she wrote home, she could feel the steady pounding of the word *deficit, deficit, deficit* in her head like the beating of a bass drum.[36]

Waves of immigrants arriving one after another compounded the economic morass. Szold had come to Palestine during the third aliyah. (The first aliyah, from about 1881 to 1904, included the Hovevei Zion groups that built some of the earliest agricultural settlements. David Ben-Gurion and others who would later become the founders of the State of Israel arrived during the second aliyah, from 1904 to 1914.) Young, single immigrants fleeing pogroms in eastern Europe—many of them penniless—made up the bulk of this aliyah, which extended from after the First World War to 1923. With the Zionist movement lacking funds to support broad settlement on the land, many of these impoverished young people, who had come as pioneers, worked as laborers, building roads throughout the country. Illnesses, particularly malaria, plagued them, and Szold wrung her hands over the fact that the immigrants arrived at a rate of three hundred a week, and the unit hospitals had to turn away dozens of them, many with high fevers, because of a lack of space. She tried to provide field hospitals near the workers' camps, but she lacked sufficient doctors and nurses to make a dent in the misery. She began preparing educational leaflets to be sent around to teach the newcomers about the diseases of the country and how to prevent them.

As the fall approached, and with it the rainy season, she became especially concerned about the immigrants living in makeshift tents, many sleeping on the ground, with flies buzzing around and spreading disease. Even though the Joint Distribution Committee provided funds to help set up and sanitize the immigrant camps, that money didn't come close to meeting the pressing needs. At times, out of sheer frustration, she lost her temper, shouting at people around her, then feeling guilty about the outburst. "I may as well confess," she wrote to Adele in October 1920, "that the life here does not make me happy. . . . Palestine now is a bundle of problems, and problems are not conducive to happiness. And it isn't conducive to happiness if we keep thinking of the hundreds and hundreds of immigrants in tents."[37]

Still, she was not altogether unhappy. It pleased her that, aware of her work with the medical unit, British government officials had expressed regret that Dr. Rubinow would be returning soon; they would have preferred that she continue. She herself felt a little sorry about his return now that her self-doubts had dissipated and she recognized that with her care and organization, the unit had become far more efficient than before. Not only that, but with a touch of vanity—or was it competitiveness with her younger sisters?—she reported that when asked to guess Szold's age, a woman had insisted it had to be no more than thirty-eight, making Szold feel young and vigorous, not yet a "nebbich."[38]

In truth, for all her complaints, much about her life gave her satisfaction. A small stone house she rented on the outskirts of Jerusalem with a social worker named Sophia Berger ranked high among her pleasures (Szold had to move after Dr. Kagan returned). Berger had come to Palestine to replace Alice Seligsberg, who had been working with war orphans. She found the house, cheerfully did all the cooking, and arranged little dinner parties and picnics, usually with Szold's closest friends in Jerusalem: Jessie Sampter; Alex Dushkin and Julia Aronson, whom Szold introduced to each other; Norman Bentwich and his sisters; Nellie Straus and her husband; and on occasion others. A guest at one of those little dinners, Pinhas Rutenberg, a Russian-born engineer, had been drawing up plans to build a hydroelectric power station on the Jordan River to conserve water. He seemed "a little too optimistic" to Szold.[39] As it turned out, within a decade that plant was built in the village of Naharayim on the Jordan, along with a string of others throughout the land. The women's entertaining usually took place in the large garden surrounding the house, an expansive area with olive, orange, almond, plum, and peach trees, and while the house, heated only by an oil stove, could become freezing in the winter, the garden compensated for many discomforts. The women were "happy as happy can be" in their lodging, Szold told her family.[40]

Then there were special events: a fancy dress Halloween

party, the first Henrietta had experienced in her life; the magnificent wedding of Herbert Samuel's son, which boasted, in addition to three rabbis, several sheikhs, Dominican priests, Russian popes, and Abyssinian clergy, and at which the sheikhs gave the couple as their wedding present an entire village, including its men, women, and children; and best of all, a surprise sixtieth birthday party for Szold, with a dinner attended by Sir Herbert and Lady Samuel, and a reception afterward for 150 guests at the Hôtel de France. Szold was inscribed in the Jewish National Fund's Golden Book, received dozens of gifts, telegrams, and letters, and delighted in the fact that so many of her well-wishers expressed the hope that she would not return to America at the end of her two years. She danced throughout the evening, one circle dance after another, until the very end. "It is wonderful to have lived from the mid-Victorian period right into the after-war upheaval," she said, "from skirts trailing in mud and dust in the streets of Baltimore to skirts above high shoe tops to escape the inevitable mud of a rainy day in Jerusalem."[41]

And running through everything Szold wrote—her diary or her letters to family and friends—shone her awe at the land itself. "What is the use of writing about the magic of the moonlight, or the brilliance of the stars, or the perfumed, clear air" she wrote home soon after arriving in Jerusalem. After her trip to Tiberias, she confessed she felt almost "overpowered by emotion. . . . The stones are soft with colorfulness, and between them spring up blossoms so curiously adapted to the peculiarity of the land that one cannot wonder enough." And as fall replaced summer, she rhapsodized over "the moonlit nights after the first rainfall, the bewildering wonder of the colors at sunrise and sunset, the delicious warmth of the sun." There would be times, later, when she longed for the woody Maryland landscape of her youth, but she always retained her love for the stark beauty of Palestine.[42]

* * *

Dr. Rubinow returned in December, and Szold humbly moved out of his large office area into a room with other employees, where she worked at a small table, although he had not asked her to do that. She eased off for a while on the long hours she had worked, and even learned to cook a little to help Sophia. They kept a kosher home, which at some point became vegetarian. Szold had remained observant, but her attitude toward the synagogue had changed. No Conservative congregations existed in Palestine, and the Orthodox synagogues she attended in Jerusalem made her feel demeaned, forced to sit behind a curtain that blocked her view of the service, except for the men's feet—reminiscent of her experience many years earlier in the synagogue in Prague. Fed up with formal services, she and her group of friends—Sophia Berger, Jessie Sampter, Alex Dushkin, Norman Bentwich, and Judah Magnes (who came to Palestine in 1922)—began meeting on Saturday mornings in Szold's or Sampter's house. They tried holding a full Sabbath service, but they "couldn't get the right spirit into it," she wrote Emily Solis-Cohen, Elvira's sister. Instead they built their service around reading the weekly Torah portion and studying the book of Jeremiah. Later they would add paragraphs from the liturgy, dropping all references to rebuilding the temple, and the women and men would sing together as a group. In the afternoon, they usually held discussions on some topic of importance that had come up during the week.

A topic that had taken on importance for Szold concerned women's role in relation to the rabbinate. The British government had given the Jewish community autonomy in terms of family law, and some women had begun protesting against the stringent anti-women rulings of the rabbinic courts, petitioning for Jewish civil courts to handle such areas as property rights, inheritance, divorce, custody of children, and others that affected them—subjects that would remain contentious for decades. Szold agreed in principle with the women's protests, yet she worried about another "cleavage" in the Jewish community. "The modification of the law must come gradually, from within," she maintained in her letter to Emily. "We must have patience." On the other hand, when she thought about how hard women had to struggle over specific issues ("shall daughters not inherit with sons?" for example), she sympathized with them. "I am dumb," she said, reluctant to offer criticism.[43]

Outside the religious realm and aside from her Hadassah work, she had agreed to head the Federation of Hebrew Women (Histadrut Nashim Ivriot), an organization that provided medical and social services specifically to women and children. Bat-Sheva Kesselman, the federation's founder, had emigrated from Odessa to the United States, where she joined Hadassah, and then moved to Jerusalem and formed the organization, largely to combat the appalling rate of infant mortality there. The group elected Szold president at its first meeting, held at the city's Amdursky Hotel on July 14, 1920. Much of the organization's work centered on aid and education for pregnant women and new mothers. A few years later it joined forces with the more feminist Union of Hebrew Women for Equal Rights to battle for women's suffrage in the Yishuv. Although Szold had not been caught up in the suffragist movement in the United States, she supported the cause here. At a public meeting in Jerusalem she charged the Yishuv to "guard and protect the principles of equality and justice which are at the core of our national enterprise."[44] More than ever before, she had become a vocal advocate for women's rights in many areas of life.

In her personal life, her friendships with women continued to strengthen her and temper her longing for her sisters. Before she arrived in Palestine, her closest friends, Jessie Sampter and Alice Seligsberg, had launched a campaign, enlisting the help of other Jewish women, to have her appointed to the Zionist Commission. Szold suspected from the start that the commission would not seat a woman, and she proved correct, but she appreciated her friends' support.[45] In her letters to Sampter and Seligsberg, she revealed some of her deepest feelings, sometimes even more fully than to her family. With their profound friendship, these women sustained one another in the difficult lives each had chosen to live in the Land of Israel.[46]

A short while after Dr. Rubinow's return, Szold took a day off from work to catch up with daily chores she rarely had time for. She reveled in washing her hair and drying it in the sun, mending her clothes, and answering letters. On other days she made time to shop for rugs to place on the icy stone floors of her house and for warm clothes to shield her from the cold that in the winter months, she found, could be even more piercing inside her house than outside. She wore long underwear and wrapped herself in a ratty secondhand fur coat someone had given her. She especially appreciated the heavy sweater her sisters had sent for her birthday. For all that, she gloried in the golden days that followed intervals of rain. The ups and downs in the weather, as she described them, seemed almost a metaphor for her responses to the world around her as 1920 turned into 1921, and she no longer carried the full burden of the unit.

She maintained her practice of visiting agricultural settlements and tent camps for immigrants and road workers, enjoying the adventure of sleeping in a tent at one place and in a kvutza (a small collective) at another. Writing home, she described the immigrants coming from eastern Europe to work the land as "wonderful," yet she could not fully accept them. "I want to—and I cannot. I love order. Disorder nauseates me. And they are system-less. They hate efficiency. . . . Yet they are heroic, not I."[47] In another letter she described a young man, a *halutz*, pioneer, she had met, originally from Galicia, who spoke of the beauty of that country but declared, "I am free here. Work has freed me here; over there I did not belong to myself." In some ways, she saw in this young halutz and others like him the culmination of the cultural Zionism she had embraced, the love of Zion she regarded as integral to Judaism. For these people Zionism was a way of life. It had its rough edges and lack of "grace," but it was heroic and "joyous," holding out hope for the kind of "rejuvenation" the Jewish people needed.[48] Nevertheless, Szold herself still grappled with the "Sturm und Drang," storm and stress, and the ups and downs of Zionist life in Erez Israel.[49]

The stresses multiplied when she found herself in the midst of a violent Arab uprising. She had been vacationing with Sophia Berger and other friends in Rehobot, a settlement outside Jaffa. They left on Sunday morning, May 1, 1921, planning to have lunch at Szold's favorite German-style restaurant in Jaffa, and ordering an automobile to take them to Jerusalem afterward. Before eating, Szold briefly visited her friend Nellie Straus, who lived in neighboring Tel Aviv. On the way she saw a procession of people carrying red flags, and learned later that they were marching in a May Day parade organized, with British permission, by Achdut Ha'avoda, the major Jewish labor party in the Yishuv. Another, smaller group of Jewish communists marched nearby, without permits. At lunch afterward she and her companions heard shots. The men at the table thought guns were being fired in the air to maintain order during the parade, but Szold felt a sickening tension that became almost unbearable when their car failed to show up.

She rushed to the Jaffa hospital and suddenly knew "there was a war on." Dead bodies lay in the courtyard and stretchers, some bearing the wounded, others the dead, formed lines outside. Inside, masses of wounded waiting to be treated packed the operating room and spread out on the floor. All had been attacked by bands of Arabs wielding clubs, knives, swords, and in some cases pistols. Sophia joined Szold, and the two stayed through the night organizing the care of the injured and assisting the crush of relatives searching for loved ones. Hundreds of other wounded and dead were at a nearby gymnasium, at another, smaller hospital, and in private homes. Szold telephoned Jerusalem for medicine and bandages as well as doctors and nurses to help at the Jaffa hospital, phoning again the next morning for food—bread and eggs—to feed the starving patients. All the shops in town had been shut tight.

Ignoring the danger to themselves, Henrietta and Sophia returned to Jerusalem, passing bands of armed Arabs. The city appeared dead, shops boarded up and merchants standing at their doors, seemingly paralyzed with fear. With no riots currently happening, Szold begged the merchants to open their stores and not give in to panic, but with little success. In an effort to mobilize the city's men to encourage the Jewish population to return to normalcy, she went to the office of the Zionist Commission and spoke to a young man, the only person she could find there. She accused Jerusalem's Jews of being "chickenhearted" when they were not, after all, in immediate danger. "Madam," the young man responded, "how many pogroms have you been through?" "None," she replied. "I have been through twelve," he said. His words, she had to admit, silenced her. These people had reason to fear.[50]

The rioting continued for almost a week and spread to a number of settlements. Nobody could say definitively what sparked the violence. Some blamed it on clashes between the two Jewish labor groups, the socialists and communists, marching on May Day, with fistfights among the marchers drawing in the Arabs. Others recalled warnings given by friendly Arabs that agitators had been planning violence against the Jews for that day. Many people spoke of the disgraceful behavior of some of the policemen, who discarded their badges and joined the mobs in beating and raping new arrivals at Bet-ha-Halutzim, a hostel for immigrants. Like many other Jews, Szold accused the British of favoring the Arabs, allowing them to be armed with clubs and knives but arresting any Jew who used a revolver in self-defense without a permit, and of censuring the Hebrew newspapers ("the editorial and . . . the news columns are almost entirely white," she wrote) but not the Arab papers.[51]

Szold had a paradoxical attitude toward arms. Her pacifist principles opposed any kind of militancy. But her Jewish sensibility insisted that Jews had a right to self-defense against Arab hostility. Some months after the Jaffa riots she wrote about an Arab "outrage" in Jerusalem on Balfour Day, November 2. She described approvingly how the Jews defended themselves "with dignity and circumspectness" and showed "restrained vehemence" at the massive funeral of five people who had been killed. Perhaps, she speculated at another time, she needed to classify self-defense differently from other forms of battle. But even if so, she had to admit, "Then I am no longer a pacifist."[52] As was the case with her Zionism and other areas of life, in the end, when practicality necessitated certain actions, it won out over cold principles.

To quell the Jaffa riots, Herbert Samuel turned to Egypt for assistance. He also infuriated many in the Yishuv by suspending Jewish immigration and sending back two immigrant ships that were on their way from Istanbul to Palestine. He told Szold personally that had he not done so, "there would have been a massacre of every Jew in the country." Yet she felt that this was a "policy of cowardice," of appeasing the Arabs at the expense of the Jews, and especially abhorrent for the Jewish high commissioner to respond in that way. She and a majority of the Yishuv faulted the British governor of Palestine, Ronald Storrs, for the same attitude—and even more so. He "despises" the Jews, she wrote after having lunch with him. In his view, the Arab was a "native"; the Jew was not. (It gave her special pleasure that he was forced to have a kosher meal because of her.) Aside from the leaders, she also believed that lower-level members of the British government who opposed the Balfour Declaration helped stir Arab anger. Nevertheless, she placed some blame on the Jews themselves for not having created better economic opportunities for both Jewish immigrants and Arab workers that might have somewhat mitigated the situation.[53]

While tensions with the Arabs raged, tensions within the Zionist movement reached their zenith. For some years there had been an uneasy peace between the American Zionists, led by Louis Brandeis, and the Europeans, headed by Chaim Weizmann, but the question of who would ultimately lead the international organization hung in the air, unaddressed openly. The charming, persuasive British chemist Weizmann, who had been instrumental in attaining the Balfour Declaration, was devoting his life to creating a Jewish state in mandated Palestine. While Brandeis and the Americans appreciated his devotion, they criticized his poor business planning and the inefficiency and fiscal sloppiness he and his supporters often displayed. Yet for all his criticisms of Weizmann, Brandeis would not fully commit his own life to running the Zionist movement. He had been to Erez Israel only once, for a short time in 1919, and although he fell in love with the land, he had no wish to do what many wanted of him: give up his Supreme Court position to be a full-time Zionist leader. He had always held that being a Zionist went hand in hand with being an American, and he believed he could fulfill both ideals best in his role as a justice of the Supreme Court.

In an atmosphere of anxiety and anticipation at the annual convention of the ZOA on June 5, 1921, held in Cleveland, Ohio, the voting went overwhelmingly in favor of the Weizmann camp on several issues, but primarily on major funding policies the Brandeis contingent had opposed. Julian Mack, president of the ZOA and Brandeis's close associate, immediately resigned his position. As people in the hall wept he read a letter of resignation from Brandeis as honorary president, which promised that he and his followers would not turn their backs on Zionism, but would remain "as humble soldiers in the ranks" while the struggle for a homeland continued. Those leaving the ZOA with Brandeis and Mack included Stephen S. Wise, Harry Friedenwald, and Nathan Straus, with all of whom Szold had close associations.[54]

"I throw my lot in with the Mack-Brandeis party," Szold wrote home a few weeks after the great schism. Placed in an untenable position, she was being pressured by both sides to sway Hadassah in their directions. She responded by refusing to choose sides for the women's organization. On the one hand, with the Weizmann victory, she did not believe she should pull Hadassah away from the international organization as a "separatist movement" (even though, in truth, the majority of Hadassah leaders backed Brandeis). On the other, she could not advise the group to accept the decisions in Cleveland "when I myself oppose them."[55]

At the heart of her opposition to the Weizmann faction lay the expansive fund-raising plan approved in Cleveland. Called the Keren Hayesod, or Palestine Foundation Fund, it was conceived as a public fund for the economic development of Jewish Palestine, a catch-all from which settlements and immigration as well as key institutions would be financed. She much preferred Brandeis's "business Zionism," as it was sometimes called, a more sophisticated arrangement that involved private investments with various safeguards under careful public supervision. From Szold's viewpoint, like that of Brandeis, the broad Keren Hayesod smacked of old-fashioned charity and, more important, opened the way to corruption by the people running it. She resented the influence the large public fund would have over the AZMU. Moreover, with Weizmann one of the leaders of the Zionist Commission, she worried that the fund would be used for political ends. Menachem Ussishkin, president of the commission, with whom she had already grappled about control of the unit, for example, wanted to put an eye specialist into one of the unit hospitals because the man once delivered a good Zionist speech, not primarily, she wrote, because he was a first-class ophthalmologist. "That sort of thing I have no interest in," she said. "That's the reason I am with the Mack-Brandeis party."[56]

Her reasons became even stronger with the machinations of Louis Lipsky. Along with Emanuel Neumann and other young leaders, Lipsky had left the Brandeis camp and joined Weizmann's supporters. With the split between the two groups, Lipsky became secretary general of the ZOA and had the additional responsibility of raising money for the Keren Hayesod. Membership in the ZOA had dropped drastically after the war and again with the split, from a high of two hundred thousand in 1918 to some eighteen thousand in 1922. Raising money for Keren Hayesod became more and more difficult. Meanwhile, Hadassah membership had continued to grow; in 1921, one out of every three members of the ZOA belonged to Hadassah. The women's organization had also begun inching its way back to more independence, creating the *News Letter* to replace the earlier *Bulletin*, which had been folded into the ZOA. Now Lipsky turned to Hadassah in his search for a Keren Hayesod source of money, demanding that its Central Committee direct the organization's chapters to turn all their collection money over to Keren Hayesod. In theory, with that money the fund would finance the health services Hadassah had been handling. In reality, as Szold pointed out, Keren Hayesod offered "no guarantee of immediacy, or efficiency, or vigor" in carrying out the practical work necessary in Palestine.[57] Aside from that, medical care in the Yishuv had been Hadassah's bailiwick from the organization's earliest days; taking direct fiscal responsibility away from it smacked of trying to deprive it of power and turn it into what Lipsky and others had always accused it of being: simply a women's philanthropy.

Seven members of Hadassah's Central Committee refused to follow Lipsky's orders. Enraged, he demanded that they resign. They, in turn, made clear that they had been elected by the local chapters, and only those chapters could dismiss them. With Szold's full support, albeit largely behind the scenes, the women rented new office space in Manhattan and sent letters with their names and Szold's as president of Hadassah to the Hadassah membership. After several bitter exchanges, the Hadassah women reached an agreement with Lipsky that essentially gave them a victory. The organization returned to the relatively semi-autonomous status it had held in the ZOA before the split, with the right to collect its own money and control its own projects. It also received representation it had not had before at world Zionist congresses. There would be more skirmishes with Lipsky, the ZOA, and the Keren Hayesod in the years ahead, but for now the Hadassah women, with Szold behind them, had shown their mettle and prevailed.

In the course of the fighting, Hadassah leaders in America pleaded with Szold to come home, handle Lipsky from New York, and run the women's group again. Brandeis and Mack insisted that she stay on in Palestine. Her character, wisdom, and commitment made it essential that she remain in the Holy Land and continue her work there, they argued. Others could run the organization at home. Although she had been heartsick about the fighting over Hadassah, she gladly followed their directions. "It would have been utterly distasteful to me to come home in order to 'save the situation,'" she wrote her sisters.[58] The Hadassah women had saved the situation on their own.

In the midst of the fighting and bitterness, and as occupied as she was with work, Szold found pleasure in both private and public events. In the private realm she held a wedding on July 4 in her garden for her two close young friends Julia Aronson and Alex Dushkin. At least 110 guests sat under groves of trees at tables decorated with brilliant garden flowers. The wedding canopy was made of unusual Bokheran silk, and Szold herself gave the bride away. "It was as charming a wedding as I have ever seen," she wrote her sisters, proud that she and Sophia had made their home a center of festivities in Jerusalem.[59] The public event, a key happening in the Yishuv, celebrated the graduation of the first class of nurses from the Hadassah Nurses' Training School in Erez Israel. Scheduled for Balfour Day, December 2, 1921, the graduation had to be postponed until December 3 because of Arab riots. The graduating nurses, twenty-two in all, filled the first three rows of the festive auditorium. Faculty, family, British officials, and prominent guests occupied the others. The entire ceremony took place in Hebrew, with even Lady Beatrice Samuel, wife of the high commissioner, who did not know the language well, nervously conferring diplomas in it.

Even so, the day held some pain for Szold. The people scheduled to speak included Dr. David Eder, head of the health department of the Zionist Commission, who did not know Hebrew. Among the guests present was Eliezer Ben-Yehuda, arguably the man most responsible for the development of modern Hebrew in the Yishuv and single-mindedly dedicated to that cause. During the course of the ceremony, Szold received a note from him on the back of an admission card, urging her not to "profane" the sanctity of the day by allowing a Jew to speak in a language other than Hebrew. When Dr. Eder rose to speak, Ben-Yehuda and his wife conspicuously stood up and marched out of the hall for all to see. Nobody else budged. Later Szold wrote Ben-Yehuda a personal note in which she granted him the right, by dint of his years of commitment to the Hebrew language, to be a fanatic. But she requested that he grant her the right, by reason of her work, to be a "fanatic for non-fanaticism."[60] She was hurt and angry that he had placed his values above the significance of the evening, especially since the program had been otherwise entirely in Hebrew.

In the keynote address Szold gave, in Hebrew, she reminded the graduates and the audience of the thousands of women in America for whom this day had been only a dream eleven years earlier when they sent the first two pioneer nurses to Palestine. It had become a reality now, a triumph for the young women who had worked hard to earn their degrees, often without adequate textbooks. And it was a triumph for those Hadassah women who had dared to dream big and whose hard work had made the dream come true.

7

◆◆◆◆◆◆

Living in Two Lands

HENRIETTA LONGED to go home to America and her family, but at every turn, her hopes were dashed. During the Hadassah-ZOA struggle, she had been figuratively "plucking daisy petals . . . should I, should I not?" before Brandeis insisted that she stay in Palestine.[1] She would be thwarted again when Dr. Rubinow announced his intention to retire from the medical unit. She had already taken full charge when he attended the Zionist Congress in Carlsbad in August 1921, and she knew that once he left permanently she would not only need to lead the unit but also help train somebody to fill his role. A small window of opportunity to go to America seemed to open in the late summer of 1922. After attending a conference herself in Carlsbad, she visited relatives in Vienna, with the idea that she might sail from there to New York for at least a brief visit. Again, it would not happen. Rubinow, who agreed to stay on the job while she was gone, barraged her with telegrams about the unit's dire financial straits. Now called the Hadassah Medical Organization (HMO), it did not even have sufficient funds to pay the doctors. Furthermore, reminding her that he had no intention of remaining much longer, he urged her to go to Paris and enlist the financial help of the Baron Edmond de Rothschild.

Dutifully, she traveled from Vienna to Paris and the baron's princely palace. Looking around at his elaborate surroundings, she had a fleeting image of him offering her "a little thing of the school of Leonardo de Vinci" to cover the unit's needs. Instead, courteously but firmly, he attacked wealthy American Jews and advised her to tell the "Guggenheims and Blumenthals and Warburgs" to do their duty. He did also praise the good work the HMO had been doing but, as she wrote her sisters, "Fine words butter no parsnips and keep no hospitals going."[2]

After another letter from Rubinow, who would leave in early December, and much soul-searching, Szold decided she had to skip America and return to Palestine. On her arrival in Jerusalem, she found the situation as grim as Rubinow had painted it. The Keren Hayesod had not come through with the monies promised, JDC funds were dwindling, and the sums raised by Hadassah in America could not make up for the extreme shortages. Rubinow had closed the hospital in Tiberias, cut down on the beds in Jaffa, reduced salaries, and discharged ninety-three employees, and still expenses exceeded the income received. "If the unit and I survive, it will be a miracle," Szold said.[3]

Suddenly, something of a miracle did happen. Nathan Straus (who had "miraculously" helped Hadassah launch its first two nurses in 1913) cabled a gift of $20,000 to Szold to use as she saw fit. The unit still suffered deep shortages, but that money would help tide it over until some of its other sources came through. Szold received a second ray of sunshine, as she called it, with the arrival in Jerusalem of Judah Magnes and his family. They moved into a house close to hers, and she and Sophie enjoyed a new arena for socializing. More important, Magnes became a great help to her, showing up at her office every day to aid and advise her in the complex work of running the unit. Sadly, in March 1923, he had to take over that office completely. She had received word that her sister Rachel was seriously ill. Nothing stopped her this time; she left for America almost immediately.

Rachel was suffering from a terminal brain tumor, and over the next several years Henrietta would torturously watch her sister's life ebb away. She stayed in an apartment at the Alexandria Hotel in New York, but spent much time in Wisconsin helping Rachel and her husband, Joe Jastrow, who had medical issues of his own. She also traveled regularly to Baltimore, where Bertha's husband, Louis Levin, died suddenly of kidney disease, leaving Bertha a widow with five children and little income. Closer to home, her youngest sister Adele turned to her for help with her problematic marriage to publisher Toby Seltzer, who courageously produced books by D. H. Lawrence that would be banned in America, but whose poor business sense put the couple deeply into debt.

Despite all those family obligations, Szold still agreed to serve as president of Hadassah a second time, feeling it her duty to do so (two years later, profoundly overburdened, she would confess privately that she was "moving heaven and earth to get out of the presidency of Hadassah").[4] The position called for traveling around the country again, recruiting new Hadassah members and opening new chapters for the ever-growing organization, whose numbers reached more than fifteen thousand in the early 1920s. This time she was far better known than in the group's early days. Word of Hadassah's work and hers in Palestine had spread through the United States—indeed, Adolph Ochs, publisher of the *New York Times* with whom she had become friendly during one of his visits to Palestine, published a piece in that newspaper about the unit and its needs. When she spoke in New York about her years in Palestine shortly after she returned, the paper covered that as well.[5]

Three thousand women attended that lecture at the Hotel Pennsylvania in New York on April 30, 1923, at a Hadassah reception in Szold's honor. Titled "Jewish Palestine in the Making," the talk optimistically affirmed that the Jews would have a center, a homeland, in Palestine unlike any Jewish center in the world, but—less optimistically—it would take several generations to fully realize that goal. "We," she said, addressing her audience, "are the generation of the desert," permitted to "fructify the earth with our ideas, with our hopes, with our very bodies," so that others who came later would be able to complete the task. This generation had the privilege of being the pioneers.[6]

In keeping with that, she described some of the problems the Jews in Palestine faced. Coming from many different lands, for example, they had not yet formed a cohesive Jewish community. There were German Jews and Russian Jews and Romanian Jews and many others, all speaking different languages. They needed to be able to communicate in the same language— Hebrew, the language of the land, which the children learned in school, but most adults still had to master. She urged her audience, the diaspora Jews, also to learn Hebrew so that they could read the Hebrew newspapers and gather firsthand information about conditions in the Holy Land. Again, she did not call on them to settle in Palestine, but she argued, as she had from her earliest Zionist days, that to fulfill their nationalist goals they needed to know Hebrew.

In this address, Szold spoke also of the demands of Jewish women in Palestine for equal rights in Jewish law. Two years earlier, when she wrote to Emily Solis about the movement for women's rights, she had waffled, concerned about changing ancient Jewish law too quickly. Now, as a leader of the Histadrut Nashim, the Women's Federation that, among other things, prepared women for political action, she placed herself completely on the women's side with their insistence on equality in family matters and inheritance rights. Now she agreed that "old Jewish law" needed to meet "the demands of modern life."[7]

Despite her reservations about the Keren Hayesod during the Brandeis-Weizmann split, in her talk she encouraged the Hadassah women to cooperate with that central fund. She aimed for peace among Jewish organizations, and even sought to calm the waters between Hadassah and the ZOA, which once again had begun grasping for control over the women's group.

A great success, the talk was printed in the American Zionist newspaper, the *New Palestine* and circulated in the Hadassah *News Letter.* It is unlikely that anyone in the general audience listening to her that day or reading the lecture later would have guessed that Szold had regarded the lecture and the public reception in her honor as "tortures," and had protested them "hand and foot" beforehand. Still shocked by how changed her sister Rachel looked because of her illness and involved in helping Bertha after her loss, Henrietta bridled at having to speak in a huge hall "full of well-dressed and well-groomed women," while she felt herself "disheveled, overwrought [and] under-prepared." She was glad to hear from Jessie Sampter, however, how well received the address had been. "I suppose," she wrote, "the essence of the matter is that if there is something to be said, it says itself, no matter how untoward the circumstances."[8] As was so often the case with Szold, she resented the pressures placed upon her (or that she placed upon herself) and felt inadequate to the moment, yet on another level found satisfaction in what she had accomplished.

During the next eight years, she would have to balance many pressures, torn as she was between her family needs, her duties as Hadassah president, and the constant demands of the organization's undertakings in Palestine. Doing so called for journeying to and from that land to America, sometimes several times a year, but never for leisurely visits there.

One of her first assignments involved helping to find and train a medical director for the HMO to replace Rubinow. The first two directors hired resigned after a short time, ill or unable to adjust to life in Palestine. The next one chosen, Ephraim Michael Bluestone, fit the bill well. Young, talented, and from a Zionist family, he had been assistant director of Mount Sinai Hospital in New York. After being interviewed by Szold in New York, he agreed to move to Palestine with his wife in 1925 for a three-year commitment. His fine qualifications notwithstanding, and even though Szold spoke highly of him, the two never enjoyed the kind of close relationship she and Rubinow had. To Bluestone, she seemed cold and distant; to her, he seemed intransigent in his opinions.[9] Nevertheless, he remained on the job for almost his entire term, and continued as a consultant to Hadassah for many years afterward. Szold formed a friendlier connection with Haim Yassky, who replaced Bluestone in 1928.

In the course of Szold's travels back and forth from Palestine, Sophia Berger married. Szold lived in various people's homes for a while, and in 1930 moved into the newly built Eden Hotel in Jerusalem. After a few months, she exchanged her tiny room for a larger one with a porch. During one of her trips to America friends in Jerusalem added attractive touches—fresh flowers, a colorful throw and cushions on the bed, and a screen that hid the washstand—turning the drab bedroom into a studio where Szold could welcome visitors. Her prized possession was a bookcase she had a carpenter make for $10, the first she ever owned. That single hotel room would be her Palestine home during most of her years ahead.[10]

Busy as she was, Szold had little time to spend in any one place in Palestine. Along with her work on the HMO and her involvement with the Nurses' Training School, she oversaw various Hadassah projects geared especially toward women and children and open, as always, to Jews, Muslims, and Christians. There were the infant welfare stations in Jerusalem and Tibe-

rias that the HMO operated and one in Haifa that it administered. Here pregnant women and those with newborn babies,
especially women from local villages and settlements, came to
learn about health and nutrition. Closely related, the Tipat
Halav, or Drop of Milk programs, offered mothers pasteurized
milk for children who had been weaned. Donkeys delivered
boxes of bottled milk to various locations, each bottle labeled
in Hebrew, Arabic, and English. There were the school lunch
plans that provided hot meals and nutrition education to hundreds of schoolchildren, partly supported by "penny lunch" programs in the United States, through which children in Jewish
religious schools donated pennies toward the cause. Other ventures revolved around caring for orphans and providing playgrounds where Arab and Jewish children could play together.

Through the Hadassah *News Letter* Szold wrote detailed
descriptions to the membership about the many enterprises
they supported in Palestine. She named the women in the organization who took direct responsibility for each project and
frequently spelled out the finances involved. As she told her
readers, she firmly believed that eventually all the Hadassah
programs should be taken over by the people in the Yishuv whom
they served. But that time had not yet come. For the moment,
Hadassah needed to continue running the Hadassah Medical
Organization and its other undertakings. The organization
had established a "system and standard," she wrote, that distinguished its activities from those of other groups, and through
their work, Hadassah women were "beginning to make of ourselves a Palestinian organization as we have been an American
organization."[11]

Spurred on by Szold's convictions and with increasing success in Palestine, Hadassah continued to grow and assert itself
as a leading Zionist institution, far surpassing the male establishment. In 1924, Szold wrote her family that "our lords and
masters were rather stunned by our appearance [at the ZOA

convention] with a paid membership of 16,500." That membership reached 34,000 in 1927. By then, the ZOA had fewer than
22,000 members.[12]

After three years of debilitating illness and false hopes,
Rachel died in September 1926, leaving Henrietta devastated
by the loss of the sister she adored and to whom she had been
closest. Her mourning lasted for months, and that same year
she resigned as president of Hadassah, worn down by grief and
overwork. She did not return to Palestine until February 1927,
and when she did, she entered a country in the depths of an
economic crisis. The economy had gone through wild swings
in the years in which Szold had been traveling to and from
America. The widespread poverty of 1923 and the exhausting
struggles to find funds for the Hadassah Medical Organization
gradually gave way a year later to a thriving prosperity that
featured ambitious construction projects throughout the land.
The change arrived with what became known as the fourth aliyah, created by a rush of immigrants from Poland, many escap-
ing new harsh economic laws and heavy taxes that particularly
hurt Polish Jews. Most of the new immigrants settled in Tel
Aviv and other towns to open shops and factories or create
business enterprises, uninterested in the agricultural ideals of
an earlier generation. The capital and entrepreneurial skills the
immigrants brought with them sent the economy soaring.

It didn't take long for the bubble to burst. Too many immigrants, too few jobs, and insufficient capital brought a halt to
the vast building ventures. Loans could not be repaid, contracts
dried up, and debts mounted. Unemployment rose to previously unknown heights, and immigration fell to new lows.

In 1927, when Szold arrived in Palestine, the crisis had
reached a peak. With the economy in ruins, every Zionist enterprise was deep in debt except for the Hadassah Medical Organization, whose good management kept it solvent. To help

counter the dismal economic conditions in the Yishuv, Weizmann and others in the international Zionist Organization, itself close to bankruptcy, sought to adopt efficient businesslike
measures along the lines Brandeis had advocated. They pared
down the Zionist Executive (which had replaced the earlier Zionist Commission) to three members, each in charge of two
areas of the Yishuv and held to a tight budget. At the Fifteenth
Zionist Congress in Basel in 1927, which Szold attended, she
was elected the first woman on the executive, and given the
education and health portfolios. A second member, the British
solicitor and well-known Zionist leader Harry Sacher, took over
responsibility for labor and settlements, and the third, Colonel
Frederick Kisch, a British officer, headed the immigration and
political departments.

Szold's feelings about the appointment, she wrote Jessie
Sampter, "can be summed up in one word—terror."[13] She had
always said she hated Zionist politics and knew nothing about
government matters, and now she would be in the center of
both. Yet in recent years, she had become increasingly drawn
to political issues, attending Zionist congresses and meetings.
It was true that terror and self-doubts went along with the new
position, but so did a deep-seated recognition that she could
handle it.

She turned her attention to the education scene first and
uncovered mayhem. Three different school systems educated
the majority of Yishuv children: religious schools, run by Mizrachi; General schools, representing the General Zionists; and
Labor Zionist schools, controlled by the Labor parties that had
come to dominate Yishuv politics and everyday life. Each stream
had its own ideology that children imbibed along with the basics of reading and writing. Szold soon learned that any attempt
to combine schools to save money or create a common curriculum that encompassed all the schools and avoided wasteful du-
plications led to furious denunciations by the parties involved.

How dare she interfere with the training of children in the ways and values of their parents!? Even worse, she found that across all the streams, teachers had not received salaries for months. Some were starving and some had desperate families dependent on them for subsistence. Many teachers went out on strike, and plans were being made to shut schools and eliminate kindergartens or complete grades to save money. Some schools did not have enough money to buy chalk.

Szold quickly realized that she needed help if she wanted to bring order into the system, and she invited a distinguished American educator, Dr. Isaac B. Berkson from the New York Bureau of Jewish Education, to join her. After receiving his acceptance, she went on a three-month fund-raising tour of the United States on behalf of the Yishuv schools. In November 1927, she and Berkson sailed together to Palestine on the R.M.S. *Carmania*. Berkson wrote his wife from the ship that while he was on deck enjoying the fresh air, Szold was in her cabin poring over education plans—typical, he would soon discover, of her round-the clock work habits.[14] The Zionist Executive appointed Berkson superintendent of the Yishuv education department, a position he held until he and his family left Palestine in 1935.

The education establishment—teachers, principals, administrators—greeted Szold and Berkson coldly, viewing them as American interlopers who would try to impose foreign ideas and methods on the land. And they denounced the deep budget cuts the two made in order to make ends meet. Attitudes changed when Szold came up with enough money from her fund-raising forays to pay the teachers and balance the budget. Although she could not eliminate the separate streams, with her organizational skills she managed to put the overall system on an even keel. In time she became known throughout the education community and among the parents of the thousands of schoolchildren as a no-nonsense administrator who got things done. She also became known as a compassionate executive willing to work her heart out to improve the lives of students and teachers.

One of Szold's money-raising successes came from an unexpected source, the British government. She approached Herbert Charles Onslow, Lord Plumer, who had replaced Herbert Samuel as high commissioner after Samuel's term ended in 1925, with a proposal for aid to both Jewish and Arab schools. Her presentation won her the first substantial grant ever given by the government to Jewish education, the sum of £20,000—and this despite Plumer's tendency to favor financing agriculture over education.[15]

Szold had a felicitous relationship with Lord Plumer, a very British-looking former general and World War I hero with a famous white bushy mustache and ubiquitous black bowler hat. She met with him frequently, finding in him a man who cared about all the people under the British mandate, Christians, Jews, and Muslims, regardless of politics. In his role as high commissioner, he gained a reputation for fairness, but also firmness. He resisted pressures from Arab leaders to undo the provisions of the Balfour Declaration, and by dint of his own personality and the authority he projected he kept peace in the land—so much so that he felt comfortable reducing the British military presence, cutting back on the number of armed units in the country.

During these tranquil years under Plumer a small group of Jewish intellectuals began meeting to discuss a plan for maintaining peace permanently. Calling itself Brit Shalom (Covenant of Peace), the group, never numbering more than one hundred, included such renowned scholars as Martin Buber and Gershom Scholem, the philosopher Hugo Bergmann, and the educator Ernst Simon. Most of its members came from central Europe or America, and many had connections with the Hebrew University. Although not a member of the group, Judah

Magnes, who had become chancellor of the university, was closely allied with it. Henrietta Szold did not formally belong to the group either, but she identified with its ideals.

The group was founded officially in 1925 at the home of Arthur Ruppin, a central figure in the development of Zionist settlements in Palestine, not as a political party but as a kind of organized "think tank" to find a road to peace between Jews and Arabs. As opposed to Vladimir Jabotinsky on the right, who viewed an open struggle between Jewish and Arab nationalism as inevitable, Brit Shalom followers sought to establish peaceful coexistence between the two peoples in Palestine. The goal they envisioned was binationalism. By this they meant that neither Jews nor Arabs would gain control of the land or dominate the other, no matter who held the majority. Both sides would share equally in economic, political, and social rights, while maintaining independent cultural lives.[16]

Many of Brit Shalom's ideals can be traced to the teachings of Ahad Ha'am, whose thoughts had influenced Henrietta Szold when she first discovered Zionism. Ahad Ha'am had emphasized the spiritual aspects of Zionism, the concept that the Land of Israel would serve as a cultural center for the world's Jews, a source of learning and creativity, not as a sovereign Jewish state. He didn't envision a binational state exactly as Brit Shalom did, but he stressed the need for fairness and morality in Jewish-Arab relations.

It has been said that although Szold maintained friendships with the group's members, she rejected Brit Shalom's views as "naïve and unrealistic."[17] The evidence suggests otherwise. At one point she spoke of herself as being in "platonic sympathy" with the group.[18] At another, she gave the first speech at the opening meeting of a "Week of the Child" celebration of Jewish children held by the Federation of Hebrew Women. In its report of the event, the Hebrew newspaper *Haam* (the "People") identified Szold as an "unofficial member of Brit Shalom," and the next speaker, Dr. Isaac Epstein, as an "official member."[19] Szold did not dispute the statement about her. She might have felt it was not appropriate at this time to officially join Brit Shalom, given her position on the Zionist Executive. Within the next decade, however, after her situation had changed, she would take an active role in a new organization with similar goals, Ihud.

Although they regarded the group as politically unsophisticated, at first Chaim Weizmann, David Ben-Gurion, and other Zionist leaders treated Brit Shalom members politely, even offering to help finance the association. Ben-Gurion particularly appreciated the introductions Magnes made for him to various Arab leaders. But when Arab rioting erupted in 1929, with many Jews massacred, Yishuv leaders as well as the general Jewish public turned fiercely against the Brit Shalom peacemakers. Arthur Ruppin, the organization's chairman, dropped out of it in despair. "What we can get [from the Arabs] we do not need, and what we need, we are unable to get," he said.[20] In fact, no Arab leader responded to Brit Shalom's overtures either before or after the riots or showed any signs of accepting a Jewish presence in the land. Brit Shalom continued its activities until 1933, when it disbanded.

Szold had been out of the country during the Arab riots, attending what turned out to be a historic Zionist congress in Zurich. At it, Zionists and non-Zionists ratified a plan to create a Jewish Agency, an overall governing body for the Jewish homeland in Palestine as provided for under the British mandate. Led by Chaim Weizmann, the plan—known as the "pact of glory"—had been worked out beforehand, allotting agency seats equally to Zionist and non-Zionists. Spirits ran high at the Zurich congress in August 1929, with such notables present as Albert Einstein, Sir Herbert Samuel, Louis Marshall, and several members of the wealthy Warburg banking family. Weizmann was elected president of the Jewish Agency and Felix Warburg became chairman of the administrative committee.[21] Szold was elected again to the Zionist Executive, now a larger body. It would be joined by a Jewish Agency Executive, an entity not yet formed.

The Arabs blamed the violence that erupted in late August in part on the creation of the Jewish Agency, maintaining that it led them to fear they were being dispossessed. Actually the grand mufti of Jerusalem, Haj Amin al-Husseini, distorted statements made at the congress to incite Arab mobs. About a year earlier there had been some skirmishes at the Western Wall, fighting that escalated after the British removed a screen separating men and women during Yom Kippur services there. The Jews were enraged at the British action and the Arabs at the Jewish claims to the wall, which the Arabs regarded as their own holy site. By August 1929, with tempers still flaring, Arabs killed a Jewish boy who had accidentally kicked a football into an Arab garden and gone to reclaim it. Within days a full-scale confrontation between Arabs and Jews burst out, with the mufti calling for a holy war. Arab mobs wielding knives, swords, and clubs murdered Jews in Jerusalem, Hebron, Safed, and other areas around the country, leaving 133 dead and some 300 others wounded. Because Lord Plumer had optimistically thinned out British security forces, and his successor as high commissioner, Sir John Chancellor, had little sympathy for the Zionist cause, it took days for the British police to establish order. When they finally did crack down, with the help of British troops brought in from Egypt, 116 Arabs were killed and 232 wounded, almost all by British actions.

Writing to Jessie Sampter a few weeks after the violence, Szold asserted that the "chief onus [for the riots] does not lie upon us," the Jews, but to a great extent belonged to the "dastardly stupid conduct of British officialdom." Nevertheless, she added, "we cannot hold ourselves guiltless." The Jewish community needed to look inward, "deep down, next to the springs of justice and wisdom," to seek an understanding of the Arabs and find a way to make peace with them.[22] And yet, for all her goodwill toward Arab aspirations, Szold reacted later with rage, as did Jews throughout the world, to a White Paper Colonial Secretary Lord Passfield published in October 1930 recommending that Jewish immigration be limited and Jewish land purchase in Palestine restricted so as not to further arouse Arab ire. To her friends in the Haganah (the underground Jewish defense force) she wrote, "I cannot bear arms, but my home is open to anything you want to leave."[23] Pacifist though she had so often declared herself, when it came to unfairness toward the Jewish people, she knew where she stood.

Szold had planned to return to Palestine from Zurich, but Weizmann convinced her that she was needed in America. She dutifully traveled to the States, where she soon found herself trapped in a "damned if she did and damned if she didn't" struggle with Felix Warburg.

Louis Marshall, who had been close to Weizmann, had died shortly after the Zurich congress. Weizmann had been grooming Marshall to lead the American Jewish community and raise big money there. With Marshall's death, the mantle passed to Warburg. Fit and aristocratic looking with a large mustache, Warburg had a generally affable manner, but could also be thin-skinned, quickly lashing out when crossed. A non-Zionist, he supported a wide range of Jewish philanthropies in Palestine and sat on the boards of numerous American Jewish organizations. In his new position with the Jewish Agency, he seemed to feel that he bore the burdens of the worldwide Jewish community on his shoulders. Szold met with him in New York on two occasions. At these meetings, Warburg reproached her for having gone to America rather than to Palestine (although she had followed Weizmann's advice in doing so), and read her a letter he had sent to Weizmann suggesting that if she did not return to Palestine very soon, Dr. Berkson, who worked with her, would be appointed in her place on the Zionist Executive. Fulfilling his directive, she headed back to Palestine, stopping off in London to see Weizmann.

When they met, Weizmann told her that Warburg was irritated with her for having gone to London without permission from his administrative committee and for having left America before a planned fund-raising campaign in which she could have been useful (although he had criticized her for being in America in the first place). Weizmann also told her that in light of the expanded Jewish Agency Executive being planned, Warburg thought she should resign at once from the Zionist Executive.

Szold confronted Warburg with this confusing and offensive array of criticisms in a straightforward letter she sent him in December. She stated politely that there were "duties, rights, and privileges" that an elected member of the executive had that could not simply be taken away by him. Furthermore, she wondered why he had not told her directly what he had conveyed to Weizmann about her. "In matters of public concern, I assure you, I can be as objective with reference to my person as though I were a thing," she wrote.[24] Later she would tell her sisters that the Warburg incident had a more powerful effect on her than she realized at the time.[25] Or, probably, more than her pride allowed her to admit to herself at that time. In truth she felt profoundly offended by the incident, and even more by Warburg's return letter to her.

Part of that letter set out an officious description of Warburg's many pressing duties as head of the Jewish Agency's administrative committee by way of explaining why he might have been "more brutally frank" with her than was otherwise his manner. Part of it offered an explanation that could have been taken as an apology for why he wanted her to resign from the Zionist Executive. Actually, he wrote, he had told Weizmann to get as many resignations from the Zionist Executive as he could before the election of the new Jewish Agency Executive. And part of it was outright insulting, even if not intended that way. Szold should turn over her education department work to Dr. Berkson and her health-care responsibilities to medical experts, he suggested, and devote herself to writing a history she had been asked to compile. By doing so, she would no longer have to sacrifice her "health and nerves" in Palestine.[26]

Szold enclosed a copy of Warburg's letter with one of her own to her sisters, along with her "summary" of what it meant: "Damn the Zionists, and as for you, get thee to a Home for Genteel Old Ladies."[27] One reaction remained unarticulated—would he have written a comparable letter to a male member of the executive?

Warburg's letter caused extra pain because the idea of Szold writing a biography seems to have come from members of Hadassah, who urged her and encouraged others to urge her, to write her autobiography. She hated that idea. The very thought of exposing her "inners" to the world was, she said, like Hadassah putting "its hand into my soul," and the fact that Warburg picked up on Hadassah's request caused her to be infuriated with the organization as well as with him.[28]

For now, Szold stayed put. While waiting for Jewish Agency Executive members to be announced, she continued her work with the education department, struggling, as always, to raise enough money to pay teachers' salaries and meet other expenses. When the announcement came, Szold's name did not appear on the list. Weizmann immediately cabled her, apologetically, but pointed out that she was still a member of the original Zionist Executive until the next Zionist congress. While she would no longer be in charge of educational activities, he hoped she might use her position to promote the work of the Zionist Organization in Europe. Although he did not say so, her exclusion from the Agency Executive undoubtedly had political overtones, prompted in part by Warburg, who wanted more non-Zionists on the executive, and by the religious Zionist Mizrachi organization, which had objected to some of the educational innovations she had made that affected their Orthodox schools.

To her, however, the exclusion seemed personal. Intensely hurt and with a sense of rejection that fed into her often shaky self-confidence, she decided to turn down Weizmann's suggestions and resign from the Zionist Executive. Remaining for her now, she wrote to her sisters, were "responsibilities and no power . . . in the awkward position of a titled, powerless functionary."[29] It was an untenable state to be in.

But if she resigned right away, what was she to do? Return to America? It seemed, for the immediate future at least, that "Warburg was going to rule American Jewish life." Under that regime, "both because it doesn't want me and because I don't want it," she said, "there is no room for me." Then again, even if she were to return in order to be near her family, she speculated to them sadly, "after all, what part do I play in your lives when I am in America? It appears that ten years of wandering away from home have loosened bonds."[30] On the other hand, "Do I want to renounce you and America definitively? Do I want to decide that for what still remains of life to me I shall live in Palestine?"[31] That's what she found herself wrestling with. Entrenched in both lands, America and Palestine, in love with both lands, yet critical of both, Szold swung back and forth between the two as she had at other times in the past. But this time, she believed, she would be making a permanent life decision. "Funny, isn't it?" she said, "to stand at the crossways at my age—to be 'unemployed' for the first time in seventy years!"[32]

She decided to wait until Weizmann returned to Palestine before making final plans. Meanwhile, she felt gratified to witness the hue and cry that arose in the Yishuv at her rejection from the Jewish Agency Executive. The teachers and principals who had so resented her at the beginning of her education work came out en masse to sing her praises. The teachers' union journal hailed her for putting education on the map in the Yishuv, the Hebrew newspapers called for her to be welcomed into the Agency Executive, and the political parties passed resolutions protesting her exclusion. Groups sent telegrams to Weizmann and daily she received laudatory letters of support from individuals and organizations. "It is absolutely embarrassing," she told her sisters, "whenever I appear, the opportunity is taken to show me distinguished honor and respect."[33] It pleased her also that the various groups she had worked with continued to turn to her for help as if her status had not changed. "I am in the position of the proverbial 'old maid' in a family—called on for all odd jobs by the public," she said.[34] An effort was being made, she rightly believed, to prove her indispensable.

For all that, Weizmann did not offer to instate her on the Jewish Agency Executive when he returned to Palestine. Nor did a trip she made to London in June for a meeting between Hadassah and the Women's International Zionist Organization change her status. At that meeting she submitted a plan to expand women's work in Palestine, without knowing how much longer she would remain in the land to see it fulfilled. In July she wrote home about an honorary degree of Doctor of Hebrew Letters she had received some time earlier from the Jewish Institute of Religion in Cincinnati, headed by Rabbi Stephen S. Wise. By September she had resigned from the Zionist Executive and come to feel that much of her work in Palestine was completed. She'd had a "change of heart and mind," she wrote her sisters, and decided that she could be "as useful or useless in America as here, while in America I can be near you."[35] In October 1930, she was back in New York.

Hadassah lured her there to discuss a new project. But the real purpose was to celebrate her seventieth birthday. Hadassah had grown in stature and power during Szold's back-and-forth years. There had been new showdowns with Louis Lipsky in the late 1920s that firmed up the position Hadassah had staked out in 1921. This time Lipsky had targeted Irma Lindheim, who had succeeded Szold as Hadassah president. While Lipsky had done poorly in raising money for the Keren Hayesod, Hadassah had raised some $750,000, from which about $500,000 would be used for its work in Palestine. And while membership numbers in the ZOA had repeatedly declined, Hadassah membership had reached 34,000 in 1927 and continued to climb. When Lindheim, backed by Hadassah, insisted that the women's organization maintain control over its own donations, Lipsky attacked her as betraying the spirit of Henrietta Szold who, he said, "recognized the proper role of women within the ranks of the ZOA."[36]

Szold responded to Lipsky's statement by demonstrating her support for Lindheim. In a message she sent to the Hadassah convention of 1928 she reminded the women that as ZOA members they had as much responsibility as the men in framing Zionist policies. "Let no one tell you that it is womanly not to exercise the right, not to fulfill the duty," she wrote. At the end of the reading of her message, the delegates to the convention rose and applauded.[37] By 1930, when Szold returned to America, Hadassah had achieved almost complete independence.

The Hadassah women celebrated Szold's seventieth birthday with lavish luncheons, dinners, and teas that raised money for them while honoring their founder. Szold was expected to speak at most of these events, and after a while, tired of the events and the endless speeches, she wondered whether life held anything more for her. Years earlier she had written to Jessie Sampter, who had achieved some recognition as a poet, that the difference between them was that Jessie had "the creative impulse," while her own life was made up of nothing more than routine details.[38] It was typical of her self-abnegation that she seemed unable to acknowledge the creativity that went into successfully fulfilling the many projects she handled. Now, however, she seemed truly at a dead end, without details or creative challenges to occupy her.

The state of limbo came to an end in February 1931. She received word that she had been elected to the executive of the Yishuv's Vaad Leumi, the National Council, a governing body that encompassed all the Yishuv's political parties and was part of the larger Knesset Yisrael (Jewish Assembly). Four months later she left for Palestine. "In the life of the spirit," she is often quoted as saying, "there is no ending that is not a beginning." She had believed her active career had ended when she returned to America. Instead she would begin a new career and a new life that kept her in the Land of Israel permanently.

8

"The Most Worthwhile Undertaking"

THE LABOR PARTY, which dominated Jewish political life in
Palestine, had not been friendly toward Henrietta Szold. She
was too American, too bourgeois for this socialist party, her
work with Hadassah too close to philanthropy and diaspora life.
Moreover, the Histadrut, the powerful labor federation that provided for all aspects of Jewish workers' lives, had its own health
clinics that did not see the need for oversight from the Hadassah Medical Organization. It therefore surprised Szold when she
arrived in Palestine to learn that the Labor party, now called
Mapai, had relinquished one of its own seats on the seven-
member Vaad Leumi executive so that she could have a place
there. She had headed the list of the Federation of Hebrew
Women, but that list did not win enough seats to be represented on the executive. Mapai's seat made the difference. Like
others in the Yishuv, the Laborites had come to realize that while

Szold might not fully share their socialist philosophy, this was a woman who made things happen.

David Ben-Gurion, head of Mapai, had developed a healthy respect for Americans, especially their efficiency and ability to raise money. Aware of the funds Szold had brought into the country in the various positions she held, he viewed her with new approval. The fund-raising expectations of Ben-Gurion and others also hovered in the back of Szold's mind, adding extra pressure to the projects she was about to begin. Nevertheless, Mapai's backing gave her work recognition and prestige among the public at large.

Her passage to Palestine took eighteen days, and her reception when she arrived was "Messianic," in her words, with everyone expecting some solution from her, whether connected to public or private matters.[1] The best welcome came from her many friends, some who traveled from Jerusalem to Jaffa to meet her at the dock, others who crowded into her room at the Eden Hotel, filling it to overflowing with flowers and plants.

Starting work, she quickly discovered that—against her will—she had become something of a tourist attraction in Palestine. A hotel scout drops her name "as a bait," she wrote her sisters, when he "goes fishing for guests" after the arrival of a train from Egypt.[2] As a result, many American tourists stayed at the Eden, and she found herself entertaining numbers of them, especially those from Baltimore. "I had twenty-two in for tea last Saturday," she wrote.[3] Then there was the Hadassah woman from Kalamazoo who accosted her "with a half-indignant, half-amazed 'Don't you remember me?'" query.[4] And aside from such intrusions, she was beset by people bringing her their problems or asking for favors. Sometimes, she said, she felt like John Adams, who wrote in his diary, "No sooner has one left the office than another enters."[5]

She still managed to work intensely, however, attending

meetings in Tel Aviv and Jerusalem within a day of her arrival, and pushing on steadily after that. For a while she set aside hours in the morning to read for enjoyment, "the first time in at least thirty years": world histories, classic novels, the letters of Abigail Adams, Emma Goldman's massive autobiography, or whatever struck her, and even found time to nap during the day.[6] That leisurely schedule evaporated as she became immersed in setting up a comprehensive social service system in the Yishuv as a large part of her work for the Vaad Leumi. Charitable organizations existed throughout the country to help the poor and unemployed, the blind, widowed, or members of a religious community. But no organized social work program systematically addressed the needs of communities and families, particularly of children who had been abandoned or orphaned, many of whom turned to petty crimes in order to subsist. In her meticulous way, Szold changed her reading habits, focusing now on books, pamphlets, and anything else that concerned social welfare in the United States, Germany, and other European countries, and began to apply the techniques she read about to the situation in Palestine.

The Yishuv had no money for social services, and without organized local communities, it had no way of levying taxes to raise money. "I feel like a squirrel in one of those barbarous cages they used to have," she wrote, going around and around and getting no place.[7] Then a modest donation came in from the Palestine Endowment Fund set up by Justice Louis Brandeis and Judge Julian Mack, and with that she got started, forming small social work centers in Jerusalem, Tel Aviv, Haifa, and later Petach Tikva. With time, as she found other sources of funding, she developed a social service department for the Knesset Yisrael, the Jewish government of Palestine, and in 1934, she founded a school for social work that trained professionals and eventually became part of Hebrew University, much as she had created the country's first school to train nurses fifteen years earlier.

While all this was going on, in the rough-and-tumble world of Mandatory Palestine, Szold's interest in abandoned and orphaned children led to her becoming deputy to the British probation officer dealing with juvenile offenders. Since the officer knew nothing about Jews, and didn't understand their language, Jewish children became her area of responsibility. Her heart broke for the young children (mostly boys) she saw in the courts and prisons who had dropped out of school and fallen into trouble with the law. The juvenile offender, she wrote home, "is so much less an offender than the people who want to reform him. They talk from start to finish in terms of reformatory institutions when all that the little wretches need is larger opportunity for recreation and for education of the hand."[8] She felt particularly disgusted by the authorities' treatment of the very young who, although "sick, defective, undernourished mentally and physically starved," were frequently placed in prisons or institutions with "big boys charged with and convicted of murder." Most shocking was that the first punishment decreed for all the offenders, young and older children, irrespective of their offenses, "according to the statute book is—flogging."[9]

Szold read booklets and met with physicians, educators, and social workers to find ways of treating juvenile offenders more intelligently and humanely. Although the British government provided little money, she managed to set up a boys' village, a kind of small farm community for young boys on probation. Eventually, the plight of young offenders became folded into the broader social work system adopted by the Yishuv.

In a tragically ironic way, as the 1930s moved on, Szold began to receive more professional social work help than she could ever have imagined. With the rise of Adolf Hitler and the National Socialist Party in Germany, German Jewish social workers, along with other professionals and working people, emigrated to Palestine, at first in small numbers and then in waves. In September 1932, Szold recorded, with some annoyance that she had to waste her time entertaining visiting dignitaries and that she was going to meet a Mrs. Wronsky, a distinguished social service worker from Berlin.[10] A year later her outlook had changed. She described spending the Sabbath with Mrs. Siddy Wronsky, who had now settled in Mandatory Palestine. Wronsky had been the archivist of the City of Berlin, editor of a number of important sociology journals, and a much sought-after lecturer. By 1933, this renowned Jewish woman had been dismissed from all her positions in Germany. She subsequently turned down a prestigious job offer from the Russell Sage Foundation in America and decided to move to Palestine. Her story, Szold wrote, "was a tale of spiritual suffering, of relinquishment of all dear values, the passion of the German Jew."[11] Wronsky planned to spend several months learning Hebrew and then devote herself to assisting Szold in organizing social services in the Yishuv. In many of Szold's later letters, she sprinkled praise of Wronsky and the enormous help she offered in that department. Wronsky is credited—along with Szold—with establishing the Yishuv's social work school and serving as its first teacher.[12]

Deeply sympathetic to the suffering of German Jews like Wronsky, Szold headed a fund-raising committee to help settle German refugees in Palestine. Fortunately, Sir Arthur Grenfell Wauchope, who became high commissioner toward the end of 1931, reopened the doors of Palestine to immigrants at this time of great need. (A letter from Prime Minister Ramsay Mac-Donald had previously rescinded many of the restrictions of the Passfield White Paper.) "The tide of German immigrants is constantly swelling," Szold wrote home. "Whole families are sleeping on the beach for want of vacant rooms."[13] And though she could not foresee the misery the future held for Jews in Germany, she seemed to grasp, before many German Jews themselves did, the hopelessness of their situation.

In one letter she wrote bitterly of the German Jewish capitalists who salvaged their fortunes and prepared to invest them "in industrial enterprises in their countries of refuge—except Palestine," not realizing that some of their "refuge" countries would soon fall to the Nazis and how crucial Palestine would be for future emigrants.[14] In another she decried those German Jews who "believe Hitler's reign will be brief and who speak of the return to Germany." Most of them were non-Zionists, she believed. The Zionists among them were more practical and realistic, as was she.[15] She had little patience for Jewish intellectuals in Palestine itself who did not become involved in the campaign to help the German Jews. "It is amazing to me," she wrote, "that some of the most thoughtful people here fail to take in the implications of what has happened and is happening in Germany." Understanding the direness of the situation, she could only hope the Yishuv leaders would not "bungle the business of absorption and adjustments" for the immigrants.[16]

Yet, in spite of her foresight in recognizing the seriousness of the German Jewish position, Szold responded slowly to early requests to help relocate German youth to Palestine. Recha Freier, a German Zionist and folklorist married to an Orthodox rabbi, first broached the subject of the young people to her in early 1932. Six German adolescent boys who had lost their jobs because of widespread anti-Jewish sentiments during a depression in Germany had asked Freier for help. It struck her that the best solution for these teenagers and others like them would be to work on agricultural settlements in Palestine. With no money to pay for the boys' transportation and no connections in Palestine, she received little support for her idea from the German Jewish community. Determined, she wrote to Henrietta Szold, as director of the Vaad Leumi's social service bureau. After consulting several Yishuv leaders, Szold turned her down. She could not imagine that German parents would send their children alone to a land they had little knowledge of. As she well knew, that land had plenty of its own orphaned and unemployed young people, with a shortage of resources and educational facilities to sustain them. German families would do better looking out for their own youth.

Freier persisted. Eventually Dr. Siegfried Lehman, director of the Ben Shemen Youth Village in Palestine—which had the support of German Jews—agreed to accept the boys and a small number of others, and to provide them with immigration certificates he had secured. The first contingent left Germany in October 1932, sent off with great excitement by German Zionist youth groups. In the course of the next months, as conditions for Jews in Germany deteriorated, Freier formed a committee of several organizations, Jüdische Jugendhilfe (Aid to Jewish Youth). Almost forebodingly, its first meeting, on January 30, 1933, took place on the day Adolf Hitler became chancellor of Germany. Later the Jugendhilfe would be organized as the Youth Aliyah department of the Berlin Palestine office.[17]

Independent of Freier, in May 1933, Chaim Arlosoroff, head of the Jewish Agency's political department, traveled from Palestine to Berlin to assess the situation of Germany's Jews. Brilliant and level-headed, he seemed destined for top leadership in the Labor party, and his recommendations that large numbers of young Germans could be transferred to kibbutzim, youth villages, and boarding schools in Palestine made a stir in the Yishuv. Because immigration certificates, issued by the Mandate government, would be needed for the German youth, Arlosoroff invited Arthur Wauchope, the British high commissioner, to visit the Ben Shemen village. Impressed by the high quality of the settlement, Wauchope informally agreed to obtain the necessary certificates for large-scale German youth immigration.

That evening, June 16, 1933, as Arlosoroff strolled on a Tel Aviv beach with his wife Sima, two men approached them. One quickly drew a gun and shot him before both disappeared into the darkness. The murder shocked Jews the world over and increased tensions within the Palestine community. The majority of the Labor party believed the assassination was a political act perpetrated by the Revisionists, extreme Jewish nationalists and at the time bitter opponents of the Labor Zionists. Szold, who had admired Arlosoroff tremendously, was profoundly distressed by his death. She wrote home that if indeed it turned out to be a political murder of one Jew by another, the "tragedy would be infinitely greater for the Jewish people," for it would mean "that the Jewish ethic has disappeared from our scene."[18] A Revisionist, Abraham Stavsky, was tried and condemned to death for the killing, but was later acquitted for insufficient evidence. The crime has never been solved.

Inspired by Arlosoroff and aware of the increasing Nazi menace, delegates to the Eighteenth Zionist Congress, held in Prague in August 1933, created a new office within the Jewish Agency Executive to deal with the settlement of German Jews in Palestine, known simply as the German Department and run in Jerusalem by Arthur Ruppin. After first refusing—yet again she had planned to move back to the States—Szold later accepted Ruppin's invitation to direct the youth bureau in the department. She had been sent to London as a representative of the Vaad Leumi to attend a conference on the German Jewish situation and at Ruppin's urging, had traveled from there to Germany. In Berlin, to her horror, she saw anti-Jewish posters everywhere—in railroad stations, on office buildings, in shops, on the streets. She met with dozens of people: Zionist leaders, heads of Jewish youth groups, and parents despondent about the future of their children in Germany. When she returned, Szold agreed to head the Youth Aliyah bureau in Jerusalem. She was seventy-three years old.

Recha Freier would resent Szold's position with Youth Aliyah for the rest of her life. She never forgave Szold for rejecting her early suggestion of transferring young Germans to Palestine, and, as the official Youth Aliyah program unfolded, she felt unrecognized for an idea she had envisioned before anyone else. Szold acknowledged Freier's role at the Nineteenth Zionist Congress, held in Lucerne in 1935. "On this occasion," she said, as part of her formal address, "I would like to express my gratitude to the woman who initiated this project, Mrs. Recha Freier. She understood this great idea and fulfilled it despite all the obstacles and hardships. We owe her a debt of gratitude for her devotion to the idea which initially found no support."[19] She repeated that tribute on several other occasions. Nevertheless, tensions between the two women remained. Szold did not involve Freier in her Youth Aliyah activities and Freier worked with various other groups in helping to rescue European Jews from Hitler. She stayed on at her work in Europe, at some risk to herself, until 1941, when she immigrated to Palestine. In recognition of her many contributions, in 1981 she was awarded the Israel Prize, that country's highest honor.

Freier may have had the vision, but she lacked administrative skills. People who knew her described her as a dreamer, a woman of many ideas but incapable of working in an organized fashion.[20] Szold, always disciplined and meticulous, quickly discovered that not only Freier but few German Zionists understood the intricacies involved in relocating children who had been separated from their parents to a country they knew almost nothing about, to do manual labor they had never done before. How to house and educate them? Train them in agriculture? Teach them a new language? Support them physically and emotionally? The "undertaking grows more and more complex every day," Szold wrote her sisters. And it was made more difficult by the "bad initial organization" that had taken place in the German Jugendhilfe.[21] She would have to work out her own system—which she did, focusing with precision on every necessary detail.

Most of the young people to be transferred from Germany to Palestine would be housed in kibbutzim, the agricultural settlements that dotted the land. They would be put up in barracks, with toilets and showers (which Szold personally inspected) and separate beds with clean linen. If a kibbutz did not have a proper structure for the children, members would have to use their own buildings for the youngsters even if that meant that they themselves slept in tents while new housing was being constructed. The children were to be trained to work the land, like the *halutzim*, the pioneers Szold had always admired, but they were also to be treated as individuals, youngsters who had left their home and parents and embarked on a new life frightening to many of them.

Ruth Halprin Kaslove, daughter of Rose Halprin, one of Hadassah's national presidents and an intimate friend of Henrietta Szold, recalled going to the port in Haifa several times with her mother and Szold to welcome arriving Youth Aliyah ships. Invariably there would be children on board who asked, in their native language, "When is mother coming?" Too frequently the answer the adults knew but would not say was "never."[22]

Szold understood the fears of the children and of the parents who let them go, and regarded her office as having "moral responsibility" for their care and safekeeping.[23] In the program she devised and then developed in cooperation with the Jugendhilfe, young people from various Jewish youth movements would be trained for six weeks at Zionist preparatory camps in Germany, supervised and taught by older counselors. At the end of that period, the counselors would leave with them for Palestine. Once there, the youth, still supervised by their counselors, would work and study on selected kibbutzim for two years, after which each group or individual would decide where to settle permanently. Generally the trainees would work on the land or do farm chores in the morning and spend four hours in the afternoon studying Hebrew, Jewish history and literature, and other subjects important to their new lives.

From the beginning, many of the young immigrants arrived with classic German books, works by Goethe or Schiller and Heine, and then felt embarrassed by those possessions or were made to feel like outcasts in the determinedly Hebrew-speaking kibbutzim they had come to. With her own Germanic background and love of German authors, Szold made a point of reassuring newcomers, often speaking to them in German, that they did not have to give up everything about their past. "Don't forget the cultural things, the fine part of Germany that you have learned," she told one group of children. "Try to forget the other things."[24]

Members of the first group selected for the Youth Aliyah project ranged in age between fifteen and seventeen, a span the British Mandate government had specified. Later Szold and others convinced the government to accept younger people in the program. As part of her responsibilities, Szold worked closely with government officials to make sure all regulations were met and all forms properly filled out so that special immigration certificates promised for Youth Aliyah youngsters could be issued. Forms included each child's medical history, with his or her mental and physical health attested to by doctors and dentists, and specific arrangements for financial support. The British were sticklers about not accepting sickly children or those whose financial upkeep could not be guaranteed. With limitations on the certificates of immigration and shortages of financial resources, Szold herself placed priorities on young people who were physically and mentally fit for the difficult task of adjusting to kibbutz life. From her viewpoint—and that of many Labor Zionist leaders—in addition to the goal of rescuing German Jewish children there was the objective of building up the land. For that, too, the quality of the candidates needed to be considered. Later, as Nazi policies became more draconian and chances for saving Jewish children grimly limited, that policy of selectivity would be severely criticized.

In 1933, when Szold began her Youth Aliyah activities for

the Jewish Agency (while still wearing her social services hat), she worked out of a small office, with just her secretary, Emma Ehrlich, at her side. Ehrlich, a young married American woman who came to idolize Szold, also became one of her closest friends and almost like a daughter to her. In an interview later in life Szold described Ehrlich's calming effect on her when the office grew in size, with many secretaries, and she would "rage and storm" at demands bombarding her from all sides. (Despite her efforts, Szold never rid herself of the sharp temper she'd had since youth.) After she'd blow up, Ehrlich would say, "Now you are going to be nice," and Szold usually was.[25]

A large part of Szold's duties involved scouting out kibbutzim and kvutzot (small settlements) appropriate as homes for the young German immigrants. Finding the right places for the children was not an easy task. Along with sleeping accommodations, each location chosen needed to have the proper facilities for schooling, dining, laundries, medical care, and other basics of everyday living. "In this little country such places are not too abundant," Szold wrote her sisters. "Besides, people are beginning to whisper to each other that the responsibility [of caring for the youngsters] is not child's play."[26] But as exhausting as she found the search, she loved traveling about the land, seeing new settlements and glorying in the scenery along the way. "The country was exquisite after the rain," she raved in one letter, "with the oranges gleaming under the dark leaves."[27] Another letter lauded the "marvelous olive groves . . . one of the most exquisite bits of scenery on earth."[28]

With few religious kibbutzim in existence at the time, placing children from the religious Zionist movements became a particular challenge for her. One settlement willing to take in the religious German children was Kvutzat Rodges, adjacent to the town of Petach Tikvah, originally founded by German religious Zionists. Szold regarded it as "primitive in the extreme" when she went to examine it, with most of its settlers living in tents without electricity, and the bathrooms far away. But its members reassured her that they would build housing for the German youth and not lower the newcomers' living standards, while giving them a "good dose of pioneering."[29] Unfortunately, a plague of typhus hit the kibbutz and when a group of religious German boys arrived, some fell ill and one died, profoundly distressing Szold, who felt personally responsible for each child she placed.

Always religiously observant herself, Szold understood the need for religious children to live in an observant environment, but she was stymied by the lack of spaces for them. The situation became even worse over time, when growing numbers of religious children lied about their backgrounds, usually with their parents' consent, in order to escape from Germany. Placed in nonreligious settlements in Palestine, some then complained that they could not practice their religion as they always had. When at all possible, Szold transferred such children to religious kibbutzim, but for the most part, she could not find places for them.[30] For many years Orthodox authorities attacked her for not settling enough religious children and accused her of discriminating against them, even though they well knew of the shortage of religious institutions to house these young people.[31]

On Monday, February 19, 1934, as an icy rain pelted her, Henrietta Szold went out to meet the first band of Youth Aliyah children to arrive in Palestine. Their ship, the S.S. *Martha Washington*, had been scheduled to dock at Jaffa, but because of gale winds and high seas, it traveled farther north to the newly opened port of Haifa. There Szold welcomed each child by name, had dinner together with all of them, and then escorted them by train to the kibbutz that would be their new home, Ein Harod. Their counselor, Chanoch Reinhold (later Rinott), who would become a well-known Youth Aliyah leader, remembered the joy with which the kibbutz members welcomed the newcomers, crowding in a circle around the dining hall and singing and dancing with excitement.[32] Szold spent two days at the kibbutz to make sure everything was in order for the new arrivals, including storage space for the mandolins, bicycles, cellos, and other paraphernalia they had brought with them.

She would repeat that pattern over the next several years, greeting every new group of Youth Aliyah children at the harbor in Haifa, and spending a day or two at the kibbutz to which they had been assigned. Her presence offered comfort; she reminded them of the Germany they had grown up in and of the parents they had left behind. This elderly woman with her dowdy clothes and no-nonsense bearing exuded strength along with warmth, helping them find the strength they needed to adjust to their new foreign lives.

Privately, she did not see herself as strong as others saw her. Her mood varied as it had each time she undertook a new project. "I alternate between gratification and self-criticism," she wrote to Jessie in the months of preparing for the first youth group from Germany.[33] On the gratification side, she had to admit, as she did to Adele, that "old as I am . . . I have not stopped growing . . . my inner world, perhaps it is my world of feeling, of instinct, expands."[34] In the self-criticism realm she sounded a tune she had before: "I have only one quality—endurance. I can peg away at details. And I do endlessly. The administration of the Youth immigration is compact of details, and I keep at them doggedly, day and night. . . . I'm a grubber."[35] But the deeper she immersed herself in the youth operation, the more she had to acknowledge, even to herself, how significant her labor was, far beyond the details that hounded her. "Even in the least attractive of the Kevuzot," she said, "the care of the children, as the pledge of a worthwhile future, is exquisite."[36] Her work made that future possible; her work saved young lives. The self-criticism died down after a while, and although the long hours and incessant pressure never let up, she came to embrace this project fully. "My Germans," she would say in speaking about the young people being brought to Palestine, as she had once spoken of "my Russians" in relation to the night school she created in Baltimore.

By the end of Youth Aliyah's first year of operation in Palestine, a dozen groups, with about five hundred young people, had arrived.[37]

In October 1934, Szold laid the cornerstone for what would become the most modern medical center in the Middle East, Hadassah University Hospital on Mount Scopus. As chair of the event, she gave a speech in Hebrew, always a nerve-wracking situation for her. Relieved to have survived the speech, she told her sisters she had the feeling throughout of being at her own funeral. Described by one speaker after another as the "mother" of Hadassah, the "founder" of Hadassah, the "inspiration" of Hadassah, and other such platitudes, she squirmed at being presented as a symbol rather than a real person who struggled to get things done. People didn't realize, she wrote, how little power she actually had.[38]

That was not quite true. Although she lacked political power, her name and reputation carried power of their own that had opened doors for her over the years in America and Palestine. For Youth Aliyah, her name would help bring in much-needed funds to make that program viable. With the Mandate government demanding a financial guarantee for each German child who entered the country, Szold had expected German parents and the German Jewish community to provide the bulk of the funding. But as the Nazi vise closed in on German Jews ever more tightly, that source of backing began to dry up. And such traditional agencies as the Jewish National Fund and the Keren Hayesod, always seeking cash themselves, had set little aside for the young immigrants. To get what Youth Aliyah needed, Szold and others involved began to spread the word about rescuing the German children outside traditional Zionist circles to groups less familiar with the operation. In time, the persistent public relations efforts paid off. Youth Aliyah committees throughout the world, many of them in Jewish women's organizations aware of Szold's achievements, made fund-raising for young immigrants to Palestine their top priority.[39]

The most important women's group of all, Hadassah, adopted Youth Aliyah as its own cause. Szold didn't push the project on the organization; in fact at first she tried to dissuade the women from taking it up. When Rose Jacobs, then Hadassah's national president, broached the subject, Szold made it clear that Youth Aliyah officials in Berlin and Jerusalem would allow no interference from America. As badly as they needed money, they would accept Hadassah's contributions only on condition that the women's Zionist organization did not have a voice in policy making. At the time, Jacobs and Tamar de Sola Pool, president of the New York chapter, were seeking new directions for Hadassah. As Szold had always insisted, Hadassah in America had turned over many of its major enterprises—hospitals, wellness clinics, school hygiene programs, and the like—to local authorities in Palestine once these people felt themselves ready to run such endeavors. The Hadassah leaders believed that assuming responsibility for the children's immigration embodied just the kind of new venture the organization needed. It would both excite the base and draw in new members. They were eager to pursue the connection, even with Szold's qualifications.

Accordingly, on August 27, 1935, with Szold's backing, Jacobs signed a confidential agreement making Hadassah the sole representative of Youth Aliyah in the United States provided that in the next two years it would cover the expenses for transferring and maintaining one hundred German and Polish youths in Palestine. Hadassah's national board in New York unanimously approved the agreement, and promised that it would raise $100,000 in the next two years—more than required. (It actually raised $250,766.76 in those two years.)[40]

Enter Louis Lipsky one more time. As chairman of the board of the United Palestine Appeal (UPA), he argued that Hadassah's exclusive right to fund-raise for Youth Aliyah in that way hurt the broader fund-raising campaigns of other Zionist organizations in America. A knock-down drag-out fight now pitted Hadassah against Lipsky and some of the most prominent male Zionist leaders in America and Palestine. In the end, with Szold's steadfast support in the background, as it had been in earlier battles, Hadassah won the exclusive right to Youth Aliyah in the United States, as originally outlined. In a compromise, it agreed to allow the United Palestine Appeal to include the money Hadassah raised for Youth Aliyah as part of the UPA financial report. With this agreement, Hadassah essentially gained full independence from the Zionist Organization of America, and finally made peace with Louis Lipsky.

In a moving newsletter to the Hadassah membership, Szold explained the goals of Youth Aliyah. Through the generations, she wrote, Jewish children have suffered—during the Spanish Inquisition, when they were sent to the island of St. Thomas; in Russia, when they were snatched from their parents and brought up in convents; and even at the present time in Mandatory Palestine, where there was not enough money to solve the many problems they faced. Yet, when she saw the boys and girls of Youth Aliyah, she thought to herself, "We are making good where the others have sinned. . . . And I went on saying to myself, That is Zionism in its truest realization."[41] In pursuit of that Zionism, Hadassah members threw themselves wholeheartedly into Youth Aliyah fund-raising and raised hundreds of thousands of dollars, most of the budget needed. The organization also enlisted prominent Americans in its campaigns, among them Eleanor Roosevelt, who accepted an honorary position with Youth Aliyah, and the popular entertainer Eddie Cantor, who became the single biggest fund-raiser for youth immigration.

Through it all, in Palestine, Szold continued her round-the-clock routine, rising at 5 in the morning and working well past midnight. People in her office marveled at how the seventy-five-year-old woman could function day after day on four or five hours of sleep a night. Sometimes she herself wondered—"I am inhuman," she wrote to Rose Jacobs.[42] In May 1935, Hans Beyth entered her life and made it more human. A successful German Jewish banker, he had been sent by the Jugendhilfe to assist Youth Aliyah in financial matters. He quickly became Szold's assistant in every aspect of her work. While he barely slowed her pace, he eased the pressure on her and shared her burdens. Two or three times a week he traveled with her on her regular visits to the settlements where the Youth Aliyah children had been placed, and he accompanied her in choosing new settlements for the groups of children arriving. A handsome, outgoing man in his early thirties, he had grown up in a well-to-do and assimilated Jewish home, becoming, like several of his friends, a Zionist as a teenager. Comfortable in his own skin, he helped make the young people he met feel comfortable and secure, speaking to them in German (he knew little Hebrew) and reassuring them in their new homes.[43]

Beyth and Szold became close friends and trusting colleagues. He never left the office before she did, and even after he married and had a family, he put in long hours working alongside her. In 1945, after she died, he replaced her as director of Youth Aliyah. Tragically, two years later he was shot and killed by Arab guerrillas while riding in a convoy from Jerusalem to Tel Aviv in connection with Youth Aliyah activities. Golda Meir, who rode in the same convoy, would later tell his son that he died in her arms.[44]

With Beyth as her loyal assistant, Szold had felt comfortable in the late summer of 1935 leaving the office to attend the Nineteenth Zionist Congress in Lucerne. She spoke there about Youth Aliyah's work and needs, appealing for more money in increasingly hard times. (It was there also that she firmed up Hadassah's involvement in Youth Aliyah with Jacobs and de Sola Pool.) At a packed public session, Chaim Weizmann, who had returned as president after being out of office for four years, presented her with an armful of red roses and announced that a new agricultural settlement would be created and named in her honor. (Kibbutz Kfar Szold was established in the early 1940s in northern Palestine at the edge of the Golan Heights.) From Lucerne, she traveled to Amsterdam to address the First World Youth Aliyah Conference, thank the delegates for the funds they had raised, and ask for more. As she wrote to Jessie, "Money, money, money" was the word that most often crossed her lips.[45]

From Amsterdam she went to Berlin. That month, September 1935, during a special session of the Reichstag held at a Nazi Party rally in Nuremberg, Hitler had presented new legislation. One part of the rules essentially decreed that Jews in Germany were not citizens. Another prohibited marriage or sexual relations between Jews and German gentiles, or Aryans, as the Nazis called them. Collectively the legislation became known as the Nuremberg Laws, one more step toward the decimation of German Jewry. The laws horrified the German Jewish community, and for the first time planted the idea of emigration into the minds of Jews who had seen themselves as solid German patriots. "The success of Zionism and Palestine is ghastly," Szold wrote her sisters.[46] By that she meant that Zionism and Palestine had become goals for German Jews only after they had been placed under ghastly pressure.

Szold was well known among German Jews, especially within Zionist circles. The *Jüdische Rundschau*, one of Berlin's most prominent Jewish newspapers, reported on her visits over the years and had congratulated her a few years earlier on her seventieth birthday. On this trip, articles about her activities appeared in the paper throughout September, and the Jewish community of Berlin welcomed her with such enthusiasm, she felt as though its members were paying her homage.[47] In light of the degradation German Jews now suffered, the meetings, lectures, and dinners they scheduled for her seemed like acts of "undaunted courage," their attempt to come as close as they could to the way life had once been.[48] Jugendhilfe leaders met with her to iron out Youth Aliyah issues and took her on trips to preparatory camps, where young people trained for their eventual immigration to Palestine. Eighty years later, journalist Tom Tugend remembered studying at a Zionist-oriented boarding school in Caputh, a suburb of Potsdam and Berlin. One evening he and other students put on a performance of Shakespeare's *Midsummer Night's Dream* in German translation for a special guest—Henrietta Szold.[49] He never forgot the thrill of that visit. Exhausted as she may have been from the day's activities, Szold made a point of attending as many such events organized by Jewish community members as she could to help bolster them in their trials.

One day she met with some eight hundred parents of Youth Aliyah children and teenagers already settled in Palestine. Packed into a small hall, the parents bombarded her with questions about their daughters and sons, and she answered as best she could, telling them how she greeted every child on arrival in Palestine and regularly visited the settlements where the children lived. "They clutched at her with eyes and hands," Emma Ehrlich, who attended with her that day, wrote. "She was the living bond" with the children they might never see again.[50] She left that evening feeling as though she were abandoning a sick child. Throughout her travels in the country, she had seen signs reading "Jews not wanted" or "Girls and Women: Jews are your depravers." Hitler will not rest, she wrote her sisters, "until every last Jew has been hunted out of Germany."[51]

From Germany she returned to Palestine for a short visit, then on to America, where Hadassah had geared up to celebrate her seventy-fifth birthday. Szold's birthdays had become important landmarks for Hadassah, not only to honor its founder but also to use the occasion for major fund-raising events. Szold never quite adjusted to these birthday bashes. She felt uncomfortable having to listen to streams of praise about herself, yet she considered the events part of her duty to the organization. This time, she went to Baltimore first, where she visited with her sisters and old friends before going on to New York. She missed the talk her friend Harry Friedenwald gave at a Baltimore Hadassah birthday party. Beyond extolling her work, Friedenwald looked back nostalgically to the early days when he would spend Sunday evenings at the Szolds' home on Lombard Street. In her letter of thanks to him, Szold picked up on that part of his talk: "Your evocations of our past, its beauty, its simplicity, its genuineness its warmth. . . . That gives me a sense of harmony, joining the latter end to the beginning, as though there had been no doubts, no hesitations, no transformations."[52] The halcyon days of Lombard Street, when she lived with her parents and sisters, remained for Henrietta Szold the touchstone of happiness in her life.

The Baltimore Hadassah chapter gave her a birthday gift of $5,000 for the children's ward of Hadassah University Hospital. She raised many more thousands for Youth Aliyah during the American trip. On the voyage back to Palestine she answered hundreds of birthday greetings she had received, and continued with more than a thousand waiting for her in Jerusalem, each note of thanks written by hand.

The Jerusalem Szold returned to had begun to feel the sting, again, of Arab hostility. A few years earlier she had written to her sisters that the Jews in the Yishuv didn't seem to realize that "the Arab question and the way they are going to solve it are the supreme test."[53] Now the swelling of the Jewish population because of German and Polish immigrants (from about 175,000 in 1931 to almost 400,000 in 1935) and the prosperity that came with it, which delighted the Yishuv, enraged the Arabs. They responded at first by isolated killings against individuals, soon escalating to large-scale attacks, burning Jewish fields and granaries and uprooting thousands of trees. Adding to that, Arab leaders declared a general workers' strike that affected all aspects of society—the buses and trucks that had Arab drivers, Jewish farms and citrus groves where Arabs worked, the port at Jaffa, run by Arab boatmen, and all manner of Arab goods and services. The strike and terror would not end, they declared, until the British stopped Jewish immigration into Palestine, forbade the sale of land to the Jews, and established a national Arab government.

In letter after letter to her family, Szold chronicled the Arab upheaval and its effect on life in the Yishuv. Concerned for the welfare of her Youth Aliyah children, she issued orders to confine them to their homes on the kibbutzim and limit travel, protecting them as much as possible from the virulence of Arab terror. And with Jews fleeing to Jerusalem from Hebron and other towns because of the violence, she took some pride, she wrote, in how well the social service systems she had put in place functioned as they cared for the now homeless refugees. She blamed the British Mandate government more than anybody for not providing adequate public security when it had ample warning of the outbreak. Why did it permit the mufti, Haj Amin al-Husseini, to incite violence without punishing him? Why did the British police search Jewish passersby for arms, but not the Arabs? Why didn't the government attempt to make peace between the two peoples instead of maintaining a neutral stand? As for the Arabs, wasn't it time for them to accept the fact that they were not alone in Palestine, that they needed to recognize Jewish claims to the land also?

Nobody could possibly blame the Jews for the riots, Szold

wrote. Moreover, Jewish defense organizations had reacted to the violence with great discipline and restraint. Even so—in a theme she had touched on in the past and would repeat in the future—"Is there no Arab side to the problem? Is it not our business to see the Arab side, too?"[54] The relationship between Jews and Arabs would always hold a central place in Szold's Zionist thinking.

In response to the disturbances, as the British called the Arab revolt, a royal commission, headed by Lord William Robert Peel, set out to investigate the situation and submit recommendations for resolving it. The Peel Commission, as it was known, arrived in Jerusalem on November 11, 1936, and for the next two months held separate hearings with Jewish and Arab leaders. Szold testified before the six-member all-male commission, but they showed little interest in her descriptions of Hadassah hospitals and health services. They aimed for big decisions, and they made them in a report published in July 1937. It recommended that the land be partitioned between Jews and Arabs, with the Jews receiving a small state in western Palestine and the Arabs holding most of the rest of the territory, more than 70 percent. The British would control Jerusalem and surrounding areas. The commission also proposed limiting Jewish immigration to Palestine to fifteen thousand a year for the next five years.

The partition recommendation created an uproar in the Jewish world, and became the most heated subject of the Twentieth Zionist Congress, which met in Zurich in 1937. Those who favored the partition plan, including Ben-Gurion and Weizmann, argued that the very concept of an independent Jewish state, small as it might be, changed the course of Jewish history, giving the Jewish people the sovereignty and freedom they had lacked for thousands of years. Those opposed, like Zionist leader Berl Katznelson, regarded the proposed area allotted to the Jews far too limited to sustain a viable state. Hadassah opposed the plan, objecting particularly to the loss of Jerusalem for the Jews and with it Hadassah Hospital and the Hebrew University. Szold's opposition went further. Like Judah Magnes, who also spoke at the congress, she still dreamed of a single state where Jews and Arabs might live together in harmony.[55]

In the end a pan-Arab congress unconditionally rejected the partition recommendation, particularly the idea of a Jewish state, and the British dropped the plan. The only part of the Peel Commission recommendation that would later be accepted concerned a limitation on Jewish immigration.

Szold left the Zionist congress early to go to Berlin for a farewell party for young people leaving for Palestine with the Youth Aliyah program. She was amazed at the change that had taken place under the Nazis in the two years since she had been in Germany. The Jews looked like "living corpses," capable now "of only one emotion—fear." Along with the parents of young people leaving for Palestine, parents of children already there again crowded around her, many with photographs of their children, pressing her for any bit of information she had about their offspring. She felt she was being torn to pieces by desperate people who had little hope for themselves, but harbored one wish above all others: "Save the young!"[56]

She returned to Palestine exhausted, spent a few weeks there, and took off again for the States, this time to Atlantic City, New Jersey, where Hadassah held its twenty-fifth anniversary convention in October 1937. The highlight for Szold was a $25,000 gift in honor of Felix Warburg to be applied to her Children's Central Fund and a birthday gift of $5,000 that she would use for the placement of children. "Worthwhile coming five or six thousand miles," she wrote to Adele.[57] To Bertha, she said, "Hadassah is an octopus, but a good one."[58] It had been a satisfying few days; she had felt distant from the organization during her years away, but felt close again now, proud of its achievements.

* * *

It was 1938, and the world had turned more chaotic than ever. In Palestine, the Arabs had begun a new round of violence in reaction to the Peel report after their earlier revolt petered out. It continued throughout the year, more viciously than before, its fury directed at the British as well as the Jews. Arab guerrillas sabotaged roads, bombed vehicles, and murdered British soldiers and Jewish settlers. The British responded by deporting Arab leaders and using military force to fight back, often brutally. The mufti, who had incited much of the rioting, fled to Lebanon, and would later collaborate with Hitler against the Jews. In Europe, the Anschluss—Germany's annexation of Austria—took place in March 1938, to the wild cheering of Austrian crowds and the despair of Austrian Jews. Four months later, at a conference at the French resort town of Evian convened by Franklin D. Roosevelt, leaders of most of the world's nations let it be known that they had little intention of increasing their quotas to accept Jewish refugees trying to escape from Hitler's onslaught. And four months after that, on November 9 and 10, Kristallnacht, Nazi mobs throughout Germany and Austria destroyed hundreds of synagogues, smashed the windows of Jewish-owned stores and homes, arrested thousands of Jewish men, and murdered nearly one hundred other Jews. If anyone had doubts about the future of Germany's Jews, the darkest predictions were affirmed that night.

With each new event, the pressures on Szold and the Youth Aliyah program mounted. Within days of the Anschluss, Austrian Jews began suffering from oppressions German Jews had experienced slowly, over months, granted at least some time to assess their lives and make plans. Austrian authorities almost immediately barred Jewish children from state-run schools and shut down Jewish businesses. Even families that had been well off fell into instant poverty. And unlike German Jews, those in Austria had not developed a large Zionist community or a strong

Youth Aliyah program. Yet, as Szold wrote her family, faced with the new reality, twelve hundred boys and girls had registered for the Youth Aliyah in an attempt to find refuge. She doubted whether even four hundred would be qualified for admission. Szold had been prepared to go to Vienna herself to try to organize the program and rescue as many young people as she could, but word came from abroad that Gestapo agent Adolf Eichmann had specifically forbade her, by name, from entering Austria on pain of making more trouble for the Jews there. Although at this point the Nazis still supported Jewish emigration from the countries they conquered, Szold may have been too prominent a personality for them to deal with as they liquidated Austrian Jewish life. "The thoroughness of the Nazis is hellish," she wrote.[59]

The British, who had cut back on immigration certificates to Palestine to placate the Arabs, had remained relatively generous with certificates for Youth Aliyah children, placing them in the more liberal category of students. But they had not changed their criteria. Housing for the young people at an educational institution needed to be assured before these youths would be given immigration certificates. As much as she wanted to get children out of Austria, Szold adhered to these standards and others that had long been established for the Youth Aliyah program. She objected, for example, when mentally or physically compromised children arrived in Palestine from Austria, reminding the Youth Aliyah office in Vienna that doctors needed to fill out detailed medical forms for each Youth Aliyah candidate before selections were made. Children with physical or mental ailments might not be able to perform the work expected of them and therefore should be carefully screened before being accepted.

Szold would be criticized as rigid and over-organized for insisting on applying earlier procedures to the current desperate circumstances not only in Austria but in all countries under

Nazi control. At one point she got into a bitter struggle with the Jewish Agency about dealing with the Mandatory government. Although the British continued to restrict Jewish immigration certificates, the category of student still remained more lenient and available. Soon, with the backing of the Jewish Agency, institutions that were not really schools began submitting applications for large numbers of young people who were not legitimate students in order to take advantage of the student certificates. Agency leaders also thought about using Youth Aliyah certificates for young people over eighteen, pretending they were younger, and allocating some to Polish youth although they were meant for German children.

Edwin Samuel, Herbert Samuel's son, who worked for the Mandatory government, warned Szold that attempting to trick the government or bypass the rules might endanger the entire Youth Aliyah enterprise. She took those warnings seriously, carefully complying with the British standards and regulations for Youth Aliyah. Jewish Agency officials argued that Szold's caution and conservatism jeopardized the lives of young people, especially those from Poland, Romania, and Czechoslovakia, and that she should confront the British boldly to expand their criteria.

Szold might indeed have followed the rules more strictly than necessary, and it is conceivable that if pushed further, the British might have made more certificates available for students and for the young in eastern European countries. Such criticisms would arise again and again.[60] Nevertheless, it is near impossible for those in the midst of a dilemma to foresee what will be. These were tumultuous times, when Nazi boots stomped across Europe faster and with more power than anybody had expected. Nobody could yet know—nobody could have imagined—that in a few years Jews in Nazi Europe would be murdered en masse through Hitler's Final Solution, and therefore had to be spirited out now under any circumstances. Then, too,

Jewish communities themselves were often mired in confusion, with Zionist groups competing against one another for money and immigration certificates. Meanwhile, the British increasingly sought to find favor with the Arabs by limiting Jewish immigration. Given these conditions, for Szold, following the rules seemed the best path to take. With limited resources, limited funds, and limited certificates, screening Youth Aliyah candidates, selecting those most likely to succeed in the land, and finding the right places for them to live made the most sense to her.

In the middle of 1938, Szold suffered angina and had to be hospitalized. The pressures of the work, the long hours, the criticisms and struggles against them—all wore her down. She recuperated in a sanitarium for two weeks and by the fall became enmeshed in work again. She resigned from her social work position, although it took months for her to get out of the many duties involved. "I was practically out, but no one else could be got in," she wrote Adele.[61] Finally freed from those obligations, she would now devote herself full-time to rescuing the young, the "most worthwhile undertaking I have ever been connected with."[62]

9

Saving Children / Seeking Peace

As THE WORLD STOOD on the cusp of war, Szold had some
reason to be pleased with the British. In early 1939, the government agreed to issue the largest number of Youth Aliyah
certificates—twenty-five hundred—that it had since the organization's beginning. Indeed, in the months between November 1938 and September 1939, Youth Aliyah brought almost as
many young Jews to Palestine as it had during the previous five
years.[1] Szold worked ceaselessly to raise the money needed and
find the places to house and educate the young immigrants.

But for thousands of adults seeking to flee the Nazis, for the
parents of Youth Aliyah children trapped in Reich-controlled
countries, for Szold's own relatives in Austria and Hungary,
that same year, 1939, would signify one of the darkest dates on
the rescue calendar. On May 17, the Mandatory government
issued a White Paper that would govern Jewish immigration to
Palestine in the years ahead. The new rules limited that immi-

gration to seventy-five thousand people over five years, a miniscule number in light of the need, after which the Arabs would have to give their consent for any further immigration. It restricted the purchase of land by Jews and stipulated that Palestine would be given independence after ten years, with the Jews a minority in that state. The Balfour Declaration, with its earnest promise of a Jewish homeland, now seemed an outworn relic of a bygone era. Cynically recognizing that under no circumstances would the Jews align themselves with Hitler, while the Arabs could go either way, the British used the White Paper to woo Arab nations to their side.

The White Paper astounded and enraged Jews throughout the world. In the Yishuv, people organized strikes, marched in protest carrying angry anti-British banners, published manifestos, and signed petitions. From national Hadassah in New York, Szold received cables of support "unanimously protesting [the] White Paper" and pledging "solidarity" in the struggle against it.[2] In turn, she sent greetings to the Hadassah convention referring to the "disappointments inflicted by the White Paper," but cited the Yishuv's "refusal to believe that escape is cut off from the innocent; and the Yishuv cannot but be right."[3] They were encouraging words, but unrealistic ones. Szold well knew that the British had no intention of rescinding their White Paper no matter how grim the situation became. And it became grimmer by the day. Earlier, in August, the Soviet Union had signed a nonaggression pact with Germany, endangering Western countries like Great Britain and France along with eastern European ones. Not long afterward, on September 1, 1939, Germany invaded Poland, triggering the Second World War.

With the British refusing to budge, continuing to limit the quota of Jewish refugees allowed into Palestine in the months before and after the beginning of the war, the Jews turned increasingly to what the Mandate powers called "illegal immigration" and the Zionists labeled "Aliyah Bet," Immigration B, an alternate form of bringing in refugees. In the dead of night, beat-up old ships that could be cheaply acquired, some cattle boats, some dilapidated vessels almost ready for the junk heap, smuggled thousands of refugees across dangerous waters to Palestine's shores. If caught by the British, the ships, with their human cargo, were returned to lands they had fled or the passengers were sent to detention camps. But many thousands of refugees escaped, among them Youth Aliyah children, and joined Jewish settlements. The Revisionists, the extreme nationalists who had broken with the mainstream Labor Zionists, led the way in organizing the illegal immigration journeys. Soon, with Palestine's doors shut tight by the White Paper, the Haganah, the Labor movement's underground military branch, followed the Revisionists' example in carrying out their own illegal immigration.

Enmity between the two groups remained, however. Attempts at reconciliation between David Ben-Gurion, Labor's head and chairman of the Jewish Agency Executive, and Revisionist leader Vladimir Jabotinsky fell through, and in 1935, the Revisionists formed their own New Zionist Organization. With that, they threw off any obligation to follow Labor directives. Ignoring Ben-Gurion's policy of *havlagah*, restraint, in response to the Arab revolt that began in 1936, they hit back hard at Arab attacks, planting bombs in crowded Arab marketplaces and bus stations and randomly killing Arab men, women, and children. By 1939, with the Arab rebellion at its height and the White Paper coming into effect, Revisionist rage seemed to know no bounds. The movement's military arm, the Irgun, struck out at Arabs indiscriminately, in one case throwing a bomb and killing innocent Arab workers who had done nothing to hurt Jews.

Distressed by the Irgun's behavior toward the Arabs, and greatly concerned about its effect on young people, who seemed dazzled by Revisionist daring, Szold decided to take action. That

July, she led the way in signing a "Manifesto against Internal Terror" circulated throughout the Yishuv. (She might actually have written much of the manifesto herself.) Addressed "to the Yishuv" and "to the youth," it declared in large black Hebrew letters, "Do Not Murder!" It went on to acknowledge the pain everyone felt at the bitter British ruling and the need to stand up against it. Nevertheless, it stated, murder—of Arabs, of the British, or of Jews—was a form of terrorism that would destroy Zionism itself. "Do not murder—this commandment from the infancy of an ancient people . . . still applies today," the manifesto stated, calling on the Yishuv to defend its national home from the "terror within" as much as from its "enemies on the outside."[4] On a separate line, above three long rows of signatures, Henrietta Szold's name appears first. The other names on that line include Berl Katznelson, the esteemed Labor leader, and the well-known Hebrew author S. Y. Agnon. Aware that her name carried weight, although she might deny the extent of her influence, Szold had become bolder in asserting her values publicly.

Amid the turmoil of 1939, Szold's sisters Bertha and Adele came to Palestine in April to visit her, aware that she could not get home to be with them. They found Jerusalem a guarded city, almost shut down, with a curfew in effect and barricades everywhere. Arab guerrillas had shot the British curator of the Rockefeller Museum as he was putting his car into the garage in what was supposedly a safe part of the city. But the sisters managed to join Henrietta and Hans Beyth on various trips to greet Youth Aliyah children arriving in Palestine and to visit some of the settlements where others lived. By the end of a day of such visits, Bertha told her family that she and Adele had dropped into bed exhausted immediately after dinner. "When one goes with Henrietta, one starts at 7 A.M. with breakfast and goes on till 6 P.M. or later," she wrote.[5]

Because Henrietta's tight schedule didn't permit her to spend all her time with them, the sisters also enjoyed themselves touring the country alone or with friends. In June they helped her move from the Eden Hotel, where she had lived for so many years, to a larger space, a furnished first-floor apartment at Glacomon House on King George Avenue, not far from many of her friends. Years earlier, after receiving a stack of letters from her sisters, Szold had written them, "The important thing is that at last I again feel that I 'belong' to someone."[6] With them close by during this difficult time, witnessing the life she led, she again felt that sense of belonging, a fundamental part of her family.

In too short a while, the family reunion fell apart. Bertha suffered a sudden heart attack in August, which filled Henrietta with anxiety. By November Bertha was well enough for Adele to return to the States and by February 1940, Bertha sailed home also, leaving Henrietta with the empty feeling she always had after separating from her sisters. Far worse, a month later, on March 16, 1940, she received the devastating news that Adele had died of an intestinal disease, something she had been suffering with for some time. Filled with grief, Szold couldn't stop herself from "brooding" constantly over her sister's death, even while continuing the grueling pace of her Youth Aliyah activities.[7] Two years earlier, in 1938, she had lost her beloved friend Jessie Sampter, a loss, she said at the time, in which "a part of myself went down with her, that part of myself which was of the best."[8] And in August 1940, just six months after Adele's death, her other dear friend, Alice Seligsberg, would pass away. That death, Szold told Rose Jacobs, meant "parting with the purest, the truest, the most stimulating of friends—with a friend in the highest sense of the word."[9] Her sisters and these close friends, both of them ardent Zionists like her, had made up Szold's most intimate circle of confidantes through much of her lifetime. With each loss, her world became narrower; with each, the knot of loneliness deep within her tightened. In spite of the widespread admiration she received, in her later years, with their "grinding, ceaseless work," as her devoted secretary Emma Ehrlich put it, she was basically alone, with "no home, no family, no personal life."[10] Indicative of that aloneness, she restlessly moved again after her sisters left Palestine, to an apartment in the Pension Romm, a two-story cottage on Ramban Street in Jerusalem, where she lived by herself (with help) for most of the rest of her days.

On the world scene, Hitler's forces swept across western Europe, conquering one nation after another: Denmark, Norway, Belgium, the Netherlands, and most of France. England courageously fought on alone, yet even in those worst of times, the British government refused to make concessions in its White Paper policy to permit Jews trying to flee the Nazis into Palestine. Clandestine immigration soared, with the British always on the lookout to capture the illegal ships before they discharged their passengers. In one tragic incident, the British transferred 1,750 passengers from two ships they had intercepted to a third, the S.S. *Patria*, in Haifa port, to be sent to Mauritius, a British colony in the Indian Ocean. Suddenly the *Patria* exploded and sank, drowning some 250 people. The Haganah had secretly planted explosives in the ship, intending to cause a small damage that would prevent it from being deported. The plan had gone horribly awry.

There had been 77 Youth Aliyah children aboard the ship. Five had lost their lives, causing Szold great anguish. In an act of compassion, the British allowed the survivors of the *Patria* to remain in the land, but first interned them for some time at the Atlit detention camp. Szold visited the detainees at Atlit, still there after eight months. She convinced the British to release 115 children who had been passengers on the ship to the care of Youth Aliyah, thus freeing them from the camp. Aware of her clout in protecting the children, the adults tried to get her to speak to the high commissioner on their behalf, but the best she could do was organize collections of food and clothing for them.

Throughout 1940, Szold had been dreading the arrival of her eightieth birthday in December, not out of fear of old age, but because her birthdays had become community-wide events in Palestine and America. As she viewed it, Hadassah in particular had turned each birthday celebration into a vulgar publicity event for its own "propaganda purposes," leaving her with an "avalanche of letters" to answer, many from people she didn't even know.[11] But this birthday became special to her, largely because of the widespread participation of her beloved Youth Aliyah boys and girls and others who had graduated from the program and were living on various farms and settlements. Delegates representing several thousand young people Youth Aliyah had rescued gathered to honor her at the Ben Shemen youth village. The Vaad Leumi organized a schoolchildren's radio program, which pleased her, with the children acting out various episodes of her life. And throughout the United States and other countries Jewish groups paid special tributes to her, with the *New York Times Magazine* publishing a feature story on the woman it called the "Grand Old Lady of Palestine."[12]

As part of her extended birthday celebration Szold donated to the Hebrew University library her father's manuscripts of his commentary on the book of Job and other writings. President Judah Magnes held a small party in the library for the occasion, with Martin Buber and other leading lights at the university in attendance. Magnes also announced a prize for the student who wrote the best essay on Rabbi Szold's work. In a brief address, Henrietta told the group that she did not know how to evaluate her father's writings, but she hoped his research would be a source of research for others.[13] She omitted saying that some forty years earlier she had enrolled in the Jewish Theological Seminary to expand her scholarly knowledge so that she might edit her father's papers herself. That experience had ended in great pain for her, and she had not touched the material since. She kept the manuscripts neatly wrapped in a metal box, but had been troubled about what to do with them. Giving them to the university library closed that circle on a happy note for her.

Hadassah gave her a check for $25,000 as its birthday gift. While she desperately needed new underwear and stockings, hard to come by during the war, as she wrote her sister Bertha facetiously, she planned to donate that money, as she always had in such situations.[14] But to whom? She agonized for weeks; so many worthy causes appealed to her for aid. She settled on creating a "Girls' Shelter," a home for young girls from poor or immigrant families, who faced many dangers in the land, particularly in war time.[15] During the same period, Hadassah allocated a sum of money for a memorial to Alice Seligsberg. For that memorial Szold suggested, and became deeply involved in planning, a Girls' Trade School in Jerusalem, in which elementary school graduates could learn cooking, sewing, secretarial work, and other vocational skills that would allow them to live independent lives.[16] Szold had given up her social service duties, but she never gave up her concern for the Yishuv's underprivileged children.

In 1941, she began using Youth Aliyah resources to help those children. By then, the Nazis no longer allowed Jews to leave the countries they occupied, and millions of Jews, including hundreds of thousands of children, remained trapped in Europe. As immigration to Palestine slowed to a trickle, Szold turned inward, toward the impoverished Jewish boys and girls living in the cities' slum areas. She developed training programs for them on kibbutzim and other institutions modeled on those created earlier for German and other European immigrants. Later, after the war, Youth Aliyah would devote itself to such youngsters.

During these war years, Youth Aliyah also turned its attention to Jews fleeing Arab lands. Persecuted Jews in Yemen escaped to the British protectorate of Aden and from there Szold had young people transferred to Youth Aliyah programs in Palestine. Vicious pogroms in Baghdad sent Jews fleeing Iraq; others escaped from Turkey, Syria, and Lebanon, in most cases entering Palestine illegally. Youth Aliyah emissaries helped place children from these lands in the kibbutzim and farms originally set up for European refugees. Between 1941 and 1943 about one thousand children entered Palestine from Mediterranean countries, cared for by Youth Aliyah.[17]

From the war's beginning, Yishuv leaders strongly encouraged Jews—pressured them, really—to enlist in the British army. Their purpose, to be sure, was to help defeat the Nazis. But they also aimed to have Jews learn from the British how to fight a war, anticipating a time when they might have a military force of their own. The Jewish Agency held enlistment drives, and by the war's end had recruited close to thirty thousand men and about four thousand women. Many of the recruits included Youth Aliyah graduates and some undergraduates determined to strike back at the enemy that had destroyed their lives. Although Szold understood their motives, she also felt responsible for each young person in Youth Aliyah. Like a parent worried about the dangers her child faced, and with her own antipathy toward fighting, she tried to temper the volunteers' enthusiasm. She and Hans Beyth met with counselors and groups of boys and girls in kibbutzim and schools to attempt to convince them to stay in their places and continue the work of building the country.[18] Nevertheless, the Yishuv recruits included many Youth Aliyah members, who felt it their duty to act.

Word of Hitler's mass extermination of Jews began to reach the Yishuv in 1942. Aside from news reports, firsthand testimony came from a group of Palestinian Jews who had been trapped in Poland when the war broke out and were part of an exchange agreement releasing German civilians in Palestine.

Even so, the idea that entire Jewish communities were being systematically annihilated seemed beyond imagination. When the truth did sink in, waves of horror and helplessness washed over the Yishuv. Just about everyone had family connections in countries under Nazi control.

As head of the Mapai party and chairman of the Jewish Agency Executive, David Ben-Gurion virtually led Palestine's Jews. Under his direction, the Agency Executive decided that in these terrible times special attention needed to be given to the rescue of children. The group reasoned that on a humanitarian basis, Great Britain and the Allies might go out of their way to help children more readily than they would adults. Moreover, it might be easier to raise funds from both Jewish and non-Jewish organizations on behalf of children. In Ben-Gurion's view, however, Henrietta Szold and her Youth Aliyah organization as it existed were not up to the task of handling the extensive rescue program that was necessary. Instead, he and the Jewish Agency Executive created a new department within the agency. It included Szold and Georg Landauer, treasurer of the original Youth Aliyah, but added three new members chosen by the Agency Executive. That arrangement would keep Szold and her Hadassah contacts available, but dilute her influence and autonomy and give the executive a greater say in the rescue and absorption of Jewish children.[19]

Hurt and resentful, Szold nevertheless accepted the new arrangements, largely because of her commitment to continuing Youth Aliyah work. She recognized also that she had organizational skills and experience with the immigration of children that the Jewish Agency Executive members lacked. She could still arrange the children's placement and education.

In expanding Youth Aliyah, Ben-Gurion envisioned rescuing thousands of children from the Nazi death machines, perhaps some four thousand from Bulgaria to begin with, then expanding to twenty-five thousand, fifty thousand, and beyond from other countries, far more than Szold had been reaching. Yet at every step of the way, his vision was thwarted. Children needed to be smuggled out of occupied lands and given passports or permits to enter still neutral territories nearby before going on to Palestine, both tasks filled with danger and difficulty. They needed adult escorts to care for them, increasing the complications. They needed seaworthy ships filled with sufficient supplies of food and other items to carry them to their destination, but ships were in short supply and money to purchase them even less accessible. They needed immigration certificates to be distributed ahead of time to enter Palestine, but the British kept a tight lid on White Paper quotas. The most potent block to the children's escape, however, were the Nazis themselves. In every country the Germans occupied and the satellite countries tied to them, they cut off the exit of Jewish children just as they did adult Jews. Hitler's Final Solution, after all, required the murder of children as well as grown-ups.

Gradually the number of Jewish children rescued during the height of the war fell from Ben-Gurion's optimistic predictions to a few thousand from Romania, Bulgaria, and Hungary and an even smaller number from other countries. Like the criticism leveled at Szold and her leadership of Youth Aliyah, attacks would be hurled at Ben-Gurion and the Jewish Agency Executive for not having saved thousands more children and adults from the flames of the Holocaust. But for them, as it was for Szold, in these years of madness and unpredictability, working from a small, powerless country under the control of a less than sympathetic colonial government and with little world cooperation too often made intentions and hopes unattainable.[20]

At the dedication of the Hadassah-Hebrew University Medical Center on the outskirts of Jerusalem in 1960, David Ben-Gurion spoke of Henrietta Szold as "not only the greatest woman American Jewry has yet produced," but also "undoubtedly one of the most noble personalities of our generation."[21] Those were not words he would have used to describe her some twenty years earlier when she was alive. During those war years, she aligned herself openly with Judah Magnes and an organization he headed that continued the ideals of the earlier Brit Shalom. Called Ihud, "Unity," it sought to achieve peace between Jews and Arabs in the Holy Land, and ultimately to create a binational state in which the two peoples lived together as equal partners. Ben-Gurion had accepted Brit Shalom for a while back in the 1920s, but had concluded, along with other Yishuv leaders, that its objectives were short-sighted and unreachable. Now Ihud, coming after the Arab uprising that began in 1936 and in the midst of the destruction of Europe's Jews (which had the support of the Arab mufti), antagonized Ben-Gurion more than had its predecessor. Szold's role in Ihud did not endear her to him at this point and might actually have been a factor in his wish to narrow her influence in Youth Aliyah.

It was an important role. Although she deplored the Arab uprising, she never stopped believing that Jews and Arabs could live together peacefully if each side made an effort to understand the other. With the war raging outside, she continued to call publicly for peace inside the land, between Arabs and Jews and Jews themselves, still torn apart by internal terrorism. In September 1941, she issued a declaration addressed to the Yishuv as a whole that appeared in all the major Hebrew newspapers. This time she used her own name only, confident enough to make her case. The declaration pleaded that for the sake of the thousands of young people who had lost their homes and families and been brought to live in the "new-old" land, the Jews in Palestine must "remove . . . violence from our midst." It ended by emphasizing that through the ages, Jews and Judaism survived not by might but by the "spirit of love and divine law."[22]

Szold received warm reactions from people who agreed with her, as she told Magnes and others. The declaration and the response to it served as a first step toward forming Ihud. Over the course of the next year, she met informally to discuss ideas with like-minded friends—many of whom had been members of the original Brit Shalom group—usually at the home of Ernst Simon. In August 1942, with Szold's help, Magnes formalized the discussions at a meeting of about a hundred people, in which the name Ihud was officially adopted. Regarding itself as an association, not a political party, Ihud aimed for a rapprochement between Jews and Arabs in Palestine through discussions and negotiations that would lead to their ideal of a binational state. Along with Szold, Magnes, and Simon, the philosopher Martin Buber became one of the leading spokesmen of the association. He joined Szold and others on the presidential board, with Magnes as president.

Ihud members published pamphlets and a periodical that spelled out their ideas, which came under attack almost immediately by the press and Zionist organizations. Ben-Gurion and other Zionist leaders hoped to increase Jewish immigration into Palestine to the point at which Jews became a majority and therefore dominant in the land. Ihud emphasized political equality between Jews and Arabs so that neither dominated the other no matter who held the majority. Some members even agreed to limit Jewish immigration for a period of years in order to reach absolute equity and avoid conflict between the two peoples. But at a time when Jews fleeing the Nazis desperately needed a place that would accept them, Ihud's critics considered such limitations a betrayal of Jewish needs and Zionist goals.

"Does the man not consider himself a Jew?" Ben-Gurion railed about Martin Buber. "If not, he has no business intervening in what the Jews are doing. If he is a Jew, he should act like one."[23] Buber, deeply committed to rescue operations, made a distinction between allowing "as many Jews as possible" into Palestine—meaning rescuing as many as possible—and seeking a majority for political purposes, a distinction Ben-Gurion and other critics ignored.[24]

Szold also came in for her share of criticism. She wrote to her sister that she and the others involved in Ihud "are being hunted down. Have you seen that some of our patriots want to read me out of the Zionist Organization?"[25] True, there was talk among mainstream Zionists of evicting her from the Zionist Organization of America. Newspapers accused her of being naïve and misguided or, as one put it, "her old age shames her youth."[26] In spite of such disapproval, however, her reputation remained largely intact. People still respected her as the woman who had organized social services for the entire Yishuv and who continued to work tirelessly deep into old age to save children from Nazi brutality.

Judah Magnes, on the other hand, was widely denounced. From the start he had not been completely accepted by the Jewish community in Palestine. In a society that valued labor Zionism, many regarded him as too esthete and intellectual as well as too extreme in his convictions. Now the word *traitor* frequently turned up in the invectives against him, and voices could be heard demanding his removal as president of Hebrew University. Magnes never backed down from his commitment to a binational state, and Henrietta Szold never backed down from her commitment to Judah Magnes and Ihud. "My relation to Dr. Magnes," she once said, "is the relation of the soldier to the officer."[27]

For several months, her commitments would embroil her in a brouhaha with Hadassah itself. Paradoxically, the incident began with total agreement between them. In 1940, Hadassah formed the Committee on Jewish-Arab Relations, charged with learning about the Arabs in Palestine and suggesting ways to improve relationships between Arabs and Jews in the country. Rose Jacobs, then Hadassah's vice president, headed the committee, which included not only Hadassah members but also the historian Salo Baron and the Zionist leader Emanuel Neumann. Jacobs worked closely with Szold, a good friend and political associate within Hadassah, in shaping and guiding the committee in its work.

In 1941, the committee invited Ben-Gurion to attend a meeting, where Jacobs explained to him that she and Szold believed Hadassah would have a significant role to play after the war when the United States would hold a predominant place in world affairs. It therefore made sense for the organization to learn as much as possible about the Arabs and offer various Zionist bodies suggestions for the future based on its findings. Ben-Gurion objected strongly. Hadassah's role, he maintained, was to educate American political leaders and the public about Zionist ideals and at the same time to counter pro-Arab propaganda. Furthermore, he insisted that while American Zionists, like the Hadassah women, had the right to deal with issues relating to the United States, they had no such right concerning the Yishuv, which they were unequipped to understand. Furious at Ben-Gurion's lack of respect for their knowledge and abilities, Hadassah members overwhelmingly opposed him and backed Szold and Jacobs on the need for research and cooperation in regard to the Palestinian Arabs.[28]

About a year later, a stunning change took place. In May 1942, delegates to a conference at the Biltmore Hotel in New York City, led by Ben-Gurion and Chaim Weizmann, openly declared the objective of establishing a Jewish "commonwealth" in Palestine, a nuanced reference to a sovereign Jewish state in that land. Hadassah fully accepted the declaration, as did other Zionist organizations. With that, Szold's identification with Ihud and its binational position became an issue for the women's Zionist organization. A series of telegrams and letters between Hadassah president Tamar de Sola Pool and Szold document the predicament. A cable from Pool in August 1942 informs Szold that Hadassah's constituency and the rest of the "American public" were confused by press reports on the purpose of Ihud, and asks for an "exposition" of the group's "aims and plans." Szold's cable in response requests that Hadassah "suspend judgment" about Ihud until it receives a long airmail letter she had sent giving its history and purpose. Back and forth the cables and letters flew with queries and explanations. Finally, a letter addressed to Szold and Magnes outlines the results of the Hadassah convention in late 1942: after heated arguments on both sides, it relates, a large majority of Hadassah members repudiated Ihud and reaffirmed Hadassah's support for the Biltmore program calling for an independent Jewish state.[29] Hadassah would continue to work for the realization of that state until its creation in 1948.

Szold felt insulted by the attacks against her and Magnes at the convention. Nevertheless, ignoring Hadassah's final position, she remained wedded to Ihud and the concept of a binational state. The Ihud society eventually failed in its aims, as had Brit Shalom, in large measure because it never found a partner among the Arabs. When, in 1946, one respected Arab leader, Fawzi al Husseini, agreed to support the concept of a binational state with the Jews, he was assassinated by Arab terrorists. "Our cousin has stumbled and received his just punishment," said a member of his family.[30]

While Ihud activities occupied Szold, she still devoted most of her long waking hours to rescue operations. One of the most dramatic of these centered on a group of ragtag immigrants from Poland known as the Tehran children. The saga began in September 1939 when both the German and Soviet armies invaded Poland, the Germans from the west and the Soviets from the east. With the fall of Warsaw to the Nazis, thousands of Jews fled Poland to the Soviet Union. They were joined by many hundreds of Poles deported by the Soviets, who regarded members of both groups as prisoners and sent vast numbers to Siberia to work in labor camps. Ill fed and plagued by typhus and other diseases, a large percentage died of sickness and starvation; others lost track of their families in the war's chaos. Children became orphaned, left on their own to forage for food and shelter. After Germany broke its pact with the Soviet Union and invaded that country in 1941, many children, among them Jewish children, were placed in Soviet orphanages throughout the land.

Now at war with Germany, the Soviets declared an amnesty for tens of thousands of Poles in the country. It also allowed the formation of a Polish army in exile, led by General Wladyslaw Anders. In the summer of 1942, the Soviet government permitted Anders and his recruits to leave the Soviet Union for Iran with the intention of joining the war against the Nazis. Thousands of civilians and children from the orphanages tagged along with the soldiers, including about a thousand Jewish children. Many of the refugees traveled by train, in overcrowded cattle cars, to Bukhara and from there to the Iranian port of Pahlavi (today Undar e-Anzalit) outside Tehran. Others reached Pahlavi by ship, under equally miserable conditions. Jewish Agency officials sent by the Yishuv met the transports in Pahlavi, where they identified the Jewish children. Once in Tehran those children, now numbering about seven hundred, were placed in a camp that became known as the "Tehran Home for Jewish Children," supervised by Zionist youth leaders, many of them refugees themselves.

The majority of Jewish children arriving in Tehran were sick, emaciated, filthy—many covered with lice—and clothed in rags. Members of the Tehran Jewish community brought them food and clothing, invited them into their homes, and took them to their synagogues. But the living conditions at the camp, administered by the Polish government, were terrible. Some of the younger children lived in barracks, the older ones in tents.

Almost all slept on mats on the ground without mattresses or sheets and just a thin blanket for cover. They lacked sufficient food and clothing, and while they might no longer have been starving, most still suffered from malnutrition. In some cases the Jewish Agency representative had to struggle to convince Jewish children to transfer from the main Polish camp to the Jewish one. Having suffered bitterly from antisemitism, these children did not want to identify themselves as Jews. And in some cases, priests had baptized the children, especially small children, and refused to let them go.[31]

The challenge now became getting all the Jewish children out of Tehran and to Palestine as quickly as possible. The most expedient route would have been to go through Iraq, but Iraq refused to have Jewish children traverse its territory. Desperate for a solution, some Yishuv leaders proposed renting a plane to carry the youngsters over or getting a British ship for the purpose. When those methods didn't work out, a committee suggested the pie-in-the-sky scheme of dressing the children in General Anders's army uniforms and passing them off as Poles.[32] In the end, the group had to take a long roundabout route, sailing to Karachi, then to Aden in British India, and on to Port Said. At Port Said they boarded a train to Palestine that carried them to Haifa. From there they were sent to the nearby detention camp at Atlit. They had left Tehran on January 2, 1943, and arrived at Atlit on February 18.

The trials of the Tehran children gripped the imagination and emotions of the Jews of Palestine. At every stop of the children's train, mobs of people came out to greet them, throw candy and flowers, and search in the gaunt faces staring out for a lost son or daughter, perhaps a neighbor's child. From their train windows the children waved little blue and white flags they had been given at Port Said, dazed at the attention they received.

Along with dozens of other people, Henrietta Szold came to the railway station in Haifa to welcome the Tehran children.

Despite the Jewish Agency's expanded role in youth immigration, she still assumed the main responsibility for placing the children in their new homes. She had been planning the logistics of their arrival since December; the enterprise, like so many others in her life, became more complex than she had imagined. Almost every political and religious group in town lay claim to the children, hoping to swell their own ranks with these new members. Some religious groups accused Szold of not knowing how to handle Polish children, many of whom grew up in Orthodox homes, because large numbers of her Youth Aliyah placements had come from assimilated German and Austrian families. Her worst headaches came from the ultra-Orthodox Agudat Israel, which insisted that every child from Poland belonged with them.

Out of "some kind of motherly feelings," Szold wrote, she understood how fragile the children were after all their suffering. "They were extremely suspicious and did not trust anybody. . . . On their long wanderings, they had got used to rely on themselves alone. If such a body received a slice of bread, he was anxious to hide it from the others." On the other hand, she found the children fiercely attached to their relatives—older ones refused to be separated from younger ones whom they had cared for and protected throughout their ordeal.[33]

When the children first arrived at Atlit, she had them sent to temporary centers around the country for five or six weeks. There, physicians, teachers, psychiatrists, educators, and other experts made a great effort to know the children as individuals and understand the lives they had led before the war. As public institutions these centers followed Jewish religious practice, serving only kosher food and observing the Sabbath and holidays, even when staff members in the centers did not adhere to tradition themselves. After much internal discussion, the Jewish Agency decided that children over the age of fourteen could choose what kind of settlement they wished to go to, religious or nonreligious. But younger children would be questioned carefully about what their home lives had been like and where their parents might have wanted them to live. Szold spent hours meeting with hundreds of the young children herself, and Hans Beyth with many others. But she was adamant, having seen the powerful attachments among brothers and sisters ("I find no words to describe how close they were") that family members not be separated, and the younger ones go with the elders wherever that led them, whether to a religious institution or not.[34] That policy sparked a barrage of angry letters from Orthodox rabbis, religious bodies, and individuals around the world, attacking Szold publicly and demanding that the children be sent to or educated in their institutions. The religious battle was "a long-drawn-out agony" for her, boiling with "devastating propaganda."[35]

After many deliberations and changes, the lists of placements were drawn up. Almost half the children went to religious institutions and settlements and slightly more than half to non-Orthodox ones. Mizrachi, a middle-of-the-road Orthodox group, sponsored most of the institutions. In a number of incidents, members of the Agudat Israel snatched children away from Mizrachi locations, forcing Szold to have them found and brought back.[36] Later, her assistant, Emma Ehrlich, would say that the respiratory disease that killed Szold began with her marathon interviews of the young children and the pressure placed on her by the religious establishment.[37]

In reality, her health had begun failing before that. There had been heart problems at times that sent her to the hospital or forced her to rest at home from her frenetic schedule. Although weakened, however, she had always managed to bounce back. After settling the Tehran children, she became involved in finding places for youngsters who survived the horrendous Transnistria massacre in Romania. The Romanian government had deported more than 150,000 Jews to Transnistria in the dead of winter in 1941 and 1942, leaving them without food or water.

Most died of hunger and cold. A few thousand children survived that and other murders in Romania, almost all of them bereft of both parents. Many were cared for in Romanian orphanages, particularly in Bucharest. After several delays, in 1944, groups of these Jewish orphans arrived in Palestine, some as young as four years old. They were all placed under the care of Youth Aliyah, overseen by Henrietta Szold.

On a pleasurable note, she participated in celebrating Youth Aliyah's tenth anniversary. With money sent from Hadassah, she made plans for a large Youth Aliyah center, with a dormitory and library and a fine reception area. In recognition of the occasion, President Franklin D. Roosevelt sent Szold a cable praising Youth Aliyah under her guidance for freeing thousands of children from German hands and "redeeming their hearts from terror and their minds from nightmare memory." He expressed his conviction that with the forthcoming liberation of Europe, Youth Aliyah would again take its place "in the forefront, as in the past" of rebuilding "shattered lives and faith."[38] And in recognition of the occasion, Boston University awarded her an honorary doctorate degree.

By then her health had begun to deteriorate seriously. Sylvia Gelber, one of the first social work students in Palestine and a good friend, recalled one of Szold's last seders. Too frail to go out, she invited Gelber, Hans Beyth, and a few other friends to a seder in her home at the pension, with Beyth leading the service. At the end, they all sang African American spirituals, which Szold remembered from her childhood in Maryland.[39] In the summer of 1944, she moved into a two-room suite in the nurses' residence on Mount Scopus. She entered Hadassah hospital in July with pneumonia, but seemed to recover enough to continue some of her Youth Aliyah work. By December she suffered a severe decline. Back in the hospital, she struggled with attacks of breathlessness and occasional confusion. Judah Magnes and

Emma Ehrlich came to see her every evening and many others, including Ben-Gurion, visited her.

Chaim Weizmann arrived one day while Magnes was visiting. The two men had been at odds because of Magnes's commitment to Ihud and pacifism, far removed from Weizmann's outlook, so Magnes waited at the doorway, allowing the other man to enter the room alone. When Szold saw Magnes, she had a nurse call him in, whereupon she took his hand. Weizmann took Szold's other hand, commenting on the fact that they were both holding her hand. It made her happy to see the two of them together, Szold told the men, and now they needed to put aside their differences. When the men left, they agreed that they must never quarrel in that way again. Szold, who had sought peace on many fronts, had cemented peace between two towering figures in the Zionist movement.[40]

Szold passed away on the evening of February 13, 1945. Emotional and loving tributes to her appeared the next day in Hebrew newspapers throughout the land where she had once had to fight to be accepted, but in the end chose as her permanent home. A joint statement in *Davar* by the Histadrut, Jewish Agency, and Vaad Leumi read: "From generation to generation they will tell of Henrietta Szold, about a mother in Israel, the likes of whom had not risen through the ages."[41]

Epilogue:
"Make My Eyes Look to the Future"

THOUSANDS OF PEOPLE from all over the country escorted Henrietta Szold to her final resting place on the Mount of Olives. Earlier, on the morning of February 14, her body, wrapped in the white shroud she had purchased in preparation for this day, lay on a bier in a large hall of the Nurses' Training School, named for her and where she had lived most recently. An honor guard of student nurses in white uniforms surrounded the bier, reciting psalms, while people paid their last respects to the woman who had become something of a legend in her adopted land. Some mourners brought flowers, others carried large floral wreaths bearing the names of their institutions. At 2:00 in the afternoon Judah Magnes recited the traditional *Kaddish* prayer for the dead before the funeral procession set out. Magnes and Chaim Weizmann were among the pallbearers, who also included Hans Beyth and David Remez, director of public works in the Yishuv. Several British government officials headed the long procession, followed by clergy members from various Christian churches and a number of Muslim sheikhs.

The mourners followed the narrow winding road from Mount Scopus toward the Mount of Olives Cemetery. Chilling rain and drizzle, broken only by occasional rays of sunshine, drenched them as they made their way. As Szold's body was lowered into the ground, the rain became heavy, as though the heavens themselves wept, one woman recalled.[1] In compliance with Szold's wishes to have no eulogies at her graveside—she had balked in her final years at the excess of praise heaped on her—a fifteen-year-old boy, Shimon Kritz, one of the Tehran children, tearfully recited the *Kaddish* prayer once again, and the body in its white shroud was covered with earth.

The Tehran children like Shimon and many others in Youth Aliyah called her "mother." It was a sad irony that this woman who never married or had children became known as a mother in Israel. In her honor, for many years Mother's Day in the state was celebrated on February 13, the anniversary of her death. Words she wrote in a letter to Jessie Sampter, "I should have had children, many children," have often been cited to demonstrate the sorrow she felt at the closing of that door after her ill-fated love for Louis Ginzberg.[2] Indeed, she did experience an emptiness in her life due to not having built a family of her own, and she did derive great pleasure from mothering the Youth Aliyah youngsters, finding homes for them, striving to solve their problems, and staying in touch with many of them after they graduated from the program.

But the phrase about children in her letter to Sampter touched on something else, even deeper and more troubling to her. It was followed by the words, "It is only in rearing children that minute service after minute service counts. In my life, details have . . . not gone to make a harmonious and productive whole."[3] Szold was a brilliant administrator. Her mastery of detail and "minute service after minute service" led, among other things, to the creation of a night school, the establishment of a medical unit, the formation of the most influential women's Zionist organization in the world, and the rescue of thousands of children from the Nazi killing machines. Yet she always questioned the value of her administrative ability. On some level she felt personally unfulfilled, not by a loss of motherhood as such but by—in her estimation—a lack of creativity. She regarded Sampter, a poet, as creative, and her own extraordinary organizational talent as stemming from the narrow demands of duty rather than from a different and far-reaching form of creativity. That is a true source of sorrow in her life: her inability to fully appreciate the greatness of the gift she possessed.

Paradoxically, insecure as she felt about her skills, she trusted her own instincts more than she trusted others'. She had a will of iron, and she pushed that will to put into effect programs and projects as she believed they should be done. She was angry and offended when Ben-Gurion made Youth Aliyah part of a larger department in the Jewish Agency, convinced that her way of handling youth immigration had been correct with no need for further input. And, as it worked out, she took control of dealing with the Tehran children's rescue in spite of the expanded Jewish Agency's duties. Modest as she was—and she was modest, routinely deflecting praise of herself to others—on occasion she allowed herself to acknowledge the uniqueness of her achievements. When she joined the Vaad Leumi, the National Council, to take over the social services department in Palestine, she told friends of her "temerity" in handling such a patchwork of different programs in that land with so little training in any of them—"When I came to Palestine, I acted as though I were an expert on medical affairs. Fate made me pretend to be an expert on educational affairs in 1927." And now, in 1931, she dared to enter yet another area that required expertise, social service.[4] Recognizing her accomplishments in other fields, she was able to enter a new one even as she questioned her qualifications.

She had the same double vision about power. If asked, she would certainly deny that she had any power at all. She hated politics, she said, and knew nothing about government, speaking of herself time and again as "befuddled" or too ignorant to take a political stand on anything. Nevertheless, she wielded enormous political power, in both America and Palestine. As founder and head of Hadassah, she guided that organization toward areas she cared about—medicine, education, social services, and later rescuing children—and raised millions of dollars through it to support those fields. She provided the backbone for the Hadassah women to stand up to male Zionist groups and achieve independence, and saw to it that its services applied equally to all factions in society: Jews, Christians, and Muslims alike. Her social circle included the most influential political leaders in Palestine—Herbert Samuel, the first high commissioner, for example, and Arthur Ruppin, who became head of the Zionist Organization's Palestine office. With great skill, she tread a thin line in dealing with British authorities in the Mandate, careful not to alienate them even when she was critical, so that she might obtain immigration certificates and other concessions when she needed them. Although she was criticized along with Judah Magnes and others who advocated binationalism, the criticism never seriously damaged her reputation. She was admired throughout the Yishuv, especially in her later years, her birthdays treated almost as communal events, and she herself frequently spoken of in hagiographic terms. While she would never admit to having power, she lent her name to Yishuv manifestos because she knew it carried weight. And she pushed the two Zionist giants, Chaim Weizmann and Judah Magnes, to reconcile, because she understood that only she could do that successfully.

Zionism governed her life. At a time when many wealthy German Jewish community leaders rejected the Zionist ideal out of fear that Jews would be accused of dual loyalty, Szold spoke freely of Zionism as crucial to Judaism and an expression of the finest Jewish impulses. But Zionism to her also meant finding a way to live with the Arabs who inhabited the same land. She blamed the British for Arab rebellions, accusing them of having gained their mandate by force and then not governing well. She blamed the Arabs for their violence, criticizing them for not acknowledging that the Jews had a right to their homeland and that there was room enough for both peoples in the land. But she also blamed the Jews for looking down on the Arabs, not acknowledging their national aspirations or making a greater effort to lift their living standards. She declared that Zionism would fail if it did not eventually find a solution to the Arab-Jewish problem.

Her solution, to a great extent, was to form a binational state. But by backing binationalism, she, like Magnes, Buber, and its other supporters, found themselves on the wrong side of history. With millions of European Jews being massacred and refugees wandering through desolate lands with no safe place to go, leaders of the Yishuv saw a dire need for an independent state with unlimited Jewish immigration. Arab intransigence about not sharing any part of the land with the Jews added to the urgency. Led by David Ben-Gurion, the Jewish State came into being. Had Szold lived long enough to witness its creation, perhaps she would have changed her thinking about binationalism; undoubtedly she would have given her support to the State of Israel once it existed. But her warnings in those early days about the dangers of not making peace with the Arabs in the land were perceptive. That elusive peace has remained one of Israel's most pressing problems.

Szold lived out her life in British Mandated Palestine, always seeing herself as an American, always on the verge of returning to the United States and her family. She wrote to her sisters every week, followed their activities assiduously, and often suffered aching loneliness away from them. Yet she didn't go back to live in America or, when she did, as in 1930, she hurried to return to Palestine when invited to be on the Vaad Leumi. She spoke of her activities in that country as simply fulfilling her duty, but one suspects that despite her loneliness and her love for family and the landscape of her youth, America no longer gave meaning to her life. She had found her soul in Palestine through the critical work she did there, and was not about to lose it again.

One question remains: does Henrietta Szold have a place in the pantheon of leaders who advanced the position of women? To be sure, on a personal level, her life evolved from an acceptance of the traditional role of women in the home to striking out on her own and, as a single woman in a decidedly man's world, heading major public and private institutions in America and Palestine. At times she questioned the male orientation of Jewish liturgy and synagogue practice, insisting on equal participation for women in the services she held with Judah Magnes, and asserting her right as a woman to say the *Kaddish* prayer after her mother's death. She was the main force in founding Hadassah, the women's Zionist organization, and through that organization she promoted women's health and educational activities. But, while she supported women's suffrage in Palestine, for example, unlike the suffragists in America, whose fierce fight to allow women the vote led eventually to the Nineteenth Amendment, or a Betty Friedan, who sparked the women's movement with its demands for women's work and pay to match those of men, Szold did not initiate broad-scale struggles for women's rights or lead masses of others to them.

She did something else, however, that created its own ripples. Under her guidance Hadassah became the largest volunteer women's organization in America as well as the largest Zionist institution in the world. That growth and the status that accompanied it empowered its membership as a group. It also opened the way for individual women to assume roles they had never tackled before or—for many—even dreamed of. Home-makers gained notice as public speakers; formerly full-time mothers shone as fiscal experts; women from all walks of life developed expertise in administration, writing, fund-raising, and parliamentary procedure. Hadassah members met with American political leaders and foreign envoys to push forward their Zionist and women's agendas. Through their activities they changed the public perception of what women could do. And they not only expanded their own lives, they laid the groundwork for the accomplishments of the women's movement. Their daughters and granddaughters, who would argue for equal pay for equal work with men, learned by example from the volunteer labor of the women who came before them to speak out with confidence and pursue their feminist agendas fearlessly.

Szold's long working hours and single-minded dedication to the causes she embraced inspired Hadassah women in their groundbreaking roles even after she officially left the organization's leadership. She may not have triggered large movements, but she had an impact on thousands of women's lives. So, yes, she belongs in that pantheon.

About a year before she died, Szold sat for a bust by the sculptor Batya Lishansky, instructing the artist to "make my eyes look to the future."[5] These words might well summarize her life and ambitions. In every endeavor she headed, whether establishing education and social services in pre-state Israel or reshaping the lives of thousands of children, she set her eyes on the future. In spite of insecurities and self-criticisms, she consistently looked ahead to expand her projects while making sure they were the best they could be in the present. Long after her death, her vision remains part of all that she created.

NOTES

Introduction

1. Emma Ehrlich, "Notes and Impressions," March 1941, RG 13, box 225, folder 5, Hadassah Archives, American Jewish Historical Society, New York.

Chapter 1. First Daughter

1. Szold to "My dear Family," July 31, 1921, RG 13, box 208, folder 3, Hadassah Archives, on long-term deposit at the American Jewish Historical Society, New York.

2. Marvin Lowenthal's interview with Henrietta Szold, December 29, 1935, RG 13, box 206, folder 3, Hadassah Archives.

3. Emma Ehrlich, "Notes and Impressions," March 1941, RG 13, box 225, folder 5, Hadassah Archives.

4. Hasia Diner, "Like the Antelope and the Badger," in *Tradition Renewed: A History of the Jewish Theological Seminary of America*, ed. Jack Wertheimer (New York: Jewish Theological Seminary, 1997), 1:30.

5. Szold to "My dear Family," January 1, 1921, RG 13, box 208, folder 3, Hadassah Archives.

6. See, for example, Eric L. Goldstein and Deborah R. Weiner, *On Middle Ground: A History of the Jews of Baltimore* (Baltimore: Johns Hopkins University Press, 2018), 90–91. See also Isaac M. Fein, "Baltimore Rabbis during the Civil War," in *Jews and the Civil War: A Reader*, ed. Jonathan D. Sarna and Adam Mendelsohn (New York: New York University Press, 2010), 181–95.

7. Jonathan D. Sarna and Benjamin Shapell, *Lincoln and the Jews: A History* (New York: Thomas Dunne Books, St. Martin's, 2015), 152–55.

8. Szold to Bertha Pearl, May 19, 1921, RG 13, box 207, folder 12, Hadassah Archives; Szold to Adele, September 6, 1921, RG 13, box 209, folder 5, Hadassah Archives; Lowenthal interview with Szold, 54.

9. Lowenthal interview with Szold, 33.

10. Sulamith, "Our Baltimore Letter," *Jewish Messenger*, January 1879.

11. Sulamith, "Our Baltimore Letter," *Jewish Messenger*, March 1878.

12. Joan Dash, *Summoned to Jerusalem: The Life of Henrietta Szold* (New York: Harper & Row, 1979), 16.

13. Irving Fineman, *Woman of Valor: The Life of Henrietta Szold, 1860–1945* (New York: Simon & Schuster, 1961), 47.

14. Lowenthal interview with Szold, 52.

15. Alexandra Lee Levin, *Henrietta Szold: Baltimorean* (Baltimore: Jewish Historical Society of Maryland, 1976), 2.

16. Alexandra Lee Levin, *The Szolds of Lombard Street: A Baltimore Family, 1835–1909* (Philadelphia: Jewish Publication Society of America, 1960), 152–55.

17. Helen Lefkowitz Horowitz, *The Power and Passion of M. Carey Thomas* (Chicago: University of Illinois Press, 1999), 230–32.

18. Marvin Lowenthal, *Henrietta Szold: Life and Letters* (New York: Viking, 1942), 8; Szold to Adele, February 16, 1933, RG 13, box 209, folder 5, Hadassah Archives.

19. Levin, *Szolds of Lombard Street*, 229.

20. Harold S. Wechsler, "Pulpit or Professoriate: The Case of Morris Jastrow," *American Jewish History* 74, no. 4 (June 1985): 338–55.

21. Alexandra Lee Levin, *Vision: A Biography of Harry Friedenwald* (Philadelphia: Jewish Publication Society, 1964), 68, 116.

22. Ibid., 134.

23. Quoted in Fineman, *Woman of Valor,* 266.

Chapter 2. "I Eat, Drink, and Sleep Russians"

1. Szold to "My dear Family," April 19, 1921, RG 13, box 208, folder 3, Hadassah Archives, American Jewish Historical Society, New York.

2. Alexandra Lee Levin, *The Szolds of Lombard Street: A Baltimore Family, 1859–1909* (Philadelphia: Jewish Publication Society, 1960), 133.

3. Irving Fineman, *Woman of Valor: The Life of Henrietta Szold, 1860–1945* (New York: Simon & Schuster, 1961), 57–58.

4. Levin, *Szolds of Lombard Street,* 139, 141.

5. Fineman, *Woman of Valor,* 46.

6. On American antisemitism and relations between German and Russian Jews, see Eric L. Goldstein and Deborah R. Weiner, *On Middle Ground: A History of the Jews of Baltimore* (Baltimore: Johns Hopkins University Press, 2018), 104–27; and Jonathan D. Sarna, *American Judaism: A History* (New Haven: Yale University Press, 2004), 135–75.

7. Szold to Rachel Szold Jastrow, October 25, 1891, in Marvin Lowenthal, *Henrietta Szold: Life and Letters* (New York: Viking, 1942), 45.

8. On the Baer Levinsohn Society, see Eric L. Goldstein, "The Practical as Spiritual: Henrietta Szold's American Zionist Ideology, 1878–1920," in *Daughter of Zion: Henrietta Szold and American Jewish Womanhood,* catalogue of an exhibition at the Jewish Historical Society of Maryland, ed. Barry Kessler (Baltimore: Jewish Historical Society of Maryland, 1995), 19–20.

9. On the night school, see Benjamin H. Hartogensis, "The Russian Night School of Baltimore," *Publications of the American Jewish Historical Society* 31 (1928): 225–28; Alexandra Lee Levin,

"Henrietta Szold and the Russian Immigrant School," *Maryland Historical Magazine* 57 (1962): 1–15.

10. Szold to Rachel Szold Jastrow, October 31, 1891, in Lowenthal, *Life and Letters*, 45.

11. Levin, "Russian Immigrant School," 6.

12. Szold to Rachel Szold Jastrow, October 31, 1891, in Lowenthal, *Life and Letters*, 46.

13. Levin, "Russian Immigrant School," 11.

14. She writes about that check—which she did not solicit—in a letter to Rabbi Joseph Hertz, October 5, 1897, RG 13, box 181, folder 6, Hadassah Archives.

15. "Russia in America," *Baltimore Sun*, July 13, 1892.

16. Szold to Rachel Szold Jastrow, November 8, 1891, in Lowenthal, *Life and Letters*, 48.

17. Sulamith, "Our Baltimore Letter," *Jewish Messenger*, October 4, 1898.

18. Levin, *Szolds of Lombard Street*, 275.

19. Lowenthal, *Life and Letters*, 53.

20. Marvin Lowenthal, interview with Henrietta Szold, December 29, 1935, 7, RG 13, box 206, folder 3, Hadassah Archives.

21. Henrietta Szold, "Early Zionist Days in Baltimore," *Maccabean* 30 (June–July 1917).

22. Szold to E. N. Solis, January 26, 1897, RG 13, box 212, folder 32, Hadassah Archives.

23. Henrietta Szold, *A Century of Jewish Thought*, originally read as a paper before the Baltimore section of the National Council of Jewish Women, January 26, 1896, and subsequently published (Baltimore: Zion Association, 1896).

24. Quoted in Lowenthal interview with Szold, *Life and Letters*, 54.

25. Joyce Antler, *The Journey Home: How Jewish Women Shaped Modern America* (New York: Schocken Books, 1997), 98.

26. See Steven J. Zippperstein, *Elusive Prophet: Ahad Ha'am and the Origins of Zionism* (Berkeley: University of California Press, 1993).

27. See Levin, "Russian Immigrant School," 15.

28. Goldstein and Weiner, *On Middle Ground*, 123.

29. Jonathan D. Sarna, *JPS: The Americanization of Jewish Culture, 1888–1988* (Philadelphia: Jewish Publication Society), 13–31.

Chapter 3. "Miss Szold" and "Dr. Ginzberg"

1. Irvng Fineman, *Woman of Valor: The Life of Henrietta Szold, 1860–1945* (New York: Simon & Schuster, 1966), 89, 95.

2. "What Judaism Has Done for Women," delivered before the Women's Parliament of the World's Congress of Religions at the 1893 Chicago World's Fair. Quoted in Alexandra Lee Levin, *Henrietta Szold: Baltimorean* (Baltimore: Jewish Historical Society of Maryland, 1995), 3.

3. Jonathan D. Sarna, *JPS: The Americanization of Jewish Culture, 1888–1988* (Philadelphia: Jewish Publication Society, 1989), 48.

4. Ibid., 133.

5. Ibid., 48, 49.

6. Ibid., 114.

7. Marvin Lowenthal interview with Henrietta Szold, December 29, 1935, RG 13, box 206, folder 3, 42–43, Hadassah Archives, American Jewish Historical Society, New York.

8. Henrietta Szold, "The Promised Land," letter to the editor of the *Nation*, August 13, 1914.

9. Szold to Elvira N. Solis, September 22, 1906, RG 13, box 212, folder 32, Hadassah Archives.

10. Alexandra Lee Levin, *The Szolds of Lombard Street: A Baltimore Family, 1835–1909* (Philadelphia: Jewish Publication Society, 1960), 343.

11. Ibid., 330.

12. Norman Bentwich, *Solomon Schechter: A Biography* (Philadelphia: Jewish Publication Society, 1938), 125.

13. Abraham E. Millgram and Emma G. Ehrlich, "Nine Letters from Solomon Schechter to Henrietta Szold," *Conservative Judaism* 32, no. 2 (1979): 29.

14. Jewish Women's Archive, "Ray Frank," n.d., https://jwa.org /womenofvalor/frank.

15. "Miss Szold to Girls," *Baltimore Sun*, June 21, 1901.

16. Henrietta Szold to Frank Schechter, August 21, 1924, Schechter Papers, Jewish Theological Seminary Archives, New York.

17. See Stephen Birmingham, *"Our Crowd": The Great Jewish Families of New York* (New York: Berkley, 1984).

18. See Mel Scult, "Schechter's Seminary," in *Tradition Renewed: A History of the Jewish Theological Seminary of America*, ed. Jack Wertheimer, 1:79–81. See also Mel Scult, "The Rabbi," *Hadassah Magazine*, June–July 1990, 23–24.

19. Szold to Elvira N. Solis, October 25, 1903, RG 13, box 212, folder 32, Hadassah Archives.

20. Scult, "Schechter's Seminary," 79–80. See also Mel Scult, "Mordecai Kaplan, the Teacher's Institute, and the Foundations of Jewish Education in America," 61–62, American Jewish Archives, Hebrew Union College–Jewish Institute of Religion, Cincinnati.

21. Herman H. Rubenovitz and Magnon L. Rubenovitz, *The Waking Heart* (Cambridge, Mass.: Nathaniel Dame, 1967), 24.

22. Scult, "Schechter's Seminary," 80.

23. Ibid., 78.

24. Szold to Elvira N. Solis, July 26, 1905, RG 13, box 212, folder 32, Hadassah Archives.

25. See Eric L. Goldstein, "The Practical as Spiritual: Henrietta Szold's American Zionist Ideology, 1878–1920," in *Daughter of Zion: Henrietta Szold and American Jewish Womanhood*, catalogue of an exhibition at the Jewish Historical Society of Maryland, ed. Barry Kessler (Baltimore: Jewish Historical Society of Maryland, 1995), 28–29.

26. The best source for that journal is Baila Round Shargel, *Lost Love: The Untold Story of Henrietta Szold* (Philadelphia: Jewish Publication Society, 1997), which reprints it in its entirety. Other sources for the relationship between Szold and Ginzberg include Fineman, *Woman of Valor*, 119–243; Joan Dash, *Summoned to Jerusalem: The Life of Henrietta Szold* (New York: Harper & Row, 1979), 47–78; and a biography by Ginzberg's son, Eli Ginzberg, *Louis Ginzberg: Keeper of the Law* (Philadelphia: Jewish Publication Society, 1966), 105–29.

27. Szold, Journal, November 17, 1908, in Shargel, *Lost Love*, 36.

28. Ibid., 46.

29. Szold to Elvira N. Solis, September 6, 1905, RG 13, box 212, folder 32, Hadassah Archives.

30. Szold to Ginzberg, July 1905, in Fineman, *Woman of Valor*, 135–37.

31. These descriptions appear in letters from the summers of 1905 and 1906, in Ginzberg, *Keeper*, 113–15.

32. Szold to Ginzberg, August 13, 1907, in Shargel, *Lost Love*, 116; Ginzberg to Szold, September 5, 1907, in Shargel, *Lost Love*, 135.

33. Ginzberg to Szold, June 1907, in Ginzberg, *Keeper*, 117.

34. Ginzberg, *Keeper*, 108.

35. Szold to Ginzberg, August 10, 1907, in Shargel, *Lost Love*, 113.

36. Szold, Journal, November 27, 1908, in Shargel, *Lost Love*, 141.

37. Ibid., 165.

38. Ginzberg, *Keeper*, 128–29.

39. Szold, Journal, December 19, 1908, in Shargel, *Lost Love*, 190.

40. Szold, Journal, November 17, 1908, in Shargel, *Lost Love*, 35.

41. See Ginzberg, *Keeper*, 107–8. See also Dash, *Summoned to Jerusalem*, 69–71.

42. Phone interview with Abby Ginzberg, Louis Ginzberg's granddaughter, April 27, 2020, and with Abby Ginzberg and extended family member Jonnie Zheutlin, May 8, 2020.

43. Szold, Journal, November 17, 1908, in Shargel, *Lost Love*, 43.

44. The letter is reproduced at https://jwa.org/media/henrietta -szolds-letter-to-cyrus-adler-july-15–1909.

45. Sarna, *JPS*, 133.

Chapter 4. Travels and Travails

1. Szold, Diary, August 2, 1909, Szold Papers, Schlesinger Library on the History of Women in America, Radcliffe Institute, Harvard University, Cambridge, Mass.

2. Irving Fineman, *Woman of Valor: The Story of Henrietta Szold, 1860–1945* (New York: Simon & Schuster, 1961), 206.

3. Ibid., 207.

4. Szold to Mayer Sulzberger, November 28, 1909, Jewish Museum of Maryland, Baltimore, http:jewishmuseummd.org/tag /judgemayersulzberger.

5. Ibid.

6. Szold's talk to women's groups after her return from her trip to Palestine in January 1910, RG 13, box 181, folder 12, Hadassah Archives, American Jewish Historical Society, New York.

7. See Rachel Yanait Ben-Zvi, *Before Golda: Manya Shochat* (New York: Biblio, 1989).

8. Szold talk to women's groups, 1910, RG 13, box 181, folder 12, Hadassah Archives.

9. Szold to Mayer Sulzberger, November 28, 1909, Jewish Museum of Maryland.

10. Szold to Alice Seligsberg, December 12, 1909, in Marvin Lowenthal, *Henrietta Szold: Life and Letters* (New York: Viking, 1942), 65.

11. Szold to Mayer Sulzberger, November 28, 1909, Jewish Museum of Maryland.

12. Szold to Elvira N. Solis, December 12, 1909, RG 13, box 212, folder 32, Hadassah Archives.

13. Szold to Mayer Sulzberger, November 28, 1909, Jewish Museum of Maryland.

14. Szold to Elvira N. Solis, December 12, 1909, RG 13, box 212, folder 32, Hadassah Archives.

15. Szold's talk to women's groups, 1910, RG 13, box 181, folder 12, Hadassah Archives.

16. Szold, Diary, March 28, 1910; March 20, 1910, Aaron Aaronsohn Papers, Jewish Museum of Maryland.

17. Michael Brown, *The Israeli-American Connection: Its Roots in the Yishuv, 1914–1945* (Detroit: Wayne State University Press, 1996), 145.

18. See Norman Bentwich, *For Zion's Sake: A Biography of Judah L. Magnes* (Philadelphia: Jewish Publication Society, 1954).

See also Arthur A. Goren, *New York Jews and the Quest for Community: The Kehillah Experiment, 1908–1922* (New York: Columbia University Press, 1970); Mel Scult, "Schechter's Seminary," in *Tradition Renewed: A History of the Jewish Theological Seminary*, ed. Jack Wertheimer (New York: Jewish Theological Seminary of America, 1997), 1:80–83.

19. See Jonathan B. Krasner, *The Benderly Boys and American Jewish Education* (Waltham, Mass.: Brandeis University Press, 2011).

20. Szold to Elvira N. Solis, July 15, 1910, RG 13, box 212, folder 32, Hadassah Archives.

21. Joan Dash, *Summoned to Jerusalem: The Life of Henrietta Szold* (New York: Harper & Row, 1979), 99.

22. Szold to Elvira N. Solis, July 11, 1910, RG 13, box 212, folder 32, Hadassah Archives.

23. Szold to Dr. Solomon Schechter, November 10, 1910, RG 13, box 199, folder 6, Hadassah Archives.

24. Szold, Diary, April 10, 1910, Szold Papers.

25. Fineman, *Woman of Valor*, 263.

26. Szold, Diary, March 17, 1910, Szold Papers.

27. Fineman, *Woman of Valor*, 259; Dash, *Summoned to Jerusalem*, 96.

28. In Jonathan D. Sarna, *JPS: The Americanization of Jewish Culture, 1888–1988* (Philadelphia: Jewish Publication Society, 1989), 133.

29. Szold to Mayer Sulzberger, June 8, 1910, Szold-Levin Family Papers, Jewish Museum of Maryland.

30. Szold, Diary, March 24, 1910, Szold Papers.

31. Szold, Diary, April 12, 1910, Szold Papers.

32. Szold, Diary, May 27, 1910, Szold Papers.

33. See Dash, *Summoned to Jerusalem*, 100. See also Baila Round Shargel, *Lost Love: The Untold Story of Henrietta Szold* (Philadelphia: Jewish Publication Society, 1997).

34. To avoid the stigma that the symptom applies only to women, the terms often used today are "conversion disorder" or "functional neurological disorder symptom."

35. Anna O. was a pseudonym for Bertha Pappenheim, whose

life in some ways paralleled Szold's. Born a year before Szold (with an older sister named Henriette), Pappenheim grew up in a well-to-do Orthodox Austrian Jewish family, was greatly attached to her father, and developed vision issues and many other physical symptoms caring for him while he was dying. Later, after she had recovered, she headed the large and influential German League of Jewish Women, which had both feminist and philanthropic aims. She also took on various social work projects. Unlike Szold, she opposed Zionism, and until the mid-1930s opposed transferring children out of Germany after Hitler came to power. She later changed her mind. She and Szold met in 1935 to discuss Youth Aliyah. Szold would not have known that Pappenheim was Anna O. That identity was not revealed until the 1950s.

36. Szold to Elvira N. Solis, June 1, 1911; June 23, 1911, RG 13, box 212, folder 32, Hadassah Archives.

37. Szold to Alice Seligsberg, July 28, 1911, RG 13, box 216, folder 3, Hadassah Archives.

38. Ibid.

Chapter 5. Hadassah

1. Quoted in Baila Round Sharget, *Lost Love: The Untold Story of Henrietta Szold* (Philadelphia: Jewish Publication Society, 1997), 319.

2. For the "circle of friendship" that existed among Szold and her women friends, see Joyce Antler, "Zion in Our Hearts: Henrietta Szold and the American Jewish Women's Movement," in *Daughter of Zion: Henrietta Szold and American Jewish Womanhood*, catalogue of an exhibition at the Jewish Historical Society of Maryland, ed. Barry Kessler (Baltimore: Jewish Historical Society of Maryland, 1995), 44–48.

3. On the influence of women's clubs, see Carol Bosworth Kutscher, "The Early Years of Hadassah: 1912–1921" (Ph.D. diss., Brandeis University, 1976), 10–14.

4. Marlin Levin, *It Takes a Dream: The Story of Hadassah*, abridged by Esther Kustanowitz (Jerusalem: Gefen, 2002), 35–36.

5. Szold to Elvira N. Solis, January 26, 1897, RG 13, box 212,

folder 32, Hadassah Archives, American Jewish Historical Society, New York.

6. See Joan Dash, *Summoned to Jerusalem: The Life of Henrietta Szold* (New York: Harper & Row, 1979), 106.

7. The—somewhat cruel—joke in the Ginzberg family was that Louis Ginzberg was the "father of Hadassah," because his rejection of Szold led her to found the organization. See Eli Ginzberg, *Keeper of the Laws: Louis Ginzberg* (Philadelphia: Jewish Publication Society, 1966), 128.

8. Marvin Lowenthal's interview with Henrietta Szold, December 29, 1935, 19, RG 13, box 206, folder 3, Hadassah Archives.

9. Levin, *It Takes a Dream*, 37–38.

10. For Friedenwald, see Alexandra Lee Levin, *Mission: A Biography of Harry Friedenwald* (Philadelphia: Jewish Publication Society, 1964), 194. For Straus, see Alan M. Tigay, "Beginnings: A Confluence of Forces," *Hadassah Magazine*, August–September 2012.

11. Mary McCune, "Social Workers in the 'Muskeljudentum': 'Hadassah Ladies,' 'Manly Men' and the Significance of Gender in the American Zionist Movement, 1912–1928," *America Jewish History* 86, no. 2 (1998): 149; see also Erica Simmons, "Playgrounds and Penny Lunches in Palestine: American Social Welfare in the Yishuv," *American Jewish History* 92, no. 3 (2004).

12. Quoted in Dash, *Summoned to Jerusalem*, 109.

13. "Why Hadassah Grows," an interview with Henrietta Szold, Hadassah *News Letter*, January 1927, RG 17, box 33, folder 8, Hadassah Archives.

14. Elma Ehrlich Levinger, *Fighting Angel: The Story of Henrietta Szold* (New York: Berman House, 1946), 65, 66.

15. Quoted in Shulamit Reinharz, "Irma 'Rama' Lindheim: An Independent American Zionist Woman," *Nashim*, no. 1 (Winter 5758/1998): 107.

16. Ernestine L. Urken, email, April 7, 2020, about her aunt's chapter.

17. Mary McCune, *"The Whole Wide World without Limits": International Relief, Gender Politics, and American Jewish Women, 1893–1930* (Detroit: Wayne State University Press, 2005), 26.

18. Lowenthal interview with Szold, December 29, 1935, 8.

19. Irving Fineman, *Woman of Valor: The Story of Henrietta Szold, 1860–1945* (New York: Simon & Schuster, 1961), 268.

20. See McCune, *"The Whole Wide World,"* 37–39, for a discussion of these issues.

21. Henrietta Szold, "Women's Zionism," *Maccabaean* 27, no. 1 (July 1915): 6.

22. Quoted in McCune, *"The Whole Wide World,"* 39.

23. Henrietta Szold, "Rose Kaplan," *Maccabaean* 31 (February 1918): 37.

24. Jane Addams in Joyce Antler, *The Journey Home: How Jewish Women Shaped Modern America* (New York: Schocken Books, 1997), 105.

25. Fineman, *Woman of Valor,* 270.

26. Levin, *It Takes a Dream,* 46.

27. Szold to Jessie Sampter, August 24, 1914, RG 13, box 212, folder 1, Hadassah Archives.

28. Ibid.

29. Szold to Elvira N. Solis, August 25, 1914, RG 13, box 212, folder 32, Hadassah Archives.

30. Dash, *Summoned to Jerusalem,* 112.

31. Szold to Mrs. Julius Rosenwald, January 17, 1915, in Marvin Lowenthal, *Henrietta Szold: Life and Letters* (New York: Viking, 1942), 84.

32. Henrietta Szold, "Zionism: A Progressive and Democratic Movement," talk at the People's Institute at Cooper Union, February 13, 1916, RG 13, box 221, folder 9, Hadassah Archives.

33. Melvin Urofsky, *Louis D. Brandeis: A Life* (New York: Pantheon Books, 2009), 406–8.

34. Ibid., 405; Dash, *Summoned to Jerusalem,* 114–15.

35. Quoted in McCune, "Social Workers in the 'Muskeljudentum,'" 140.

36. Quoted in Carol Bosworth Kutscher, "The Early Years of Hadassah, 1912–1921" (Ph.D. diss., Brandeis University, 1976), 158.

37. Levin, *It Takes a Dream,* 58–59.

38. Szold to Cyrus Adler, December 1, 1915, in Lowenthal,

Life and Letters, 90; Szold to Mayer Sulzberger, December 1, 1915, in Jonathan D. Sarna, *JPS: The Americanization of Jewish Culture, 1888–1988* (Philadelphia: Jewish Publication Society, 1989), 135.

39. Szold to Elvira N. Solis, August 22, 1916, RG 13, box 212, folder 32, Hadassah Archives.

40. The entire letter is in Lowenthal, *Life and Letters*, 92–93.

Chapter 6. Palestine

1. Szold to Jessie Sampter, March 8, 1917, RG 13, box 212, folder 1, Hadassah Archives, American Jewish Historical Society, New York.

2. Ibid.

3. Norman Bentwich, *For Zion's Sake: A Biography of Judah L. Magnes* (Philadelphia: Jewish Publication Society, 1954), 102–4.

4. Quoted in Naomi Lichtenberg, "Hadassah's Founders and Palestine, 1912–1925: A Quest for Meaning and the Creation of Women's Zionism" (Ph.D. diss., Indiana University, 1995), 170–71.

5. Quoted in Melvin I. Urofsky, *Louis Brandeis: A Life* (New York: Pantheon Books, 2009), 496.

6. Quoted in Carol Bosworth Kutscher, "The Early Years of Hadassah, 1912–1921" (Ph.D. diss., Brandeis University, 1976), 163.

7. Szold to Jessie Sampter, December 20, 1917, RG 13, box 212, folder 1, Hadassah Archives.

8. Szold to Jessie Sampter, April 7, 1917; May 4, 1918, RG 13, box 212, folder 1, Hadassah Archives.

9. Kutscher, "Early Years of Hadassah," 166.

10. Szold to Jessie Sampter, March 16, 1918, RG 13, box 212, folder 1, Hadassah Archives.

11. Szold to Jessie Sampter, March 17, 1917; March 16, 1918, RG 13, box 212, folder 1, Hadassah Archives.

12. Szold to Jessie Sampter, January 1, 1918, RG 13, box 212, folder 1, Hadassah Archives.

13. Szold to "My dear Ones," July 1, 1922, RG 13, box 208, folder 4, Hadassah Archives.

14. *Hadassah Bulletin*, August 1918, RG 17, box 59, folder 4, Hadassah Archives.

15. Emanuel Neumann, *In the Arena: An Autobiographical Memoir* (New York: Herzl, 1976), 42–43.

16. Quoted in Marvin Lowenthal, *Henrietta Szold: Life and Letters* (New York: Viking, 1942), 115.

17. The AZMU is described at great length in Marlin Levin, *It Takes a Dream: The Story of Hadassah*, abridged by Esther Kustanowitz (Jerusalem: Gefen, 2002), 57–80; see also Joan Dash, *Summoned to Jerusalem: The Life of Henrietta Szold* (New York: Harper & Row, 1979), 125–28.

18. Alexandra Lee Levin, *Mission: A Biography of Harry Friedenwald* (Philadelphia: Jewish Publication Society, 1964), 268.

19. Years later, when Bertha moved to a smaller house and had to dispose of household items from the Szold's family home she had stored, Henrietta advised her about what to keep, but wrote, "And I'd burn, without opening it, a bundle containing a record about myself." Neither she nor Bertha did. August 25, 1941, RG 13, box 207, folder 16, Hadassah Archives.

20. Szold to Mrs. Leon M. Solis-Cohen, March 13, 1921, RG 13, box 212, folder 32, Hadassah Archives.

21. Meir speech commemorating tenth anniversary of Szold's death, March 14, 1955, 85092 12429, Henrietta Szold Foundation, Jerusalem.

22. Szold to Alice Seligsberg, November 30, 1919, quoted in Lowenthal, *Life and Letters*, 117.

23. Szold to Rabbi Joseph Hertz, November 20, 1897, RG 13, box 181, folder 6, Hadassah Archives.

24. Quoted in Eric L. Goldstein, "The Practical as Spiritual," in *Daughter of Zion: Henrietta Szold and American Jewish Womanhood*, catalogue of an exhibition at the Jewish Historical Society of Maryland, ed. Barry Kessler (Baltimore: Jewish Historical Society of Maryland, 1995), 23.

25. Szold to "My dear Ones," April 15, 1920, RG 13, box 208, folder 2, Hadassah Archives.

26. Szold to "My dear Family," May 11, 1920, RG 13, box 208, folder 2, Hadassah Archives.

27. Szold to "My dear Family," May 13, 1920, RG 13, box 208, folder 2, Hadassah Archives.

28. Szold to "Dear Family," May 26, 1920, RG 13, box 208, folder 2, Hadassah Archives.

29. Szold to Harry Friedenwald, March 16, 1921, in Lowenthal, *Life and Letters*, 169.

30. Szold to "Dear Family," May 26, 1920, RG 13, box 208, folder 2, Hadassah Archives.

31. For more on his love affair, see Dash, *Summoned to Jerusalem*, 151.

32. Szold to "My dear Ones," June 3, 1920, RG 13, box 208, folder 1, Hadassah Archives.

33. Szold to "My dear Family," June 21, 1920, RG 13, box 208, folder 1, Hadassah Archives.

34. For more on her eulogy, see Irving Fineman, *Woman of Valor: The Life of Henrietta Szold, 1860–1945* (New York: Simon & Schuster, 1961), 289.

35. Storrs quoted in Dash, *Summoned to Jerusalem*, 153; Szold on Ussishkin in letter to "My dear Ones," June 3, 1920, RG 13, box 208, folder 2, Hadassah Archives.

36. Szold to "My dear Ones," July 25, 1920, RG 13, box 208, folder 2, Hadassah Archives.

37. Szold to Adele, October 26, 1920, RG 13, box 209, folder 5, Hadassah Archives.

38. Ibid.

39. Szold to "Dear Family," November 22, 1920, RG 13, box 208, folder 2, Hadassah Archives.

40. Szold to "My dear Ones," October 30, 1920, RG 13, box 208, folder 2, Hadassah Archives.

41. Szold to "My dear Family," January 1, 1921, RG 13, box 208, folder 3, Hadassah Archives.

42. Szold to "My dear Family," May 11, 1920; June 21, 1920; to "My dear Ones," November 13, 1920, RG 13, box 208, folder 2, Hadassah Archives.

43. Szold to Emily Solis, February 22, 1921, RG 13, box 212, folder 32, Hadassah Archives.

44. Quoted in Deborah S. Bernstein, ed., *Pioneers and Home-makers: Jewish Women in Pre-State Israel* (Albany: State University of New York Press, 1992), 270.

45. Joyce Antler, *The Journey Home: How Jewish Women Shaped Modern America* (New York: Schocken Books, 1997), 118.

46. On Szold's friendships, see Joyce Antler, "Zion in Our Hearts: Henrietta Szold and the American Jewish Women's Movement," in *Daughter of Zion: Henrietta Szold and American Jewish Womanhood*, catalogue of an exhibition at the Jewish Historical Society of Maryland, ed. Barry Kessler (Baltimore: Jewish Historical Society of Maryland, 1995), 45–47.

47. Szold to Adele, April 28, 1921, RG 13, box 209, folder 5, Hadassah Archives.

48. Szold to "My dear Family," April 19, 1921, RG 13, box 208, folder 3, Hadassah Archives.

49. Szold to Adele, September 29, 1933, RG 13, Box 209, folder 5, Hadassah Archives.

50. Szold to "My dear Family," May 18, 1921, RG 13, box 208, folder 3, Hadassah Archives.

51. Szold to "My dear Ones," June 26, 1921, RG 13, box 208, folder 3, Hadassah Archives.

52. Szold to Jessie Sampter, November 6, 1921, RG 13, box 212, folder 1; Szold to Bertha, November 21, 1921, RG 13, box 207, folder 12, Hadassah Archives.

53. On her lunch with Storrs: Szold to "My dear Ones," August 4, 1921; on British response to the violence, Szold to "My dear Ones," June 26, 1921, both in RG 13, box 208, folder 3, Hadassah Archives.

54. For a full description of the split, see Melvin Urofsky, *American Zionism from Herzl to the Holocaust* (Lincoln: University of Nebraska Press, 1975), 246–98.

55. Szold to "My dear Family," June 22, 1921; Szold to "My dear Ones," July 13, 1921, both in RG 13, box 208, folder 3, Hadassah Archives.

56. Szold to "My dear Ones," June 26, 1921, RG 13, box 208, folder 3, Hadassah Archives.

57. Szold to Alice Seligsberg, June 20, 1921, quoted in Donald Herbert Miller, "A History of Hadassah, 1912–1935" (Ph.D. diss., New York University, 1968), 123; see also 124–32. For more about the Lipsky-Hadassah fight, see Urofsky, *American Zionism*, 342–45.

58. Szold to "My dear Family," October 7, 1921, RG 13, box 208, folder 3, Hadassah Archives.

59. Szold to "My dear Ones," July 13, 1921, RG 13, box 208, folder 3, Hadassah Archives.

60. Szold to "My dear Ones," December 9, 1921, RG 13, box 208, folder 3, Hadassah Archives.

Chapter 7. Living in Two Lands

1. Szold to "My dear Family," September 17, 1921, RG 13, box 208, folder 3, Hadassah Archives, American Jewish Historical Society, New York.

2. Szold to "My dear Family," October 10, 1922, RG 13, box 208, folder 4, Hadassah Archives.

3. Szold to "My dear Family," November 1, 1922, RG 13, box 208, folder 4, Hadassah Archives.

4. Szold to Jessie Sampter, June 10, 1925, RG 13, box 212, folder 1, Hadassah Archives.

5. "Women's Aid to Palestine," *New York Times*, May 21, 1922; "3,000 Greet Woman Palestine Leader," *New York Times*, May 1, 1923.

6. Szold, "Jewish Palestine in the Making," talk given on April 30, 1923, printed in *New Palestine*, May 4, 1923. Reprinted in Hadassah *News Letter*, June 1923, RG 17, box 33, folder 5, Hadassah Archives.

7. Ibid.

8. Szold to Jessie Sampter, August 10, 1923, RG 13, box 212, folder 1, Hadassah Archives.

9. See Joan Dash, *Summoned to Jerusalem: The Life of Henrietta Szold* (New York: Harper & Row, 1979), 188–93.

10. Szold to "My dear Sisters," March 14, 1930; July 12, 1930; June 5, 1931, RG 13, box 208, folder 6, Hadassah Archives.

11. Hadassah *News Letter,* May, 1924; June, 1924, RG 17, box 33, folder 5, Hadassah Archives.

12. Cited in Mary McCune, *"The Whole Wide World without Limits": International Relief, Gender Politics, and American Jewish Women, 1893–1930* (Detroit: Wayne State University Press, 2005), 104; Melvin I. Urofsky, *American Zionism from Herzl to the Holocaust* (Lincoln: University of Nebraska Press, 1975), 345.

13. Szold to Jessie Sampter, November 1, 1927, RG 13, box 212, folder 1, Hadassah Archives.

14. Telephone conversation with Carmel Berkson, Isaac Berkson's daughter, August 5, 2021.

15. Rose Zeitlin, *Henrietta Szold: Record of a Life* (New York: Dial, 1952), 78; Tom Segev, *One Palestine Complete: Jews and Arabs under the British Mandate* (New York: Henry Holt, 1999), 291.

16. Joseph Heller, *From Brit Shalom to Ihud: Judah Leib Magnes and the Struggle for a Binational State in Palestine* [in Hebrew] (Jerusalem: Hebrew University, 2003).

17. See Dvora Hacohen, *To Repair a Broken World: The Life of Henrietta Szold, Founder of Hadassah* (Cambridge, Mass.: Harvard University Press, 2021), 208.

18. Quoted in Susan Lee Harris, *The Bi-national Idea in Palestine during Mandatory Times* (Tel Aviv: Ben Nun, 1970), 171–72.

19. "The Jewish Child and the Involvement of Brit Shalom," *Haam,* July 26, 1931. Szold's name also appears in a list drawn up by the group—"Roll of Sympathisers of the Brith Shalom Society, 1931," along with those of Judah Magnes, Manya Shochat, and others. A187/9, Central Zionist Archives, Jerusalem.

20. Quoted in Anita Shapira, *Ben-Gurion: Father of Modern Israel* (New Haven: Yale University Press, 2004), 85.

21. Ron Chernow, *The Warburgs: The Twentieth Century Odyssey of a Remarkable Jewish Family,* 2nd ed. (New York: Vintage Books, 2016), 300–301.

22. Szold to Jessie Sampter, September 13, 1929, RG 13, box 212, folder 2, Hadassah Archives.

23. Quoted in Zeitlin, *Henrietta Szold,* 118.

24. Szold to Felix Warburg, December 23, 1929, RG 13, box 212, folder 27, Hadassah Archives.

25. Szold to "My dear Sisters," June 17, 1930, RG 13, box 208, folder 6, Hadassah Archives.

26. Felix Warburg to Szold, January 10, 1930, RG 13, box 212, folder 27, Hadassah Archives.

27. Szold to "My dear Sisters," February 6, 1930, RG 13, box 208, folder 6, Hadassah Archives.

28. Ibid.

29. Szold to "My dear Sisters," May 7, 1930, RG 13, box 208, folder 6, Hadassah Archives.

30. Szold to "My dear Sisters," June 17, 1930, RG 13, box 208, folder 6, Hadassah Archives.

31. Szold to "My dear Sisters," July 8, 1930, RG 13, box 208, folder 6, Hadassah Archives.

32. Szold to "My dear Sisters," May 7, 1930, RG 13, box 208, folder 6, Hadassah Archives.

33. Ibid.

34. Szold to "My dear Sisters," June 17, 1930, RG 13, box 208, folder 6, Hadassah Archives.

35. Szold to "My dear Sisters," September 9, 1930, RG 13, box 208, folder 6, Hadassah Archives.

36. For Irma Lindheim's report to the 1927 convention, see "Annual Convention of Hadassah Opens," *Baltimore Sun*, June 24, 1927.

37. Hadassah *News Letter*, August, 1928, RG 17, box 33, folder 5, Hadassah Archives.

38. Szold to Jessie Sampter, August 24, 1924, RG 13, box 212, folder 1, Hadassah Archives.

Chapter 8. "The Most Worthwhile Undertaking"

1. Szold to "My dear Sisters," June 5, 1931, RG 13, box 208, folder 6, Hadassah Archives, American Jewish Historical Society, New York.

2. Szold to "My dear Ones," September 2, 1932, RG 13, box 208, folder 7, Hadassah Archives.

3. Szold to "My dear Sisters," July 31, 1931, RG 13, box 208, folder 6, Hadassah Archives.

4. Szold to "My dear Ones," September 2, 1932, RG 13, box 208, folder 7, Hadassah Archives.

5. Szold to "My dear Sisters," June 5, 1931, RG 13, box 208, folder 6, Hadassah Archives.

6. Szold to "Dear Sisters," July 3, 1931, RG 13, box 208, folder 6, Hadassah Archives.

7. Szold to "My dear Sisters," July 31, 1931, RG 13, box 208, folder 6, Hadassah Archives.

8. Szold to "My dear Ones," June 9, 1932, RG 13, box 208, folder 7, Hadassah Archives.

9. Szold to "My dear Sisters," July 29, 1932, RG 13, box 208, folder 7, Hadassah Archives.

10. Szold to "My dear Ones," September 22, 1932, RG 13, box 208, folder 7, Hadassah Archives.

11. Szold to "My dear Sisters," September 20, 1933, RG 13, box 208, folder 7, Hadassah Archives.

12. Ayana Halpern, "Jewish Social Workers in Mandatory Palestine: Between Submission and Subversion under Male Leadership," *Nashim* (2019): 82.

13. Szold to "My dear Sisters," September 20, 1933, RG 13, box 208, folder 7, Hadassah Archives.

14. Ibid.

15. Szold to "My dear Sisters," September 29, 1933, RG 13, box 208, folder 7, Hadassah Archives.

16. Szold to "My dear Sisters," June 9, 1933, RG 13, box 208, folder 7, Hadassah Archives.

17. Brian Amkraut, *Between Home and Homeland: Youth Aliyah from Nazi Germany* (Tuscaloosa: University of Alabama Press, 2006), 45.

18. Szold to "My dear Sisters," June 23, 1933, RG 13, box 208, folder 7, Hadassah Archives.

19. Quoted in Leah Rosen and Ruth Amir, "Constructing National Identity: The Case of Youth Aliyah," *Israel Studies Forum* 21, no. 1 (Summer 2006): 45.

20. See Sandra Berliant Kadosh, "Ideology vs. Reality: Youth Aliyah and the Rescue of Jewish Children during the Holocaust Era, 1933–45" (Ph.D. diss., Columbia University, 1995), 45.

21. Szold to "My dear Sisters," December 29, 1933, RG 13, box 208, folder 7, Hadassah Archives.

22. Ruth Halprin Kaslove, "Memories of Rose Luria Halprin," in *American Jewish Women and the Zionist Enterprise*, ed. Shulamit Reinharz and Mark A. Raider (Waltham, Mass.: Brandeis University Press, 2005), 329.

23. Amkraut, *Between Home and Homeland*, 54.

24. Marlin Levin, *It Takes a Dream: The Story of Hadassah*, abridged by Esther Kustanowitz (Jerusalem: Gefen, 2002), 142.

25. Marvin Lowenthal's interview with Henrietta Szold, December 29, 1939, 60, RG 13, box 206, folder 3, Hadassah Archives.

26. Szold to "My dear Sisters," July 27, 1934, RG 13, box 208, folder 8, Hadassah Archives.

27. Szold to "My dear Sisters," December 29, 1933, RG 13, box 208, folder 7, Hadassah Archives.

28. Szold to "My dear Sisters," August 3, 1934, RG 13, box 208, folder 8, Hadassah Archives.

29. Szold to "My dear Sisters," December 29, 1933, RG 13, box 208, folder 7, Hadassah Archives.

30. See Amkraut, *Between Home and Homeland*, 85–86.

31. Dvora Hacohen, *To Repair a Broken World: The Life of Henrietta Szold, Founder of Hadassah* (Cambridge, Mass.: Harvard University Press, 2021), 273.

32. Chanoch Rinott, "Looking Back on Youth Aliyah" (London, 1979), sent to author by Lynne Reinhold Irvine.

33. Szold to Jessie Sampter, September 26, 1933, RG 13, box 212, folder 2, Hadassah Archives.

34. Szold to Adele, February 8, 1934, RG 13, box 209, folder 6, Hadassah Archives.

35. Szold to Adele, June 22, 1934, RG 13, box 209, folder 6, Hadassah Archives.

36. Szold to "My dear Sisters," August 3, 1934, RG 13, box 208, folder 8, Hadassah Archives.

37. Levin, *It Takes a Dream*, 140.

38. Szold to "My dear Sisters," October 19, 1934, RG 13, box 208, folder 8, Hadassah Archives.

39. See Amkraut, *Between Home and Homeland*, 72–75.

40. Levin, *It Takes a Dream*, 143–44.

41. Hadassah *News Letter*, October, 1935, quoted in Melvin Urofsky, *American Zionism from Herzl to the Holocaust* (Lincoln: University of Nebraska Press, 1975), 396.

42. Ibid., 151.

43. For a description of Beyth, see Irving Fineman, *Woman of Valor: The Life of Henrietta Szold, 1860–1945* (New York: Simon & Schuster, 1961), 376.

44. Ralph Martin, *Golda—Golda Meir: The Romantic Years* (New York: Scribner, 1988), 297.

45. Szold to Jessie Sampter, September 24, 1935, RG 12, box 212, folder 2, Hadassah Archives.

46. Szold to her sisters, October 1, 1935, in Marvin Lowenthal, *Henrietta Szold: Life and Letters* (New York: Viking, 1942), 286.

47. *Jüdische Rundschau*, September 17, September 20, and September 27, 1935. My thanks to Benjamin Kuntz for sending these articles.

48. Szold to her sisters, October 1, 1935, in Lowenthal, *Life and Letters*, 284.

49. Email to author from Tom Tugend, March 21, 2020.

50. Emma Ehrlich, "Notes and Impressions," March 1941, RG 13, box 225, folder 5, Hadassah Archives.

51. Szold to her sisters, October 1, 1935, in Lowenthal, *Life and Letters*, 286.

52. Alexandra Lee Levin, *Mission: A Biography of Harry Friedenwald* (Philadelphia: Jewish Publication Society of America, 1964), 369.

53. Szold to "My dear Sisters," June 22, 1934, RG 13, box 208, folder 8, Hadassah Archives.

54. Szold to her sisters, June 5, 1936, quoted in Alexandra Lee Levin, ed., *Henrietta Szold and Youth Aliyah: Family Letters, 1934–1944* (New York: Herzl, 1986), 15. Letters relating to the Arab re-

volt appear on pp. 10–17. On the theme of Arab-Jewish relations, see also Lowenthal, *Life and Letters*, 310–13.

55. For Szold's position, see Joan Dash, *Summoned to Jerusalem: The Life of Henrietta Szold* (New York: Harper & Row, 1979), 265–66.

56. Szold to her sisters, August 27, 1937, in Lowenthal, *Life and Letters*, 327.

57. Szold to Adele, October 29, 1937, RG 13, box 209, folder 6, Hadassah Archives.

58. Szold to Bertha, October 29, 1937, RG 13, box 209, folder 6, Hadassah Archives.

59. Szold to her sisters, June 3, 1938, quoted in Levin, *Henrietta Szold and Youth Aliyah*, 30.

60. For many contemporary and later criticisms of Szold, see Kadosh, "Ideology vs. Reality."

61. Szold to Adele, October 26, 1938, RG 13, box 209, folder 6, Hadassah Archives.

62. Szold to her sisters, August 15, 1935, in Lowenthal, *Life and Letters*, 282.

Chapter 9. Saving Children / Seeking Peace

1. Brian Amkraut, *Between Home and Homeland: Youth Aliyah from Nazi Germany* (Tuscaloosa: University of Alabama Press, 2006), 121.

2. Hadassah cable, May 19, 1939, RG 13, box 216, folder 24, Hadassah Archives, American Jewish Historical Society, New York.

3. Szold, "Greetings to a Hadassah Convention under the Shadow of War!" RG 13, box 225, folder 28, Hadassah Archives.

4. "Do Not Murder!" reprinted in *Davar*, July 7, 1939.

5. Bertha Levin to family, April 19, 1939, quoted in Alexandra Lee Levin, ed., *Henrietta Szold and Youth Aliyah: Family Letters, 1934–1944* (New York: Herzl, 1986), 36.

6. Szold to "Dear Sisters," December 7, 1934, RG 13, box 208, folder 8, Hadassah Archives.

7. Szold to Bertha, June 14–17, quoted in Marvin Lowenthal, *Henrietta Szold: Life and Letters* (New York: Viking, 1942), 335.

8. Szold to Sampter's sister, quoted in Joyce Antler, *The Journey Home: How Jewish Women Shaped Modern America* (New York: Schocken Books, 1997), 126.

9. Szold to Rose Jacobs, November 20, 1940, quoted in Lowenthal, *Life and Letters*, 336.

10. Emma Ehrlich, "Notes and Impressions," March 1941, RG 13, box 225, folder 5, Hadassah Archives.

11. Quoted in Antler, *Journey Home*, 128.

12. Kathleen McLaughlin, "Grand Old Lady of Palestine," *New York Times Magazine*, December 15, 1940.

13. "Papers of Rabbi Benjamin Szold of Blessed Memory to the University," *Haolam*, February 6, 1941.

14. Szold to Bertha, February 12, 1941, RG 13, box 207, folder 16, Hadassah Archives.

15. Ibid.

16. Szold to Bertha, September 26, 1941, RG 13, box 207, folder 16, Hadassah Archives.

17. Statistic from Dvora Hacohen, *To Repair a Broken World: The Life of Henrietta Szold, Founder of Hadassah* (Cambridge, Mass.: Harvard University Press, 2021), 306.

18. Emma Ehrlich Levinger, *Fighting Angel: The Story of Henrietta Szold* (New York: Berman House, 1946), 167.

19. Tuvia Friling, *Arrows in the Dark: David Ben-Gurion, the Yishuv Leadership, and Rescue Attempts during the Holocaust*, 2 vols., trans. Ora Cummings (Madison: University of Wisconsin Press, 2004), 1:150–51.

20. Ibid. For an in-depth discussion of attempts and failures to save children, see 1:153–69.

21. Ben-Gurion's speech at dedication of Hadassah-Hebrew University Medical Center, *Jewish Telegraphic Agency Daily News Bulletin*, August 4, 1960, jta.org/archive/ben-gurion-lauds-hadassah-pays-tribute-to-henrietta-szoldpremier.

22. "To the Yishuv," signed Henrietta Szold, *Davar*, September 15, 1941. The reference to the spirit of love comes from the phrase in the biblical book of Zechariah (4:6): "Not by might nor by

power, but by My Spirit says the Lord of Hosts." The Ihud group used it frequently.

23. Quoted in Tom Segev, *A State at Any Cost: The Life of David Ben-Gurion*, trans. Haim Watzman (New York: Farrar, Straus & Giroux, 2019), 309.

24. Paul Mendes-Flohr, *Martin Buber: A Life of Faith and Dissent* (New Haven: Yale University Press, 2019), 247.

25. Quoted in Levin, *Family Letters*, 65.

26. See Joan Dash, *Summoned to Jerusalem: The Life of Henrietta Szold* (New York: Harper & Row, 1979), 298.

27. Quoted in Rose Zeitlin, *Henrietta Szold: Record of a Life* (New York: Dial, 1952), 140.

28. See Zohar Segev, "From Philanthropy to Shaping a State: Hadassah and Ben-Gurion, 1937–1947," *Israel Studies* 18, no. 3 (Fall 2013): 133–57.

29. Some of the letters and cables can be found in RG 13, box 215, folder 14, Hadassah Archives.

30. Quoted in Walter Laqueur, *Dying for Jerusalem: The Past, Present and Future of the Holiest City* (Naperville, Ill.: SourceBooks, 2005), 179.

31. See Mikhal Dekel, *Tehran Children: A Holocaust Refugee Odyssey* (New York: Norton, 2019), 253–58.

32. Friling, *Arrows in the Dark*, 1:150.

33. "A Statement on 'The Tehran Children' and on Religious Education for Youth Immigration," by Miss Henrietta Szold, Director of Youth Aliyah, Jerusalem (New York: United Palestine Appeal, n.d.), RG 13, box 221, folder 70, Hadassah Archives.

34. Ibid.

35. Szold to Rose Jacobs, June 7, 1942, quoted in Antler, *Journey Home*, 127.

36. Sylvia M. Gelber, *No Balm in Gilead* (Ontario: Carleton University Press, 1989), 192.

37. Dash, *Summoned to Jerusalem*, 311.

38. "Roosevelt Hails Aid to Jewish Children," *New York Times*, March 9, 1944.

39. Gelber, *No Balm in Gilead*, 192–93.

40. Judah Magnes, "Last Days," diary entry for December 27, 1944. See Dash, *Summoned to Jerusalem*, 314.

41. "Statement of the Major Institutions," *Davar*, February 14, 1945.

Epilogue

1. Sylvia M. Gelber, *No Balm in Gilead* (Ontario: Carleton University Press, 1989), 193.

2. Szold to Jessie Sampter, August 23, 1917, RG 13, box 212, folder 1, Hadassah Archives, American Jewish Historical Society, New York.

3. Ibid.

4. Szold to Alice Seligsberg, July 14, 1931, in Marvin Lowenthal, *Henrietta Szold: Life and Letters* (New York: Viking, 1942), 232.

5. Miriam Freund, "Make My Eyes Look to the Future," *American Jewish Historical Society* 49, no. 3 (March 1960): 158–72.

ACKNOWLEDGMENTS
_____

I WAS FORTUNATE to have researched much of the material I
needed for this book before the coronavirus pandemic shut down
archives and libraries. I'm grateful to two people who gathered
many of those materials for me: Miriam Wallerstein in New York
and Dr. Boaz Lev Tov in Israel. Miriam spent many days at the Center for Jewish History, where the Hadassah Archives are on deposit
at the American Jewish Historical Society, assembling Henrietta
Szold's letters and writings and examining related documents. I
thank her for her dogged work and fine suggestions. Boaz, head of
the Department of History at Bet Berl College, devoted hours to
finding material by and about Szold in the Central Zionist Archives
in Jerusalem, most of it in Hebrew, and online in historical newspapers. He also shared his extensive knowledge of pre-state history
with me in long cross-continent telephone conversations. I so appreciate his erudition and friendship. I also thank the staffs of the
Hadassah Archives, Central Zionist Archives, and American Jewish Historical Society for their aid in locating letters and documents,

and the staff at the Jewish Museum of Maryland in Baltimore for their graciousness and knowledge in responding to my queries.

Thank you to Ina Cohen of the Jewish Theological Seminary Library for her invaluable help in discovering articles and dissertations about Szold and Hadassah and making them accessible to me. And deep gratitude to Jennifer Fauxsmith, research librarian at the Schlesinger Library on the History of Women in America, part of the Radcliffe Institute of Harvard University, for making available Szold's personal journal of 1910, both handwritten and typed. Thanks also to Hagai Tsoref for his kindness and help with the Israel State Archives.

I thank Professor Anita Shapira, co-editor of the Jewish Lives series, for inviting me to contribute to this prestigious group of biographies and especially to write about Henrietta Szold. Anita's friendship and encouragement mean a great deal to me. My gratitude also to the team at Yale University Press for their care and commitment as they ushered this work from manuscript to finished book: Heather Gold, Mary Pasti, and Elizabeth Sylvia. And special thanks to Robin DuBlanc for her careful and thoughtful copyediting.

A heartfelt thank you to the many Hadassah members who generously wrote to me in response to a small notice I placed in *Hadassah Magazine* about this project. Space did not allow me to include all the memories and stories I received, but every one of them contributed to my overall view of Szold and my appreciation for her long-standing relationship with the women of Hadassah.

Finally, as always, I thank my husband and family for their patience, love, and understanding as I put other matters aside to focus on Henrietta Szold and her times.

INDEX

JEWISH LIVES is a prizewinning series of interpretative biography designed to explore the many facets of Jewish identity. Individual volumes illuminate the imprint of Jewish figures upon literature, religion, philosophy, politics, cultural and economic life, and the arts and sciences. Subjects are paired with authors to elicit lively, deeply informed books that explore the range and depth of the Jewish experience from antiquity to the present.

Jewish Lives is a partnership of Yale University Press and the Leon D. Black Foundation. Ileene Smith is editorial director. Anita Shapira and Steven J. Zipperstein are series editors.

Jerome Robbins: A Life in Dance, by Wendy Lesser
Julius Rosenwald: Repairing the World, by Hasia R. Diner
Mark Rothko: Toward the Light in the Chapel, by Annie Cohen-Solal
Ruth: A Migrant's Tale, by Ilana Pardes
Gershom Scholem: Master of the Kabbalah, by David Biale
Bugsy Siegel: The Dark Side of the American Dream,
    by Michael Shnayerson
Solomon: The Lure of Wisdom, by Steven Weitzman
Steven Spielberg: A Life in Films, by Molly Haskell
Spinoza: Freedom's Messiah, by Ian Buruma
Alfred Stieglitz: Taking Pictures, Making Painters, by Phyllis Rose
Barbra Streisand: Redefining Beauty, Femininity, and Power,
    by Neal Gabler
Henrietta Szold: Hadassah and the Zionist Dream,
    by Francine Klagsbrun
Leon Trotsky: A Revolutionary's Life, by Joshua Rubenstein
Warner Bros: The Making of an American Movie Studio,
    by David Thomson
Elie Wiesel: Confronting the Silence, by Joseph Berger

FORTHCOMING TITLES INCLUDE:

Abraham, by Anthony Julius
Hannah Arendt, by Masha Gessen
The Ba'al Shem Tov, by Ariel Mayse
Walter Benjamin, by Peter Gordon
Franz Boas, by Noga Arikha
Bob Dylan, by Sasha Frere-Jones
Anne Frank, by Ruth Franklin
George Gershwin, by Gary Giddins
Ruth Bader Ginsburg, by Jeffrey Rosen
Jesus, by Jack Miles